FROM HUSSAR TO MAYOR:
JOHN THOMAS GODDARD O.B.E., M.C., J.P.

A Biography

by

Ronald D. Knight

Also by the Author:

THOMAS HARDY O.M. AND SIR EDMUND GOSSE LITT.D.
(First edition 1968; second revised edition 1975)
HAMBLEDON'S CRICKET GLORY Series: Volumes 2-19 & 26-28
(1974-2000 discontinued)
THE KNIGHT FAMILY 'JOURNAL' (Quarterly) (1979-1986 discontinued)
COLONEL T. E. LAWRENCE (Lawrence of Arabia) VISITS MR. & MRS.
THOMAS HARDY (1985)
T. E. LAWRENCE AND THE MAX GATE CIRCLE
(First edition 1988; second revised edition 1995)
T. E. LAWRENCE: HIS ORDERS, DECORATIONS AND MEDALS
(First edition 1989; second revised edition 2006)
THE HOME FRONT Life in Dorset 1939-1944 (An Evacuee's Experience)
(1999)
T. E. LAWRENCE'S IRISH ANCESTRY AND RELATIONSHIP TO SIR
WALTER RALEIGH (2000)

© Ronald D. Knight 2007

Published by the author:
Ronald D. Knight
18 Manor Road
Redlands
Weymouth
Dorset DT3 5HR

ISBN: 978-0-903769-29-7

CONTENTS

ILLUSTRATIONS 2
PROLOGUE & ACKNOWLEDGEMENTS 3
INTRODUCTION 5
THE EARLY YEARS 1879-1898 7
THE BOER WAR 1898-1902 14
MARRIAGE 1903-1905 29
INDIA 1906-1914 39
THE GREAT WAR: 1915 44
THE GREAT WAR: 1916 50
THE GREAT WAR: 1917 53
THE GREAT WAR: 1918 59
POST-GREAT WAR 1919-1924 62
PUBLICAN 1925-1930 68
POLITICIAN 1931-1938 72
MAYOR 1938-1939 76
WAR-TIME MAYOR: 1939 85
WAR-TIME MAYOR: 1940 95
WAR-TIME MAYOR: 1941 101
WAR-TIME MAYOR: 1942 113
WAR-TIME MAYOR: 1943 122
WAR-TIME MAYOR: 1944 133
WAR-TIME MAYOR: 1945 144
THE END 1945-1946 157
EPILOGUE 164
APPENDIX I: THE GODDARD FAMILY GENEALOGY 172
APPENDIX II: TRANSCRIPT OF WEYMOUTH'S GOODWILL MESSAGE
                      TO U.S.A. 12th NOVEMBER 1941 175
APPENDIX III: ANCIENT ORDER OF FORESTERS 179
BIBLIOGRAPHY 182

ILLUSTRATIONS

Between pages 38-39

Map of Wednesbury 1890 (Ordnance Survey-© crown copyright); Dudley Street, Wednesbury c.1887 (Sandwell Library); St. James' Street, Wednesbury 1933 (Sandwell Library); Rear of Foster Street, Wednesbury 1933 (Sandwell Library); 'Dark Satanic Mills', Wednesbury 1904 (Sandwell Library); St. James' School, Wednesbury 2003 (Author); Newbridge Barracks, Ireland (Lawrence, Dublin); Relief column entering Ladysmith 1900 (Author's collection); Map of Boer War (Museum of Lancashire); Map of Aldershot 1895 (Ordnance Survey-© crown copyright); 14th (King's) Hussars sergeant - Review Order (Gale & Polden); 14th (King's) Hussars - Proceeding on Manoeuvres (Gale & Polden); Cavalry Gates at Aldershot - Then c.1910 (G.B.Newby, Aldershot) and Now 2004 (Author); 14th Hussars 'At Stables' (Author's collection); 14th (King's) Hussars Review Order (M.Ettlinger & Co.); Mount Pleasant, Redan Hill, Aldershot 2003 (Author); Presbyterian Church, Aldershot 2003 (Author).

Between pages 64-65

14th Hussars Regimental Medal (Museum of Lancashire); R.S.M. John Goddard (Museum of Lancashire); 'Battle of Umm-al-Tabal' 1915 (Museum of Lancashire); 'Withdrawal from Kut' 1915 (Museum of Lancashire); Surrender of Khazimain 1917 (Museum of Lancashire); Map of Mesopotamia and Persia (*The War Illustrated* 29th April 1916); R.S.M. John Goddard on horseback (Goddard family); R.S.M. John Goddard with medals (Goddard family); 14th/20th Hussars Revolver Team 1925 (Weymouth RBL).

Between pages 144-145

Royal Adelaide Hotel exterior and Coffee Room c.1930 (Weymouth RBL); Weymouth Celebrities in Caricature 1933 (*Sunday Graphic*); John Goddard elected Mayor 1938 (Weymouth Library); Mayor Goddard laying foundation stone (*Dorset Daily Echo*); Trowel and Key (RBL); Mayoress and granddaughter (Goddard family); Mayor, Mayoress and Royalty (Weymouth Ref. Library); Mayor with King George VI (Weymouth RBL); Mayor and Mayoress with mobile kitchen (Weymouth Ref. Library); Mayor and Mayoress with American serviceman (*Dorset Daily Echo*); *Royal Adelaide Hotel* bomb damage 1941 (Acutt); *Adelaide Court* 2003 (Author); Mayor Goddard and Lady Mountbatten (Acutt); Goddard service-women (Goddard family); Mayor and Mayoress Goddard collecting money (Weymouth Ref. Library); VE street party (Audrey Judge); Goddard Challenge Snooker Cup (Weymouth RBL); Weymouth Hospital's Goddard plaques (Author); Mayor and Mayoress Goddard portraits (Goddard family); John Goddard's medals (Goddard family); Re-dedication of British Legion's Goddard Room (Goddard family).

PROLOGUE & ACKNOWLEDGEMENTS

It was whilst being Honorary Secretary of the Weymouth Branch of The Royal British Legion, that I received a telephone call out of the blue in March 2001. The call was from his granddaughter, Ann Goddard, who initially enquired whether there was still a 'Goddard Room' at *Legion House* in Weymouth. At the time the name meant nothing to me, nor any knowledge of a 'Goddard Room'; but after searching through the Legion Branch archives, and the Weymouth Reference Library, something of a full picture quickly began to emerge of who was John Thomas Goddard, and his above average abilities and achievements.

There had been a 'Goddard Room' at *Legion House*, but it had disappeared many years ago in various renovations and alterations within the building. This situation was however to be quickly remedied, as will be seen in the EPILOGUE.

As well as a subsequent further growth in a collection of photographs, newspaper reports, and other Goddard memorabilia, the culmination was the resurrection of a sound recorded goodwill message on a 78 r.p.m. gramophone record, given by John Goddard to Weymouth in Massachusetts, U.S.A., made in November 1941 when he was Mayor of Weymouth in Dorset, UK.

Unfortunately the Army Personnel Centre of the Ministry of Defence has lost - or at least has twice failed to locate - John Godddard's army service records. Thus some aspects of his time in the Hussars can only be conjecture, as ascertained from the several published 14th and 14th/20th Hussars' *Histories*.

Acknowledgements and grateful thanks for help in compiling the John Thomas Goddard story are gratefully given to various members of his extended descendant family: Ann Goddard, Pamela and Alvin Tull, Tony Woodford; Claire S. Harris and Keith MacDonald from other branches of the family. Also to Peter Goddard and others of The Goddard Association of Europe; two members of the Weymouth Branch of The Royal British Legion: Bill Roper for his considerate rescuing of several relevant artifacts from removal and destruction, and Ted Sturmey for advising me of the John Goddard plaques in the Weymouth Community Hospital; Mr Cross of the Weymouth Community Hospital for allowing me to photograph these plaques; the Branch Committee of the Weymouth Branch of The Royal British Legion for extensive use of its archive material and permission to publish; the late Committee of The Royal British Legion (Weymouth) Club Ltd for kindly consenting to the re-dedication of a 'Goddard Room'; Maureen Attwooll, ex-Reference Librarian at Weymouth Public Library, for her encyclopaedic knowledge of local history, and tracking down of the 1941 goodwill recording; Geoffrey Pritchard of Weymouth & Portland B.C. for initially suggesting the recording's existence; Jack West, previous curator of Weymouth Museum, for loaning the gramophone record for transcription; Alderman 'Andy' Hutchings for referring me to D.G.F.Acutt's book; Sherrens Printers of Weymouth for consent to reproduce material from Acutt's book; the Reference Library of Weymouth Public Library with its collection of Goddard material, and both Weymouth and Dorchester Reference Libraries for extensive use of their reading and print-out facilities of microfilms of old local newspapers; Dorset History Centre, Dorchester, for permission to publish material held in Weymouth Reference Library; the Friends of Weymouth Library for allowing me to give an illustrated talk on John Goddard in February 2003; Richard Samways, archivist of Weymouth Museum; Betty Cornick, 'Dick' Noakes, and Audrey Judge for their reminiscences of John Goddard, particularly the latter for her permission for use of a VE-Day street party photograph; Sandwell Community History & Archive Service at Smethwick Library, Smethwick, West Midlands for information and photographs of late 19th century Wednesbury, and permission to publish; Dr. Stephen Bull, curator of The Museum of Lancashire, Preston, Lancashire, for details of John Goddard's army career in, and history of the 14th (King's) Hussars, and permission to publish; Patrick Dwyer of 'Hussars Research'; the Aldershot Military Museum; Aldershot Public Library; F. David Scadden of the Honorary Court Highclere of the Ancient Order of Foresters Friendly Society, Weymouth; Mr Dunford of Weymouth Drama Club; Peter Marks, Curator, Dorset Masonic Museum; Diane Clements, Director, The Library and Museum of Freemasonry, London; Robbie Feltham, Past-Chairman Weymouth Licensed Victuallers Association; Kelly Chambers of Rushmoor Borough Council's Crematorium & Cemeteries; Weymouth Crematorium for allowing me to look through their Books of Remembrance; Sidney Farmer for some back copies of Black Country newspapers; Steve Johnson, *Birmingham Evening Mail*; the *Dorset Echo* for its frequent publicity, etc. in recent years about John Goddard, and to David Murdock the Editor for permission to publish contemporary articles from its predecessor the *Dorset Daily Echo*. There are inevitably other people and institutions who have assisted in some way, and my apologies to those inadvertently omitted.

Finally, I must profusely thank my wife, Iris, for her forbearance for those times I have been away from home researching, or in my study compiling the manuscript. Also my thanks for taking my photograph for the back cover.

Many illustrations and photographs have been obtained through kind individuals, various archives and libraries, and the Internet. Unfortunately it has only been possible to reproduce a fraction of them.

Responsibility for content and publication is solely my own, and is being undertaken at my own expense, with no expectation of financial gain.

August 2007   Ronald D. Knight
                                                         Weymouth

INTRODUCTION

From his humble beginnings in the late 19th century slums and squalor of Wednesbury, in the aptly named Black Country, John Goddard rose to what could be justly considered the appropriate top of his chosen career in the army - Regimental Sergeant Major of a prestigious cavalry regiment. In the vast open spaces of South Africa in the Boer War, and similarly later of Mesopotamoia and Persia in the Great War, he would have shared the dangers and privations of his fellow hussars. With perhaps a more conducive family background, coupled with his obvious natural drive in his chosen profession, he might even have achieved officer status. Such promotion from the ranks has been quite possible, especially during wartime.

His peaceful retirement as a publican in Weymouth, and then a town councillor, was shattered with the coming of World War Two in 1939. By then he was Weymouth's first citizen, the Mayor, and was to be continuously chosen to lead and encourage the townspeople all through that almost six-year conflict.

Like many others he suffered from having his home bombed, being lucky not to have been killed. But with his resilience and determination he was soon again at the head of the town's war efforts. This received due recognition from Buckingham Palace with the award of an O.B.E. With the eventual successful ending of the war he could gracefully step down from his arduous task. A grateful Weymouth rewarded him with its highest accolade, to become a Freeman of the Borough. But fate - in the form of 'the grim reaper' - was to deny him the pleasure and honour of physically receiving his reward. It was sadly devolved on his faithful widow to accept on his behalf.

By 2001 there were hardly any memorials to him around Weymouth, with not many people realising their significance - including the author. Whilst most Weymouth locations associated with John Goddard remain, there is not a lot now at Wednesbury due to wholesale redevelopment. To see Wednesbury as it was one has to peruse the photographic collection at Smethwick Public Library, or purchase old picture postcards, and books of collections of them. It was in an endeavour to remedy these defects of knowledge and remembrance that widespread research into his life was quickly undertaken. Eventually it was realised that only some form of publication could adequately do justice as a lasting memorial to John Goddard's personality and achievements.

There must inevitably be plenty of untapped primary source material not researched. The records of Weymouth Town Council are an example. But as much of John Goddard's political career had been chronicled in the local Press during his lifetime, it was considered of no great exclusion not to have methodically gone through a myriad of Council minutes, etc.

As has already been noted, a possible useful source has been denied us by the apparent loss by the M.O.D. of his Service records.

No apologies are made for what may appear to be over-fulsome newspaper and other published extracts. For these not only contain episodes in the life of the subject, and equally of immediate life and events around him, but also show examples of his own thoughts and utterances - as well as what others close to him thought of him. As it is inevitable that further information could be forthcoming, including hopefully his missing armed service record, no claim can therefore be made for this to be a definitive biography.

So although this may possibly be the nearest there will be for a biography of John Goddard, at least for some time, at least it is more than just a bare bones chronology of dates and events. Something of the character of the man is displayed. In fact it shows that he *was* a 'character', and it is hoped it has been able to do him justice. This hope is extended to include his loyal wife Hilda, who appears to have lived to a certain extent in his shadow, but was apparently still able to be her own person.

THE EARLY YEARS

1879

John Thomas Goddard was born on Thursday, 28th August 1879, at the family home of 12 Dudley Street, Wednesbury, Staffordshire. According to a *Certified Copy Of An Entry Of Birth* his parents were William Goddard, a Railway Labourer, and Catherine. She was not to register the birth until 23rd September, and signed with an 'X'. According to Census records, William Goddard had been born about 1837, at Hounslow, Surrey [sic]. Catherine's *Birth Certificate* shows she had been born 15th July 1846, at 8 Gas Street, Leamington, Warwickshire, being the daughter of William Clark (Saddler) and Fanny (née Clayton), with the latter also signing with an 'X'. Royal Leamington Spa is some 30 miles south-east of Wednesbury. William Goddard (when a Porter, aged 27), and Catherine (Servant, aged 21) had been married by banns at St. Peter's Church, Coventry, on 21st July 1867, with both shown on the Marriage Certificate as living at Paynes Lane, Coventry, and again Catherine signing the Register with an 'X'. William Goddard senior was shown as a Labourer. Witnesses were: John Boddington and Sophie Boddington ('X').

Dudley Street in Wednesbury at that time was close to two sets of railway tracks, with their sidings, and passenger and goods stations. William Goddard would thus have had no difficulty in finding employment in what was then a labour-intensive industry.

Wednesbury (locally pronounced 'Wensbury') had grown up around a hill, some eight miles north-west of Birmingham. There may well have been a village on the hill over 2,000 years ago. The 'bury' part of the name means fort, suggesting there was a defended settlement on the hilltop in the Iron Age. Little is known about Wednesbury in the Roman period. The 'Wednes' part of the name refers to the pagan Anglo-Saxon's god Woden, and who called the place 'Weadesbury' (or Wodensborough).

Wednesbury in medieval times was a rural village consisting of a church (St. Bartholomew), manor house, and a cluster of dwellings, surrounded by strip-cultivated fields, and beyond them heathland used for grazing animals. Wednesbury's industrial development began in the Middle Ages (c.1315), when coal and iron were mined, and later clay for pottery. Metal objects and textiles were also made. In the 17th century, pottery made in Wednesbury ('Wedgbury ware') was being widely sold in the Midlands, but this was to be eclipsed by the Stoke-on-Trent potteries. Local white clay was also used to make tobacco pipes. Limestone was worked, leaving several uncharted subterranean caverns liable to collapse. By the 18th century the main occupations were coal mining and nailmaking.

But the largely still rural aspect of Wednesbury remained until the great canal to Birmingham was dug out in 1768. The construction of canals led to a drastic reduction in the price of Wednesbury coal for nearby Birmingham's growing industries. Local coal mines yielded a superior kind of coal, which from its great heat was very suitable for the forges. It was, however, prone to spontaneous combustion, with consequently some ground in the town smoking and fuming from underground fires, and even causing resultant ground collapses.

In its own way Wednesbury was to be part of the 19th century Industrial Revolution. Coal mining and iron production in Wednesbury declined somewhat in the 1860's and 1870's, but metal manufacturing industries increased. Edge tools, mainly large hand tools, were being made from 1817; and from 1838 axles, wheels, rails and boiler plates for the rapidly growing railway network. Then from 1854 Wednesbury itself was to be served by three railway companies, each with its own station. Tube making - particularly gun barrels - was also important throughout the 19th century, and gave Wednesbury the name of 'Tube Town'. The town's innumerable tall chimneys belching out noxious smoke helped it to become part of the justly named 'Black Country'.

Whether the living conditions of the working classes in Wednesbury at the time of John Goddard's childhood were in anyway similar to those deplorable ones portrayed so graphically in the *Royal Commission on the Employment of Children* 1847, the author is not competent to comment. However, it may be noted that purely on the mode of dress of the women and children as depicted in contemporary photographs, matters seem to have improved somewhat in the intervening 30-40 years - though not necessarily in the way of housing accommodation.

There was a market on Fridays, open from 5 a.m. to 8 p.m., and on Saturdays from 6 a.m. to 11 p.m.; and fairs on 6th May and 3rd August for cattle. This original market town, before it was to become eventually absorbed in the massive conurbation of Birmingham, was to grow from a population of 4,160 in 1801 to 11,625 in 1841; 14,281 in 1851; 21,968 in 1861; 25,030 in 1871; 24,566 in 1881; 25,347 in 1891; and to 26,554 in 1901. The rapid population growth during the 19th century generated overcrowded slums, as photographs show. Two new ecclesiastical parishes were formed in 1844, St. James and St. John, with St James church being built in 1847/8.

The then main road which still runs through the town, Holyhead Road, was a section of the famous 'Parliament' coaching route laid out by Thomas Telford in the 1820's. Even up to 1900 fields still came in quite close to the town.

1881

A transcription of the 1881 Census, taken on Sunday, 3rd April, gives details of the Goddard household at the time as:

Address: 26 Great Western Street, Wednesbury, Staffordshire

	Married	Age	Sex	Birthplace
William Goddard	Head M	43	M	Hounslow, Surrey
				Fitter [...] (Railway Trackman)
Catherine Goddard	Wife M	35	F	Leamington, Warwickshire
William Goddard	Son	15	M	Leamington, Warwickshire
				Labourer in Ironwork
Frances Louise Goddard	Dau	10	F	Birmingham, Warwickshire
				Scholar
Henry Goddard	Son	8	M	Reading, Berkshire Scholar
Moses Goddard	Son	5	M	Reading, Berkshire
John Goddard	Son	1	M	Wednesbury, Stafforshire

This shows that within two years the family had moved to a different street, though in the same immediate location.

Frances had been born on 6th December 1870 at Wharf Street, Birmingham, but with her second name registered as Louisa, and father as a Railway Servant; Henry, born 6th February 1873 at 53 Hosier Street, Reading, Berkshire, was registered by his mother as "Harry", and father a Railway Truck Fitter; Moses, born on 7th November 1875 at 7 Coley Street, Reading, (was to be known as "MOSS"), with father shown as Railway Waggon Fitter, and mother Catherine still signing with an 'X'.

John Goddard was to be known as "DID" by family and grandchildren, but why is not known. The earlier Goddard ancestry, and circumstances for the move from Hounslow to Leamington, Birmingham, Reading, and eventually Wednesbury have not been determined - though there were other recorded Goddards in the Wednesbury area.

A further son, Charles, was to be born at 26 Great Western Street, Wednesbury, on 14th October this year, with father William now shown as a 'Railway Labourer', and mother signing with an 'X'.

1884

On 30th November yet another son was to be born to the Goddards, Frederick. This birth was at a further new family home of 4 St. James Street, with father

William now shown as a 'Road Labourer'. The mother, Catherine, was still responsible for registering the births, this time some six weeks after the event, and signing with an 'X'. St. James Street was only a stone's throw away from Great Western Street, just the other side of Dudley Street. Were these moves to larger premises to accommodate the increasing family?

John's fifth birthday had been in the August, so it could be expected that he started school at about the same time. It can be assumed that he would have attended the one in St. James Street. The contemporary *Diary* or *Log Book* for the St. James's Boy's School survives, currently kept at Sandwell Community History & Archive Service at Smethwick. The school had re-opened in July 1884 as a Boys' and Girls' School, having previously been just for girls. There were some 200 pupils, rising to about 250. Although it was noted in the School *Log Book* when new pupils joined, unfortunately names were not given. Names were only given for unusual occurrences and punishments, and John's does not appear for any reason.

Subjects apparently taught were Reading, Writing, Arithmetic, Geography, and Religious Knowledge. Her Majesty's School Inspectors and Diocesan Inspectors, plus the rector, made regular respective visits and reports, which were generally 'Good' to 'Excellent'. The Rev. John Hopkins had become rector of St. James sometime during 1884.

Around the middle of May several boys had been absent owing to the prevalence of measles. On 7th November it was noted: 'Several of them owing to breakings out in the head have been obliged to keep their hats on.' Would this have been ringworm? There were many absences during December because of sickness.

1885

Early in the year 'A disease of the eye which is catching' caused several school absences. In March two boys were imprisoned by magistrates for a day, and received five lashes, for stealing money from a shop.

Absences from school could be for many other reasons: Funerals, inclement weather, annual fairs, parish and Sunday School excursions, Parliamentary and other elections, unveiling of the statue of a prominent citizen, the Wednesbury Flower Show, a travelling circus. However, on one occasion a boy pupil was fined five shillings by the magistrates, plus costs, for continued absence.

Every morning during Lent the pupils went across the road to St. James' church; and of course on other church festival days, when the afternoons could be half-day holidays.

1887

On 21st June was Queen Victoria's 50th 'Jubilee Day' holiday. After being given commemorative medals at school, Wednesbury pupils were all marched to the New Park, where the Mayor declared it 'open'. After singing the National Anthem they were all then marched to a field at Wood Green for buns and tea, with festivities lasting until 6·30 p.m.

Also about this period, in Dudley Street and Holyhead Road, there was some trench digging for the laying of a deep sewer. This apparently reached down into a coal seam, showing how relatively near the surface was coal in the area. Photographs were taken at the time of local residents in the act of coal-picking. It may well be that one or more of the children photographed could have been Goddards.

1888

On Sunday, 23rd December, John Goddard's elder sister Frances married George Coombes at Moxley, Staffordshire. Their ages were given as 20 and 21 respectively. The father of George was Henry Coombes. Moxley is at the northern end of Holyhead Road, about a mile from the area of the various Goddard residences.

1890

In June the Upper Standard boys at St. James' School started going to the Wednesbury Public Baths on one afternoon a week during the summer season. There was a school football team which entered the Wednesbury & District Football Challenge Shield, which they were to win one year. Whether any Goddard boys played is not known.

1891

The winter of 1890/1891 was to be one of the most severe of the century, which doubtless hit hard the poorest sections of the community.

The 1891 Census, taken on Sunday, 5th April, takes one a further ten years along the life-story and composition of the Goddard family. It had moved yet again, this time back to Dudley Street, Wednesbury, where they had been in 1879, but this time at number 22.

		Age	Birthplace	Occupation
William Goddard	Head	53	Surrey, Hounslow	General Work
Catherine Goddard	Wife	46	Warwickshire, Leamington	
William Goddard	Son	25	Warwickshire, Leamington	Ironworks Labourer
Henry Goddard	Son	18	Berkshire, Reading	Ironworks Labourer
Moses Goddard	Son	15	Berkshire, Reading	Ironworks Labourer
John Goddard	Son	11	Staffordshire, Wednesbury	Scholar
Charles Goddard	Son	8	Staffordshire, Wednesbury	Scholar
Frederick Goddard	Son	6	Staffordshire, Wednesbury	Scholar

Since the 1881 Census two further children (sons) had been born; and unsurprisingly the only daughter, Frances, had now left home on marriage. For some unknown reason the eldest son, William, aged 25, is shown at home although the 1901 Census appears to show that he was apparently married by 1881 with family. All this may mean that the move was again due to the increasing number of family members. Also, since 1881 William senior seems to have changed to more menial employment. Neighbours in the street were similarly employed by the ironworks and railway.

1893

As John Goddard had been born in August 1879, he would have thus become 14-years' old this year, and left school for some as yet unknown employment.

1894

In July, Standard 6 and 7 boys at St. James School started to attend the Technical School for two half-days a week.

1895

From the beginning of February free breakfasts were given to the poorest children while the severe weather lasted. About forty school pupils were so treated for at least a week. Would the remaining Goddard boys still at school have qualified?

1896

Both Goddard parents were to die before their expected time. Catherine was to be the first, on Tuesday, 19th May, at 42 Foster Street, Wednesbury, aged 51. The cause of death was stated on a *Certified Copy of an Entry of Death* to be 'Tubercular Disease of Heart. Ascites'. Her daughter, Frances Coombs of 1 Court, St. James Street, Wednesbury, was present at and registered the death. Catherine was to be buried on 23rd May, in the Wednesbury Cemetery in Wood Green Road. There had been yet another change of the family's address.

William senior died only a few weeks later, on Saturday, 20th June 1896, aged 60, at the same address as his wife. He died of 'Pneumonia. Syncope', with his occupation now being stated as 'A Chemical Works Labourer'. Again, daughter Frances was present at and registered the death. William was also to be buried at the Wood Green Road Cemetery, on 27th June, apparently in the same grave as his wife, which is now unmarked and unlocatable. According to a correspondent to the *Black Country Bugle* in January 1990, regarding a funeral of that period, it cost three guineas (£3. 3s. 0d) - about three weeks' wages.

There were seemingly three relatively young orphans now still living at home - John aged 16, Charles 13, and Frederick 11, with the latter two presumably still attending school.

It is not surprising that both parents died when they did. According to a contemporary map the family's various homes in Wednesbury were all in fairly close proximity to, and surrounded by a combination of coal-burning railway steam locomotives; foundries; iron, tube, and brass works; a smithy; a shaft, axletree and wheel works; a gas, steam, and water cock manufactory; cylinder and coil works; and an unspecified engineering works. Contemporary illustrations show that these works had tall chimneys pouring out a doubtless mixture of noxious smoke and fumes - for it was part of the aptly named 'Black Country'. Health and Safety was not a major concern at that time, as it was to be a century later. Being latterly a 'Chemical Works Labourer' would doubtless have brought William Goddard's life also to an inevitable premature end.

The 1901 Census appears to throw some light on the future of the suddenly bereft Goddard siblings. Frances and William junior appear to be living next door to one another in Leabrook Road, which is a continuation south-westwards of Dudley Street. At No. 6 is a George Coombs, age 32, a General Labourer, born in Birmingham, his 30-year old wife [Frances] Louisa, and six children, the eldest aged 11; plus Frances's brothers Moses, Charles and Frederick, all General Labourers. Whilst at No. 7 is William, aged 34, born at Leamington; with his wife Emma(?), also aged 34; plus five children, the eldest aged 14.

THE BOER WAR

c.1898

John Goddard is believed by the family to have joined the 14th (King's) Hussars in 1898, when he was aged 19 years. But without his official Service Record being available for verification this is not certain, though Goddard's later comments seem to substantiate this.

What John's previous employment was is not known, and why the army as an ultimate career can only be conjecture. And why it was this particular regiment is again not known, especially as the 14th's main recruiting area was apparently the south of England. Although there were only horse-drawn vehicles about at the time, there would not probably have been much available horse-riding in Wednesbury to have persuaded him to join a cavalry regiment. However, there was a well-known local town personality, Alderman, J. A. Kilvert, who had joined the 11th Hussars when aged 17, and had been at Balaclava during the Crimean War (1854/1856). Then in 1893 there had been the erection of a Drill Hall in Bridge Street, Wednesbury, where the local Volunteers in their resplendent uniforms could further fire the imagination of the town's boys and young men. It has been suggested that a certain percentage of recruits would have been drafted into the cavalry, with or without any knowledge of horsemanship.

The premature death of his parents a couple of years or so previously may have also been a contributory reason for enlisting. It has been said (*A Handbook of the Boer War*) that 'an existing or prospective War always keeps the recruiting sergeant busy, but the object of a War is a matter of indifference to the recruit.' In the Sudan, Lord Kitchener was leading an expeditionary force against the self-elected Messiahs - the Mahdi and Khalifa. During this campaign the battle of Omdurman was the first in which the cavalry fought in the new dress of khaki drill. The blue of the lancers, and the scarlet of the dragoons were never again to be seen in action, though still to be worn on special or ceremonial occasions.

Whatever the reason, young John Goddard must presumably have been in a fit enough condition to have been accepted into this prestigious regiment. And moving away from heavy-industrial Wednesbury must have given him a new lease of physical life.

The 14th Hussars had originally been raised in the Midlands in 1715, at the time of the Jacobite Rebellion, under the name of Dormer's Dragoons. Dragoons were mounted infantry. The regiment was to have a somewhat chequered history. In 1776 it was renamed the 14th Light Dragoons; in 1796 the Duchess of York's Own Light Dragoons; in 1830 the 14th King's Light Dragoons; and finally in 1861 the 14th (King's) Hussars. Hussar was a 15th century Hungarian word meaning 'one in twenty', and related to the conscription then of one man in twenty from every village. The regiment was to be engaged in the Peninsular War against Napoleon, and in India during the Mutiny. The uniform towards the end of the nineteenth century was a blue Atilla tunic with gold looped frogging, red facings, gold piping, buttons, epaulettes, pointed cuffs with gold lace Austrian knots, short white gloves, gold shoulder sash with red central stripe (left-to-right), blue pants with white stripes, black kolpack (short hussar busby) with white plume, a yellow bag on the right side, black ankle boots.

Three Squadrons of the Regiment ('A', 'B', 'D') and H.Q. at this time were stationed in cavalry barracks at Newbridge in Ireland, plus Squadron 'C' at the nearby Curragh Camp, with a total strength of some 23 officers and 591 other ranks. According to the experiences of a non-cavalry recruit (W.H.Price) in 1914, and which may possibly be unchanged from the late 1890s:

'So eventually off we went to catch the night mail train Euston to Holyhead. . . We embarked on the mail boat about 4.00 p.m., the sea being very choppy and rough. There being many cavaliers aboard and there being no seats available i settled down on the deck and went to sleep. . . [Arriving at Dublin] We found we were bound for Curragh Camp, near Dublin and entrained for the nearest station (Newbridge). From Newbridge we marched three miles to Curragh . . . In those days the Curragh was mainly a large Cavalry Camp with a few battalions of infantry. We were soon fitted out with uniforms, etc.,
'Through the cold and wet winter months we soldiered on. The Curragh Camp being on high ground was very exposed and we felt the full force of the many winter gales, but our food was very good and varied.'

The small market town of Newbridge is some 25 miles south-west of Dublin, being a garrison town during the British occupation. It had grown since the building of extensive cavalry barracks in 1816. These spacious barracks consisted of two parallel ranges of buildings, connected by a central range at right angles; and were capable of accommodating two regiments, with officers' apartments, a hospital and married quarters. Just south-west of Newbridge is The Curragh, a fine undulating down, six miles long and two miles broad, lying in a direction from north-east to south-west. It is in fact an extensive sheep-walk of above 6,000 acres

'forming a more beautiful lawn than the hand of art ever made. Nothing can exceed the extreme softness and elasticity of the turf, which is of a verdure that charms the eye, and is still set off by the gentle inequality of the surface: . . . The place has long been celebrated as the principal race-ground in Ireland',

and it would thus seem an ideal place for cavalry training.

A usual term of army engagement would be seven years with the colours and five years in the reserve, with an option to extend as appropriate. Some may have gone the whole way and signed-on for 21 years. Which choice John Goddard made is unfortunately not known. According to the service record of a London recruit in the 14th Hussars who enlisted some ten years previously, John Goddard would have apparently been immediately vaccinated - a practice which would continue. After two years service good conduct there could have been a grant of a penny added to the shilling a day.

Because of his relative lack of education John Goddard is said by the descendant family to have attended night school whilst in the army. Even after the passing of Foster's Education Act in 1870 many army recruits remained illiterate, and from 1871 attendance in Army schools was compulsory for all new recruits. Apparently there were four levels of Army Education Certificates, the lowest (4th class) involved just reading and simple arithmetic. From 1889 the possession of 2nd and 1st class certificates were among the requirements for promotion to corporal and sergeant respectively. In the *Historical Record* of the regiment mention was often made of the many Certificates of Education achieved by men of the 14th Hussars.

As a lowly Private, John naturally had to clean out the horses. According to a descendant family member he was apparently once caught-out taking apples from an officer's horse called 'Beauty', and presumably being suitably punished.

The cavalry rank of Private Gentleman, Private Man or plain Private had been in use for nearly three centuries, but was not to be officially redesignated Trooper until 1924. However, Privates in the cavalry had prior to this date been known unofficially as Troopers for many years.

1899

At the outbreak of the Second Boer War in South Africa in early October, the Regiment was mobilised, with strength now up to a total of 687 officers and men. Embarkation could not take place, however, until a serious outbreak of influenza and 'pink-eye' amongst the horses had been overcome. The Regiment was thus not able to be inspected until Thursday, 26th October at Newbridge by Field-Marshal Lord Roberts, Commander-in-Chief in Ireland. He was soon to be appointed - at the age of 67 - as Supreme Commander in South Africa, following several setbacks there. The Regiment for this occasion was in service marching-order, ready for active service, all dressed in khaki uniform. Eventually three service Squadrons of the Regiment ('A', 'B', 'C') and H.Q., of 585 officers and men were able to leave Newbridge on Thursday, 16th November, leaving their horses behind - with a reserve Depôt Squadron being left at the Curragh Camp. Private John Goddard is believed to have spent just over a year in Ireland, according to a cooment in the *Dorset Daily Echo* of 21st November 1931.

After travelling by steamer and train they arrived on the 17th at the West Cavalry Barracks, Aldershot, where they were provided with fresh horses.

Aldershot's three cavalry barracks housed a brigade of three horsed cavalry regiments. West Barracks (to be renamed Willems Barracks in 1909) consisted of four two-storey troop stables, officers' and sergeants' messes, a riding school, plus a guardroom and cells. The spot has since been redeveloped into a Tesco supermarket and Travel Inn complex, and housing. However, the original gateway still survives the 1964 demolition, facing the A325 Farnborough Road roundabout. Presumably the Regiment now started to take well-earned leave.

Aldershot (originally spelt Aldershott in a *Hampshire Gazetteer and Directory* of 1859) was originally just a village with some 875 inhabitants. But in 1854 a large tract of land northwards was bought by the government, and an extensive military camp started to be built. North Camp was mainly of long ranges of wooden huts, but South Camp consisted of Cavalry, Infantry, and Artillery Barracks, a Riding School, etc. Resulting from an influx of civilian support and entrepreneurial facilities such as shops, trades, and public houses, Aldershot's population soon rose to 3,000 by 1858 - exclusive of an average of 7-8,000 military personnel.

Every minute of the day was strictly organised, with different bugle calls detailing each part of the routine. Aldershot Military Museum has a copy of a 'Cavalry Soldier's Routine 1898':

06·00 hrs Reveille (wake up).
            Night Guard Dismissed (night guard look after stables).
06·15 hrs 'Dress' sounded - men go to Stables.
            Roll call at stables. Remove litter from stall.
            Horses taken to water.
07·30 hrs 'Stables' sounded. Inspection by orderly troop sergeant, and Officer of
            the Day. Horses fed, and Bedding weighed out by Quartermaster and
            drawn from store.
07·45 hrs 'Feed' sounded. Each horse is fed three feeds of corn per day, and three
            feeds of hay.

08·00 hrs 'Dismiss' sounded. Then 'Breakfast up'. Breakfast taken - Tea and
            bread in barrack rooms.
08·15 hrs 'Dress' sounded. Recruits prepare for riding school. Other men
            exercise horses, and undertake other duties.

08·30 hrs 'Fall in' sounded for riding school. Riding school exercise for two
       hours. Other men take out horses for exercise for two hours.
11·00 hrs 'Orderly Room' sounded. Guard turns out.
11·15 hrs 'Stables' sounded. Men work until 13·00 hrs.
12·45 hrs 'Feed' sounded. Horses fed.
13·00 hrs 'Dinner' sounded. Men eat dinner in barrack rooms.
14·00 hrs 'Dress' sounded.
14·25 hrs 'Fall in' sounded for foot parade for recruits.
14·30 hrs 'General parade' sounded. Regiment on parade. Dismounted foot and
       weapons drill practised until 15·45 hrs.
14·45 hrs 'Dress for guard' sounded.
15·00 hrs Day Guard Dismissed/New Day Guard Mounted (look after main
       gate).
15·45 hrs School lessons and fencing classes.
17·00 hrs 'Tea' sounded. Men eat tea in barrack rooms.
17·15 hrs 'Dress' sounded. Men prepare for stables.
17·30 hrs 'Stables' sounded for last time.
18·00 hrs 'Dress for Guard' sounded.
18·15 hrs 'Feed' sounded. Horses fed. Night Guard posted.
18·30 hrs 'Dismiss' sounded. Men free to leave barracks or go to the canteen.
       Most men will spend at least two hours in the evening cleaning arms
       and accoutrements in preparation for work the following day.
21·15 hrs 'First post' sounded.
21·30 hrs 'Last post' sounded. Canteen closes. Men return to their barrack rooms.
22.00 hrs Orderly sergeants check all men are in rooms, and report absences to
       the guardroom. Main gate locked.
22·15 hrs 'Lights out' sounded.

'A' and 'C' Squadrons and H.Q. travelled in four trains to Southampton, embarking and sailing on the s.s. *Victorian* on Wednesday, 13th December, in cold and snow conditions. The *Victorian* of 12,000 tons belonged to the Allan Line, which normally plied between the U.K. and Canada. (Private) John Goddard was seemingly in 'B' Squadron, which left Aldershot on the 19th and sailed on the 21st, in the s.s. *Cestrian*, and was to experience very rough weather during the voyage. This ship of 8,823 registered tons, had been built in 1896, and to be owned by F.Leyland & Co. (1900) Ltd. According to *The Times* of 22nd December 1899, the 14th Hussars contingent on board were 165 men and 161 horses, with a captain, two lieutenants and two 2nd-lieutenants. There were also the Royal Horse Artillery and several other small units. The ship arrived at Las Palmas on 27th December.

Letters home from Imperial Yeomanry troopers listed the daily routine on board during the three week journey of a cavalry troopship. This consisted of kit inspections, church parades, stable duties, games, lifeboat drill and meals. The hammocks were a source of much trouble, as two separate home-letters testified:

"We sleep in hammocks slung up as close together as we can get them, 200 in one mess, and I can tell you it gets pretty hot."

"There was great fun when the hammocks were introduced, many of us slept on the floor."

Apparently on one of the ships carrying the 14th Hussars there was complaint of the poor fare (tinned meat and Dutch cheese) provided for them. On shore for half an hour at Las Palmas, however, they were able to buy oranges at 50 for a shilling.

It is not the purpose in this biography to either discuss the pros and cons of the Boer War, or cover the whole campaign, but only to chronicle as far as can be ascertained something of John Goddard's participation in it. There are already plenty of books covering that whole particular topic, some of which have been included in the BIBLIOGRAPHY.

1900

'A' and 'C' Squadrons arrived at Cape Town in South Africa on 1st January, and then going on to Durban. 'B' Squadron eventually reached Cape Town on Wednesday, 10th January, and then travelled by rail to arrive at De Aar on the 18th, said to be the most dusty spot in the whole of the country. This was of course the Southern Hemishpere summer period. Here there was to be great difficulty in watering horses. The Squadron whilst here was engaged on occasional reconnaissances and escorts. They then marched on horseback to the Orange River ("dusty" and where the temperature around the previous Christmas was "105 degrees in the shade"), and arriving at Zoutpans Drift on 4th February to join the 1st Cavalry Brigade, as part of the Cavalry Division commanded by Major-General French. The rest of the Regiment initially served under General Sir R. H. Buller. The 14th Hussars as a whole were continuously to be actively involved in both large and small scale skirmishes, as well as being involved in the later guerilla phase of the conflict.

Queen Victoria had initiated a scheme for her troops in South Africa, that for Christmas each man there should receive a tin box of chocolates. Thus 100,000 tins were ordered. The rectangular boxes measured some 6 inches by 3½ inches, and 1 inch deep. The hinged lid had a red background with a gilt medallion in the centre bearing the Queen's head. On the left-hand side of the lid was the Royal and Imperial monogram **VRI** surmounted by the Crown in gilt, blue and white. On the right-hand side were the words **SOUTH AFRICA 1900**. Along the bottom of the lid, in facsimile of the Queen's handwriting, were the words *I wish you a happy New Year. Victoria R.I.* The chocolate boxes had been designed by Barclay & Fry Ltd, and manufactured by Barringer, Wallis & Manners Ltd. The chocolate was supplied by J.S.Fry and Sons (40,000 boxes), Rowntree's (40,000) and Cadbury's (20,000 boxes). The chocolate was made in blocks 3 inches square, being sub-divided into three 1-inch wide pieces. Four such blocks were wrapped in silver paper, and packed in each of the greaseproof paper-lined tins. It was the Queen's express wish that only her soldiers should have these tins, and orders were consequently given for the destruction of the dies once the required number had been manufactured. The Queen's chocolate reached South Africa about mid-January, and issue started almost immediately.

Thus on 9th February, this Queen's chocolate was issued to all ranks of 'B' Squadron before they moved off the same day to take part in the relief of Kimberley. Some tins issued during the campaign were sent home unopened to their families by the recipients, or the tins themselves kept as precious souvenirs. Such tins regularly come up for sale or auction on the Internet, but the author's acquired item is unfortunately not a good specimen.

After taking part in several engagements, during which a patrol fired 'B' Squadron's first shots in an encounter with the enemy Boer, the members of the Squadron were apparently the first troops to reach and relieve beseiged Kimberley on the 15th February. There followed 'B' Squadron's involvement in the engagement, 10-day siege of (partly in very bad weather), and subsequent capture of a Boer army at Paardeberg (a prominent hill) on the 27th February. Meanwhile, the other Squadrons of the 14th Hussars were to earn the Regiment the Battle Honour of 'Relief of Ladysmith' for their part in that operation on 28th February. Ladysmith was a garrison town inside British territory, having been under siege for 118 days. To the British public these two victories heralded what was mistakenly considered the end of the war, but to the Boers it was now only just about to begin.

There was continuous heavy rain, but also a shortage on both sides of clean drinking water, and food, though British half rations could now be increased to three-quarters rations. Further reconnaissance and engagements resulted in the 14th Hussars being involved in the capture/surrender of Bloemfontein on 13th March. According to the South African Field Force *Return of Troops Marching into Bloemfontein on its Surrender, 13th March 1900*, the 14th Hussars detachment consisted of seven officers, 108 other ranks, and 74 horses.

This defeat by the Boers was to usher in their guerilla, or second period, of the war.

As well as short rations for the cavalry horses, and the troops being in a tattered, hungry and exhausted condition, there was also a shortage of medical staff and supplies. The latter deficiency was important because of increasing dysentry, fever and disease amongst the soldiers. Only a third of the exhausted horses were still in commission. It was opined in *A Handbook of the Boer War* that 'horse casualties, due to want of water, forced marches, and ignorance of horsemastership on the part of all ranks, who were inclined to regard cavalry work in the light of a steeplechase, were so heavy . . .' The latter accusation could not surely be laid at the door of the 14th Hussars.

As an illustration of conditions at the time, *The Graphic* newspaper of 13th October 1900 carried a drawing by its special artist, C. E. Fripp R.W.S., signed and dated "Sept 1900". This depicted a dead horse being dragged from out of a river, with its disconsolate kit-laden rider looking-on. The cavalry regiment concerned was diplomatically not mentioned. The legend beneath read:

'Many a starved animal, weak from over work, is ridden by an 'absent-minded beggar' into the muddy dam to drink. The sticky mud holds the poor beast with a tenacity with which it cannot in its exhausted condition cope. In its struggles to escape it falls, and then it is usually done for. If not left to expire of suffocation and pollute the dam - usually the case on the march - it is hauled to the bank as shown in my sketch, the trooper meanwhile cursing his luck at having got his kit wet and having to foot it until a remount is found somewhere.'

Back in England, at Wednesbury, there were meetings of support, and funds were started for families, and sick and wounded soldiers of local Regiments, Reservists and Volunteers. Schoolgirls knitted socks, and other presents were sent out to South Africa. With letters later being sent home confirming the bad conditions experienced by their writers, parcels of clothing and food were to be sent out, plus tobacco which was often used as currency. These parcels did not always arrive, or were greatly delayed.

Whether such support was given to Wednesbury regular soldiers scattered amongst non-local Regiments is not known, but they were to need it as much as the newly enlisted men. It would be interesting to learn whether John Goddard wrote to any of his siblings at Tipton; and whether they were in any financial position to send him anything.

In a letter sent home by one local soldier, possibly in the December, he wrote:

"They [the Boers] dread the cavalry with lances, they run for miles. They don't like cold steel."

Presumably they would have been equally scared of the sword-brandishing Hussars.

At Bloemfontein on the 27th March the Cavalry Brigade took part in the ceremonial visit by His Excellency Sir Alfred Milner, the Governor and Commander-in Chief of the Cape of Good Hope and its Dependencies, and who was also High Commissioner for South Africa. 'B' Squadron provided an escort for him. This was followed on the 30th by the Squadron attending the funeral of a previous 14th Hussars commanding officer, Colonel the Hon. G. H. Gough, who at the time was on the staff at Bloemfontein. On 14th April the whole Regiment met up together again at Donkershoek, 8 miles north of Bloemfontein, as part of the 4th Cavalry Division, under the now Lieutenant-General French. The 14th Hussars was detached for a while as escort to Field Marshal Lord Roberts, Commander of the British Army in South Africa. The 14th were also on burial duties, resulting from bad drinking water.

On 18th April, the horses of the Brigade were out grazing, with not all of them being hobbled. It was then that the whole Regiment of the 17th Lancers, who were not part of the 4th Brigade, came galloping through the grazing area on exercise. In consequence, many of the tethered horses being utterly scared stampeded and galloped off towards Bloemfontein. It took several days to collect them again, with some never being recovered. The 14th Hussars lost about 53 horses, and were thus understrength for the relief of Wepener which was completed on 25th April, during which the cavalry passed through a swarm of locusts. During prior and subsequent engagements there were casualties to men and horses, including from insanitary conditions at times, the cold weather with the onset of the Southern Hemisphere winter, and lack or loss of supplies.

In the same Squadron as John Goddard was Corporal John Spring, who had joined the Hussars in 1888, some ten years before Goddard. At the hotly contested action at Roodekop on 24th April, the 14th Hussars had to dismount and run up a hill, just beating the Boers doing the same. 'B' Squadron immediately came under heavy enemy fire for twenty minutes, and Corporal Spring became one of several casualties when he was shot through both legs. Corporal John Goddard helped to carry him from the field. Spring was invalided home, but was later to return to the Regiment as saddler sergeant-major, and discharged in 1910. These two hussars were later to meet up again in 1925 following Goddard's own discharge.

Here in 1900, after only two or three years, John Goddard's ability had thus already well placed him on the promotion ladder, having obviously attained the requisite Education Certificate. Until 1910 the 14th Hussars was to be the only Regiment to have German silver eagle arm badges authorised for Corporals. These were of white metal, oval, 43·0 mm high, 35·6 mm wide, with a hachured raised rim, loops NS 34mm.

After several more engagements the 14th Hussars were to be part of the Cavalry Division which left the area of Bloemfontein on 7th May in the direction of Kroonstad, which was reached on the 12th. During this period there was to be frost at night. After being in the rearguard of Field-Marshal Lord Robert's force, with successful skirmishes and engagements, the 14th Hussars were involved on 31st May in the surrender by the Boers of Johannesberg. The 14th Hussars were also in the rearguard in the final push which reached Pretoria on 4th June, when the 300 miles march and engagements from Bloemfontein to Pretoria was carried out in 36 days. Then for 48 hours, on 11th-13th June, the dismounted 14th Hussars were amongst those in considerable fighting in the engagement at Diamond Hill, south of Pretoria.

After these hostilities there was a further fresh supply of horses, in between patrols and outposts. A further issue of Queen's Chocolate took place on 6th July, some of which was sent home, but most eaten at once as a welcome change from the very unvaried diet.

During this spell an officer of the 14th Hussars brought along his pet baboon, to be named *Kruger*, which he had just bought in Pretoria

On the 11th and 12th July the 14th Hussars and others had to beat off Boer attacks at Derdepoort. They were being continuously fired upon by the Boers' artillery and musketry. The British carbines were found to be not equal to the Boers' rifles which had a longer range.

From 17th July the British force, including the cavalry, commenced a series of marches eastwards in an endeavour to encounter the main large concentration of some 5,000 Boers. On the 25th July the 14th Hussars, now became attached to the 1st Cavalry Brigade in other actions. By 1st August the 14th Hussars had been given a very long line of outposts to hold, of some 5 miles, at a place called Blinkpan, 14 miles south-west from Belfast. This line was held by just 340 men and 250 horses, with 110 men on guard and outpost duty every night. As the Boers had denuded the land of forage on the grass veld, this resulted in a high loss of horses, plus those shot in action, and needing to be replaced. The British had to rely on what could be taken from denuded farms, or bought from local shops. Losses of both men and horses also resulted from exposure to the rain and cold.

The men and horses were subject to tedious and incessant marches. One cavalryman was to record:

'This is the time when the monotony becomes terrible. In two's or four's, or in troop, as the case may be, you plod, plod, plod, on till about 12 o'clock, with perhaps two or three short halts of a few minutes, during which you dismount and lie in the shade of your horse, or, if he will only stand, go to sleep at once, only to be awakened in a minute or two by that dreaded cry of "Stand t'yer 'orses". Then "Prepare to Mount", "Mount", and plod, plod, plod, on again. At about 12 you off-saddle for an hour or so, feed, collect fuel, finish the remnants of biscuit and bully, and on-saddle, to plod, plod, plod on till 5 or 6 at night. While on the march there is no change or excitement, no nothing to while away the weary hours but one's pipe, and how fond one grows of that.'

A photograph was published in a contemporary publication, captioned 'Swords being sharpened in the field'. It depicts three large circular grindstones, each attended to by two men - one turning the handle whilst the other is sharpening a sword on the turning stone. Each stone is also accompanied by a small tin bath, presumably to hold water to wet the stone.

The 14th Hussars continued to be frequently found either in the vanguard, or on an exposed flank, and thus generally in some form of action. Sometimes they were having to be dismounted, as the horses were too exhausted, or when up along mountain tracks too dangerously narrow to be ridden. They were also open to sniping and other forms of enemy attack. From 26th August the Cavalry, with the 14th Hussars in the advance-guard were involved in actions leading to the Battle of Belfast, which was the last the Boers fought as an army, indulging thereafter largely in guerilla warfare.

During September and October the 14th Hussars were still frequently in skirmishes over rugged ground. Although sometimes action was hot, fatal casualities in the 14th Hussars of men and horses were few. There were also reconnaissance duties.

On 21st October, during a halt at Bethel, Lieutenant-General French, commander of the Cavalry Division, ordered a parade of the 14th Hussars. This was in order to particularly compliment the Regiment on its fine record during the long trying marches and arduous campaign, when they were often suffering from shortage of rations, exposure in hot weather, and harrassing outpost duty. But he overstepped his thanks when he said: ". . . but the war is nearly over, and can only last a few weeks longer - perhaps for you only a few days."

On the 26th October, after Boer harrassment, and being short of rations and horses, the Cavalry reached Heidelberg for a short well needed rest. Many men were without boots. On the 30th, all the dismounted men of the different regiments (including many of the 14th) left Heidelberg by train for Pretoria, in open trucks. The mounted Cavalry Division column marched to Pretoria, taking four days, in heavy rain and with very little or no food. They were also again harrassed by the Boers, and lost many animals. The whole force was in a pitiable state. No new clothing had been issued since the start of the campaign, and many men were wearing Boer clothes and strange footwear bought or commandeered. All wore beards. Here the 14th Hussars had its first occasion to use tents since leaving Bloemfontein six months earlier; and all regiments were now to be re-equipped. Diaries of soldiers in other regiments confirm the general pitiable state of both men and horses.

At Pretoria they had three weeks rest, with fresh horses arriving. At the same time, after a year, the campaign was believed to be nearly over, such that on 28th November Lord Roberts left by train for England, having apparently considered he had beaten the Boers in the field, and occupied their country: an opinion not shared by the Boers. Part of the 14th Hussars was used to help protect the train from any attack, and as a guard along a section of the railway line. Lord Kitchener took over from Lord Roberts, to mop up the extremists and guerillas. Also to clear Boer farms and capture their forage and stocks of cattle, sheep and goats. The driving of these captured animals was to be an onerous task. Boer families were put together in concentration camps.

Whilst collecting fruit in a farm orchard a Troop disturbed the beehives there, which promptly cleared the orchard, but the angry bees followed. Brigade Headquarters had to move indoors, where an officer was attacked whilst in the bath. The field hospital luckily contained only a couple of light cases, but everyone had to clear out. Unfortunately two tethered horses were stung to death. It was lucky that during this confusion there was not a Boer attack.

The 14th Hussars in the 4th Cavalry Brigade, on 22nd November was now to return to Heidelberg, clearing out the country of marauding bands of Boers. These were to be now engaged in last ditch guerilla warfare, which the cavalry were best able to deal with. The British were now equipped with new long rifles having double the range of their previous carbines.

On the 17th December the 14th Hussars marched from 1-30 a.m., arriving at Elansfontein Station by 6-15 a.m. 'A' Squadeon, and part of 'B' (160 men and 250 horses) boarded the first train at 7-10 a.m. The remainder of 'B' Squadron and the rest of the regiment (200 men and 250 horses) boarded the second train; with all arriving at Krugersdorp later that afternoon.

At 2-45 a.m. on 19th December the regiment paraded in pouring rain and joined the 1st Cavalry Brigade at the rear of the column. The next day 'B' Squadron was detached for six days to General Clement's column. Thus the year ended with this extended exercise, plus clearing the scattered farms, and collecting the cattle, sheep, horses and other provisions for British own use. There was also the capturing of prisoners-of-war, with the 14th Hussars in the forefront of it all. The year ended with the regiment now divided amongst three different Brigades, and to continue

'adding fresh lustre to their already high and distinguished reputation.'

1901

The 14th Hussars continued with engagements against parties of Boers led by their able leaders, with one such sucessful commando force being led by Jan C. Smuts (later to be the General Smuts leading South African forces for the Allies during WW2). There was also convoy escort duty. All this was often in heavy rain, and muddy and swampy conditions, and lack of supplies, taking its toll of men and horses of both sides. There was the continuing rounding-up and capture of Boer prisoners, livestock, and with more Boer families being removed to concentration camps.

On 1st January 'B' Squadron joined 'A' at Ventersdorp as part of General Babington's column. There was some hot action over the next few days, before taking duties of guarding the drifts over the Vaal at Rooikraal. On 8th March somed horse-sickness broke out in 'B' Squadron. Then on 27th a troop of 'B' Squadron joined 'A' in General Babington's column. The rest of 'B' for seven weeks from 2nd April were on eventful weekly convoy escort duty.

British troops were now extensively using the slouch-hat, originally the Boer trademark.

Part of Kitchener's strategy was the use of many multi-columned drives to harrass the Boer commando bands of guerillas. Individually or in concert these columns were to criss-cross the open veld of the Transvaal, Orange Free State, Orange River Colony, and Cape Colony. This strategy was not always successful in catching the elusive Boer bands.

The 14th Hussars operated in trying conditions at times, and being also short of water and food. Thus foraging parties were used, augmented by 68 boxes of Queen's Chocolate in March. This time it was Queen Alexandra's present in the style of the late Queen Victoria. During the South African winter there was sometimes a "sharp frost at night". In spite of these difficulties, the 14th Hussars continued to receive glowing reports from Column Generals.

On 30th May 'B' Squadron entrained at Potchefstroom for Klerksdorp, to join 'A' Squadron as part of General Hickie's Column, acting as flank guards. On 20th June both Squadrons left the Column, going to Krugersdorp, and arriving at Newcastle on the 24th to rejoin the rest of the 14th Hussars who were there. From 31st July the Regiment was to be distributed at Broefly in Northern Natal, with the main body of 'B' Squadron at Koningsberg, and a detachment at Jack's Hill.

'B' Squadron and HQ joined General Poultney's Column in the rear guard, at Utrecht, on 15th August. They were to be involved in stiff engagements during the next few weeks. Throughout all this the Boers were continuing their sniping.

The advent of another South African summer in September brought with it mist, fog, cold drizzle, torrential rains, and resultant impassable rivers across the veld.

On Christmas Day, when possible, there was another distribution of chocolate, plus a plum pudding, beer, and a pipe of tobacco to follow.

1902

At the beginning of the year the 14th Hussars were still engaged in continued driving operations against Boer commandos and guerilla units, and the farms which they used. These actions included the digging and manning of trenches as part of the trapping of Boers. This the 14th sometimes did alone, or as part of a large Column. In February the total strength of the Regiment was 480 officers and men.

Spring brought its own hazards, e.g. wasps and mosquitoes at times, plus further mist and fog.

Peace was declared on 1st June. A few days later a party of the 14th Hussars had to go to England to represent the regiment at the coronation of King Edward VII, but this did not include Corporal John Goddard. The rest of the regiment remained in South Africa for the rest of the year. Thus he was not able to participate in the rejoicings back at Tipton/Wednesbury following the Peace Declaration, and the triumphant return of the conscripts and volunteers. On 25th October and 11th November there were satisfactory Generals' Inspections

When the Regiment was in India during the Second Sikh War of 1848-1849, it was awarded the unofficial nickname of 'The Ramnuggur Boys' following their glorious charge at Ramnuggur on 22nd November 1848. Since then the event was to be celebrated on this date, but obviously not at times when the regiment was fighting out in the field. But now in peacetime it was able to be celebrated again on 22nd November, in a Kroonstad hotel.

John Goddard seems to have come through this War unscathed, as his name does not appear amongst the list of war wounded, nor for any honour or award, or any mention at all up to this date in the *14th Hussars Historical Record*. It is not known whether he caught any of the prevalent diseases and illnesses resulting from sunstroke, poor sanitation and hygiene, polluted rivers, etc. However, for their participation in the South African Wars, combattants could be awarded the two South African medals.

The first was Queen Victoria's South African Medal, with its red, blue and orange ribbon, and 26 possible bars for the many actions which took place there.

John Goddard was awarded six of these bars - those for the RELIEF OF KIMBERLEY, PAARDEBERG, DRIEFONTEIN, JOHANNESBERG, DIAMOND HILL, BELFAST, which corresponds with the earlier actions of Squadron 'B'.

The other medal was King Edward's South African Medal, with its green, white and red ribbon, and two bars inscribed SOUTH AFRICA 1901 and SOUTH AFRICA 1902.

MARRIAGE

1903

The Regiment was ordered back to England on 12th March, after ironically having to hand in or sell all their horses to the Boers. On 24th March the Regiment left Kroonstad, and embarked in the s.s. *Dunera* at Cape Town on the 28th. This ship of 5,414 tons was another built - in 1891 - for British India, and capable of 14 knots. Sailing via the Suez Canal they arrived at Southampton on 4th May.

They then went by train to Aldershot, as had many units since the end of the Boer War. On their arrival at the railway station the Regiment was presented with a cream-coloured horse for the Kettle Drums from King Edward VII. The Regiment attracted some considerable attention with their now full-grown baboon mascot 'Kruger', which walked behind the Band as they marched from the Government Siding. They marched to the West Cavalry Barracks, where they had been previously quartered at the outbreak of the War, to form part of the 1st Cavalry Brigade.

On 26th June two Squadrons took part in a Review at Aldershot. Then on 5th July, General Sir John French, now Commanding Aldershot Army Corps, presented South African Medals to the Regiment, and made a most flattering speech. The author has a picture postcard also showing the hero of Mafeking 'Major-General S. S. Baden Powell presenting S. African Medals on Cavalry Parade', with everyone in full dress uniform. Only a few years hence he was to turn his energies to forming the Boy Scout movement.

On Wednesday, 8th July, there was a Grand Review before King Edward VII, and President Loubet of France. The Regiment provided the escort to the Royal carriage. According to a copy of the 6d *Official Programme* in the Aldershot Military Museum, the event took place on Laffan's Plain, Aldershot. The Troops had to form up at 2-45 p.m., although the train conveying the Royal party from London Victoria was not due to arrive at Farnborough Station until 3-30 p.m. It seems the Regiment may not have taken part in the Grand Review itself, but did form part of the Grand March Past.

The Regiment was on 26th August to be inspected by General Baden-Powell, the Inspector-General of Cavalry, and who expressed himself satisfied, including with the progress of the training. This was followed by manoeuvres about Newbury Down between 10th-19th September, and visits by foreign generals.

1904

On Saturday, 23rd April, there was a further inspection of the Regiment by General Baden-Powell. Then on Monday, 9th May, they were part of the Cavalry Brigade in cavalry actions held before King Edward VII.

It was whilst stationed at Aldershot that John Goddard seems to have romantically met Hilda Constance Margaretta Elliott. She had been born on 18th October 1879, to George William Goddard (a Grocer and Baker) and Eleanor (née Dixon) at 96 High Street, Aldershot. According to the 1881 Census taken on Sunday 3rd April, the Elliott family was still at the Baker's Shop, 96 High Street, Aldershot. George W. Elliott is shown as aged 30, born at Gosport in Hampshire, a Baker & Grocer, and Eleanor (aged 32, born at Great Harksly [*sic*] in Essex). Children shown were Albert E.G. (aged 7, a scholar, born at Great Harksly), Hector P. (aged 5, also a scholar and born at Great Harksly), Ethel E. (aged 3, born at Aldershot), and finally Hilda (aged 1 year, also born at Aldershot). There were also two late teenage servants: Thomas E. Timms (Cook Servant) and Annie Smith (General Servant). With the latter's birthplace given as Gosport, was she a relation of George Elliott?

The son Hector Peek was actually born at 5 Park Place, Aldershot on 28th January 1876, with father George shown on the Birth Certificate as a Confectioner. Eleanor Ethel Gertrude was born at 96 High Street on 26th December 1877, with father George now shown on her Birth Certificate as a Grocer.

Before the advent of the Army in 1853, Aldershot was just a windswept, remote little village, well off the beaten track. with a High Street running N-S some 100 yards either side of the railway bridge which was not built until about 1870. Using an 1890s large-scale Ordnance Survey map of Aldershot, from the 1881 census enumerator's description nos. 1-5 Park Place was situated at the southern end of a block of buildings on the western side of the original section of the High Street, just south of the railway bridge, between what is now St. Michaels Road and St. Georges Road East. Northwards, next door to 1 Park Place was 97 High Street (a Shoe Shop), and next to that no. 96 (a Baker Shop - George W. Elliott and family). As these buildings do not appear on an 1855 map of Aldershot, it may be safely assumed that they were the beginnings of civilian development to cater for the army influx.

One also wonders why George left Gosport for Essex. Great Harksly is undoubtedly Great Horkesley, a small village in Essex, some four miles north-westwards of Colchester on the A134 road. According to Lewis's *Topographical Dictionary* of 1844, "it was pleasantly situated south of the River Stour, 3,083 acres in extent, with 730 inhabitants, a National School, and All Saints church with its embattled tower."

It is not hard to guess that George Elliott left Essex to take advantage of the trading opportunities opening up with the Army. On a visit to the Army Museum at Aldershot in 2003, the author noticed a small exhibit of particular interest on a wall. It was a framed original handwritten Order, issued by the Assistant Quartermaster General's Office, 'Q' Lines, South Camp, Aldershot:

'Head Quarters
3rd Division
5 Army Corps

Permit the bearer George Elliott to pass between the lines for the purpose of supplying the troops with Fish, Fruit, Pastry and Sherbert.
5th July 1876

Herbert[?] Smith
Lt. Col.
Asst. Dn. Qr. General'

Sherbert was a name for soft drinks.

Assuming this to be the same George Elliott, it would seem that it was *circa* 1875 when the family moved from Essex to Aldershot. *Kelly's Directory* of 1877 shows he had moved a few doors up to 96 High Street as a Grocer; and in 1879 as a Grocer & Baker.

By the time of the 1891 Census, taken on Sunday, 5th April, one result of the development that had been going on in Aldershot over the past couple of decades or so, was the building of new shops in the newer part of the town in the northward extension of the High Street. This was the complete renumbering of properties in the older section of the High Street, and quite possibly their rebuilding. For whatever reason, the Elliotts were now living at 5 Mount Pleasant Terrace, Redan Hill, Aldershot. Redan Hill is an area north off the old High Street, approached by a road running parallel immediately south of the railway line, firstly named Cemetery Road but renamed Redan Road in 1948.

This Census entry reads: George W. aged 40, Grocer Master; Eleanor, 43; Albert E.G., 17, Grocer; Hecter P., 15, Grocer's Assistant; Hilda E.M., 11, Scholar; Hamilton G, 8, Scholar; John X., 4, Scholar; Ethelbert I.G., 2; Ethel A, 1 year; but no note of any servants this time. There does, however, appear to be on the same premises a James Doherty from Ireland (with occupation unclear except for the letters R.A. which would imply that he was a soldier), his wife Mary, and young child Annie.

The enumerator's description, when compared with the 1890s map, does not make it clear where Mount Pleasant Terrace was. The recorded description of properties were: Mount Pleasant Hotel, 1-4 Mount Pleasant Cottages, 5-18 Mount Pleasant Terrace. It can only be assumed that all these buildings were those at the top of Redan Road and into what is now Mount Pleasant Road. A descendant family member recalls visiting her great-grandmother Elliott at the large premises on the corner of Windmill Road and Mount Pleasant Road. With the now increasing family numbers a large house would have been necessary.

At that time, Redan Hill was a favourite spot for walking and picnics, with views over the Camp area and Government sidings. This recreational site when visited by the author in 2004 was overgrown with trees and bushes, with most views blocked by foliage, and subject of a 2000 joint regeneration programme by Hampshire County Council and Rushmoor Borough Council. The camping area and sidings by the nature of things have gone, and been re-developed.

George Elliott senior was to die on 30th October 1893 of "Bronchopneumonia 10 days", aged 43 years, at Redan Hill, Aldershot. He was shown as being a "Grocer Master". His wife Eleanor was present at time of death. George was buried on 3rd November, in Redan Road Cemetery, Division B, number 35. Similar to several others there it was in unconsecrated ground. This would have been due to the Elliott family being Presbyterian, as the consecrated ground there was reserved for the burial of people christened Church of England. The Elliotts' 8-year old daughter Eleanor had been similarly buried in Redan Road Cemetery, in Section A, reserved for the burial of children, and being now completely lawned with no headstones or memorials. (See also 1926)

Kelly's Directory for 1895 shows Eleanor Elliott as a Shopkeeper at Redan Hill. The 1901 Census, taken on Sunday, 31st March, shows Eleanor (aged 52, widow) as the Head, and as a General Shop Keeper at the 5 Mount Pleasant Terrace premises; with Hilda (21), described as a Music Teacher; plus sons Oswald (14, Van Boy); Ethelbert L.G. (13); daughter Ethel A. (10); and a boarder, William Lummon, (40, Canvas Tent & Sail Maker).

According to a *Certified Copy Of An Entry Of Marriage*, John Goddard and Hilda Elliott were married on Thursday, 2nd June 1904, at a Presbyterian Church of England. Both were aged 24 years. Witnesses were J. Hampson and Kezia Clarke. John Goddard is shown as 'Sergeant 14th Hussars, Cavalry Barracks, Aldershot'. Thus after possibly barely six years' service John was progressing well up the promotion ladder. Hilda was not shown with any profession, but still at 5 Redan Hill, Aldershot. It is noted that John's late father is shown as having been a Carpenter, though as a Chemical Worker on his death certificate in 1896.

The Goddard-Elliott marriage was extensively reported in *The Aldershot Military Gazette.*

'MARRIAGE OF MISS ELLIOTT

'On Thursday afternoon the marriage of Miss Elliott, eldest daughter of the late Mr. George Elliott, of Aldershot, and of Mrs. Elliott, of Redan House, Aldershot, and Sergeant John Thomas Goddard, son of the late Mr. William Goddard, of Staffordshire, was solemnised at the Presbyterian Church, Aldershot, in the presence of a very large circle of friends and relations. The bride is a native of Aldershot, and enjoys the friendship of many, whilst the young bridegroom is one of the smartest and most popular non-commissioned officers in a most decidedly popular regiment. The wedding was solemnised by the pastor, the Rev. R. A. Stewart, and the happy bride was given away by her brother, Mr. H. Elliott. She wore a dress of cream crepe de chine, trimmed with silk insertion, lace and chiffon, and which became her charmingly. She wore also a wreath of orange blossoms and a tulle veil, her only ornaments being a gold watch and long gold guard. Her wedding bouquet was composed of white roses, geraniums, and marguerites. Her bridesmaids were Miss Ethel Elliott, sister, Miss Kizzie Clarke, cousin of the bridegroom, and Miss Kitty Goode. Miss Elliott and Miss Goode wore dresses of cream nun's veiling and carried baskets of white roses and pink geraniums, their ornaments being gold brooches, the gift of the bridegroom; and Miss Clarke was attired in a gown of cream cashmere trimmed with silk, and a black picture hat trimmed with black ostrich tips. She, too, carried a beautiful bouquet of white roses and geraniums. The bouquets were each tied with ribbons of the regimental colours of the 14th Hussars, namely, blue and yellow. The duties of best man devolved upon and were discharged by Sergt. Hampson, of the 14th Hussars, and at the close of the pretty service it was interesting to note that the brother non-commissioned officers of the bridegroom's regiment formed an archway from the church portals to the carriage with their crossed swords, 'neath which Mr. and Mrs. Goddard happily passed. A reception was subsequently held and breakfast served at the home of the bride's mother, quite fifty guests being present. At a later hour of the day the newly married couple left to spend their honeymoon at Leamington, in Warwickshire, the bride's going away dress being of pale green cloth, with a black picture hat trimmed with black ostrich tips, whilst she also wore an ostrich feather boa that had been sent home to her as a wedding gift by her soldier brother from South Africa. The presents were numerous, and included the following:-

'Mrs. Elliott (mother of the bride), wedding dress and household linen; Staff Q.M.S. A. Elliott (brother of the bride), cheque and one dozen knives; Miss A. Elliott, trinket set; Mrs. A. Elliott, silver spoons; Master Ted Elliott, tea cloths; Mr. H. Elliott (brother of the bride), cheque; Miss May Elliott (neice of bride), table cloth; Mr G. Elliott (brother of the bride), South Africa, cheque; Mr. O. Elliott (brother of the bride), electro-plated jam dish; Master E. Elliott (brother of the bride), set of china jugs; Mr. R. Elliott (uncle of the bride), silver salts; Miss Kizzie Clarke (cousin of the bridegroom), silver table and salt spoons; Mr. Clarke (cousin of the bridegroom), silver plated forks; Sergt. Hampson, 14th Hussars, silver teapot, silver match box, and pictures; Mrs. Hyatt (aunt of bride), silk ties; Sergt.-Major and Mrs. Perks, A.S.C., handsome table cover; A Friend, a cheque; Mrs. Chanticy, silver cruet; Mrs. Hewitt, sugar sifter and basin; Mrs. Wilkinson, glass dishes; Mrs. Chandle, toast rack and silver cream jug; Mrs. Sexton, salt cellars; Miss Holmes, afternoon tea cloth; Mr. and Mrs. Pritchard, serviettes and tray cloths; Mrs. Goodman, cheese dish; Mrs. and Miss Gale, vases; Misses L. and B. Chant, photo frames; Mrs. Goods, cut glass biscuit barrel; Miss Kitty Goode, silver jam spoon; Mrs. and Miss J. Collins, silver apostle jam spoon; Mrs. Matthews, vases; Mrs. L. and M. Bard (Croydon), cruet; Miss Webb, china flower vases; Pte. Sutton, case of silver fish knives and forks; Corpl. and Mrs Kie, silver teapot and cosy; Sergt.-Major and Mrs Harmer, toilet set; Mrs. Mitchelson (cousin of the bride), cheque; Mr. and Mrs. W. Stiff, silver plated cruet; A Friend, silver match box; Miss H. Lloyd, (Cardiff), dessert dish; Mr. and Mrs. McCheer, silver butter and jam spoon; the Sergeants of B Squadron, 14th Hussars, marble timepiece; Messrs. Phillips, spoons and sugar tongs; Mrs. Berry (aunt of bridegroom), jam dish and spoon; Miss Berry, half-a-dozen wine glasses and half-a-dozen cut tumblers, old china, and cake; Mr. & Mrs. Lewis, cushion cover; Mr. Solomon, pair of pictures; Corpl. Cox (Malta), picture.'

This report raises several points. Firstly, by heading the report just 'MARRIAGE OF MISS ELLIOTT' could pre-suppose that she was a well-known figure in Aldershot, or at least within the local Military. With the earlier death of her sister Eleanor, Hilda would now have been the eldest daughter. Was this yet another address given for the Elliott residence? It would have to be of a substantial size to have seated some fifty wedding guests. *Redan House* could well have been the the same large building earlier identified by the descendant relative. Nobody from the Goddard family in Wednesbury or Tipton area seems to have been involved, except possibly the 'Miss Kizzie Clarke' whose details have still to be determined. She apparently signed her name as a witness to the wedding as 'Kezia Clarke'. A descendant family member does recall her mother talking about 'Kezia'. By only giving christian name initials to other family members there is some doubt as to all their identities.

The Presbyterian Church involved was presumably that at the time on the south side of Victoria Road, just east of its junction with Station Road. Building of the church had begun in 1863, and completed 1869. In 2004 it still had its two distinctive square towers, though the Manse alongside had long gone. The building is now used by the Aldershot Branch of the New Testament Church of God. This end of Victoria Road in 1904 was primarily residential, but has since been redeveloped into business premises. It would thus have been a 10-15 minutes sedate walk from Redan Hill to church.

The honeymoon location of Leamington was the birthplace of John Goddard's late father and grandmother, so there may presumably have still been residual family there.

Since 1867 the 14th Hussars' Sergeants had had an oval embroidered or metal sterling silver Prussian Eagle arm badge, worn above their chevrons. At about this time (1904) the metal oval arm badge of a Sergeant was backed by a red cloth backing with a saw tooth or serrated edge, in all orders of dress. The arm badge was of black metal, with gilt crown, *FR* Cypher, orb, sceptre and trefoils on the wings; 50·7mm high, 39·4mm wide, two loops 25mm.A Sergeant's mess dress was adapted from the stable jacket which was worn open but looped at the collar, with a stiff white collar and shirt and a cummerbund. There is a photograph of a Sergeant taken about this date, wearing full dress with a black Eagle arm badge, and authorised white metal collar badges.

Eight days after the marriage, on Friday, 10th June, the 14th Hussars were in attendance at a Review in honour of H.I.H. the Archduke Francis Ferdinand of Austria, who complimented the regiment on its march past. This was the same Archduke whose murder at Serajevo in 1914 was to precipitate the Great War. Whether Sergeant Goddard would have been required on parade, such that it may well have been a short honeymoon, is not known. During the summer the 14th took part in operations around the Aldershot area.

On the night of Saturday/Sunday 3rd-4th September occurred another stampede, the worst in the Regiment's history. This took place on Baddesley Common, just north of Southampton. The *Southern Echo* of 5th September carried the following report:

'On Saturday the cavalry and mounted infantry, with several batteries of light and field artillery, and the pontoon train of the Royal Engineers, attached to the 1st Army Corps, under the command of Lieut.-Gen. Sir John French, which is to embark at Southampton today, Monday, for conveyance to the East Coast for the autumn manoeuvres, marched into camp on Baddesley Common, which is connected by means of portable field telegraph with the camp on Southampton Common.

'During the night one of the horses of the 8th Hussars was kicked by another, and had its leg broken, and it was determined by a veterinary officer to put the animal out of its misery.

'It is stated that he endeavoured to accomplish this end with a silent pistol; but that did not act, and he accordingly used an ordinary one.

'In the stillness of the early morning, about half past two, when it was pitch dark, a shot rang out in the lines of the 8th Hussars and immediately the stampede occurred.

'There was nothing to stop the maddened rush of the affrightened steeds.

'The ground was soft from the heavy rain of the previous morning, and it was a comparatively easy matter for the horses to pull the pegs from the earth . . .

'The stampeded horses dashed out of the enclosure, most of them jumping a fence in which was barbed wire, breaking down one or two posts supporting the same. The majority of the maddened creatures . . . dashed along towards Chilworth . . .

'The roadway bore traces for a considerable distance of the direction taken by the frightened animals by the large quantity of blood that had dropped from their legs, pieces of string with which their ankles had been tied, broken pegs, and blankets with which they had been covered for the night littering the roadway.

'Some of the horses halted after going some distance, either through the injuries to their legs, or having got over their frenzy, and were captured.

'Others dashed off in the direction of Chandler's Ford or Winchester, but it is computed that about 300 galloped down the magnificent avenue which intersects Southampton Common . . .

'Downwards the horses galloped, but as they neared the more thickly-populated parts of Southampton they disappeared in various directions.

'About 100 dashed through Above Bar-Street, and a police constable made a gallant attempt to stop the animals, but finding that they continued their mad stampede, and that his efforts had no effect, he wisely beat a retreat.

'Through the Bargate the terrified creatures tore, some being crushed against the sides of the structure, down to the Town Quay . . . All the morning mounted men were returning to Baddesley Common with batches of the runaways.

'Some were discovered by the roadside with such serious injuries that it was necessary in mercy to put an end to their sufferings.

'It was reported in the camp at midday that 47 horses had to be shot at different places to put an end to their misery. A good number had been returned to camp about noon, but such a small percentage belonging to the 8th Hussars were fit to ride that the gallant regiment was practically reduced to the position of an unmounted troop . . .

'The incident was bad enough in all conscience, but the wildest stories got into circulation. One of these was to the effect that many of the horses in their desperate flight dashed over the Town Quay and were drowned, but this was not the case.

'. . . At the bottom of The Avenue the horses' weight and impetus was such that some of them were unable to turn into London-road without fouling the ornamental iron fences and low walls in front of the houses in College-place and some of the cast-iron fences were broken off . . .

'When [a witness] saw them in the picket lines in the morning many of them had patches of skin and hair scraped off and various cuts and bruises . . .

'The first tramlines were being laid in Southampton at the time and, as "there was no road round the Bargate in those days, all the horses converged on the narrow road under the Bar, fell into the trenches made for laying the lines, and many suffered broken legs and had to be destroyed."

'This was in the days when a narrow pedestrian arch was either side of the Bargate, and what a fearful mess it was to see blood stains at each opening.'

According to the *Historical Record*'s account of the incident, instead of the horses being tethered to a long rope, they were each held by a shackle and a single peg to the fore-leg only. Unfortunately this was not the usual hard ground, but sandy soil. Some horses soon pulled out their pegs, and being startled by the sound of a wounded horse being shot, and then being frightened by their loose pegs hitting them, they started a general stampede. Some horses were later found back at Aldershot, and as far away as Basingstoke some 30 miles distant. Others were found in Southampton Docks four or more miles away. Over 100 horses were killed, injured, and missing. All this played havoc with the manoeuvres. Presumably sergeant John Goddard would have been some how involved in all this rounding-up, hence the inclusion of this event in detail.

Equestrian, rifle, etc. events were held during the year whilst the Regiment was at Aldershot, with some Regimental success, but detailed results not known. In the meantime, Regimental Races, and Point-to-Point Meetings, and participation in Tournaments had now resumed after the South African War.

On 26th September the Regiment began to leave Aldershot by route march, with Squadrons billetting at Redhill the first night, Tonbridge Wells the second, and Ashford the third. All arrived by 2nd October at the Somerset Barracks, Shorncliffe, the south coast town in Kent.

Posted by a Corporal Mason from Shorncliffe, in December, was a picture postcard showing the 14th Hussars on a King's Birthday Parade, but not giving any date or location.

1905

In January the Regiment was inspected by Eastern Command Generals, including Baden-Powell, and found to be extremely efficient. The Regiment, still at Shorncliffe, was to form part of the newly-formed 2nd Cavalry Brigade in June.

On 12th August was the birth of the Goddards' first child, Eleanor Pearl Catherine. She was born at the Female Hospital, Shorncliffe Camp, Sandgate. Place of residence was shown on the birth certificate as being the Camp. Thus it would appear that Sergeant Goddard's wife had travelled with him, and in married quarters.

On Friday, 1st September, the Regiment marched to Aldershot to take part in manoeuvres, and being inspected by Generals French and Baden-Powell; after which they apparently returned to Shorncliffe.

1890 Map of Wednesbury showing the general location of Goddard residences
and surrounding industries

Dudley Street, Wednesbury. Coal picking from trench when deep sewer was laid.
c. 1887

St. James Street, Wednesbury. Rear of Nos. 7-10, showing Nos. 1-5, Court 1. Slum clearance. 1933

Foster Street, Wednesbury. Rear of Nos. 21 - 26. Slum clearance. 1933

"Dark Satanic Mills" - Messrs. J. Bagnall & Sons' Lea Brook Ironworks.

St. James School,
St. James Street,
Wednesbury, 2003.

The Barracks, Newbridge, Co. Kildare, Ireland.

Relief column entering Ladysmith, lead by the 14th (Kings) Hussars,
3rd March 1900.

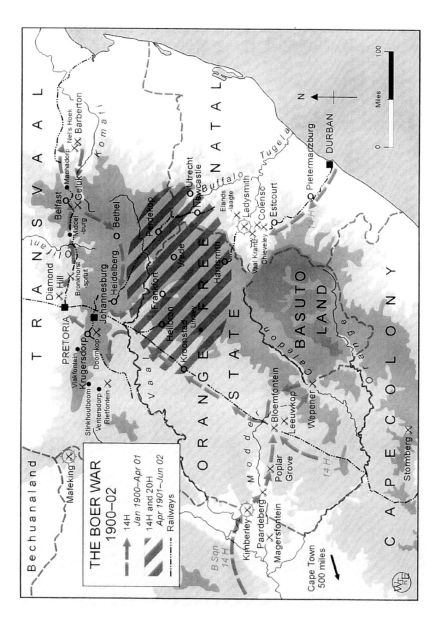

Map of the Boar War 1900 - 1902 showing 14th Hussars routes and engagements.

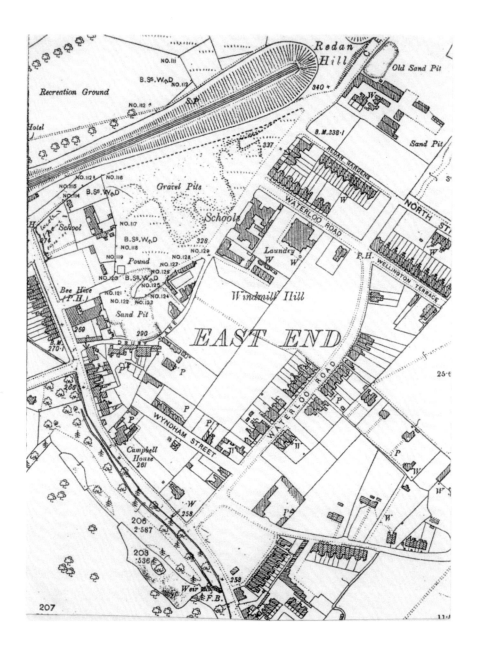

Map of Aldershot with 1895 revisions. Northern section of Waterloo Road since renamed Mount Pleasant Road. Earlier Elliott shop and residence opposite the Bee Hive public house.

14th (King's) Hussars proceeding to manoeuvres.

14th (King's) Hussars sergeant in Review Order.

Gateway of West Cavalry Barracks, Aldershot c. 1910

Remaining gateway of West Cavalry Barracks, Aldershot 2004

14th (King's) Hussars at stables.

14th (King's) Hussars in Review Order

Mount Pleasant Road, Redan Hill, Aldershot 2003. Elliott residence believed to have been the large corner building on the left.

The old Presbyterian Church, Victoria Road, Aldershot 2003.

INDIA

1906

During the year there were the usual Regimental, Army and Military competitions entered into, again with some success, but details not given.

On 6th June was the first of what was to be an Annual Regimental Dinner for past and present Officers, N.C.O.'s and men at the *Holborn Restaurant*, London.

The 14th Hussars were later to be ordered to sail for India. There was furlough before they eventually left Somerset Barracks at Shorncliffe, at 7 a.m. on Monday, 5th September, and marched to Shorncliffe railway station. They subequently embarked at Southampton on board s.s. *Assaye*, which sailed at 5 p.m. This ship of 7,376 tons, built in 1899, was capable of travelling at 16 knots, and belonged to the Peninsular and Oriental Steam Navigation Company. 577 officers and men sailed, plus 51 'ladies' and wives, and 58 children, including presumably John Goddard's wife and one year old daughter Eleanor.

The Regiment reached Bombay on 26th September, joining the Cavalry Brigade at Bangalore on the 29th, where lines were set up. The Regiment had last been here in 1870. Time was then spent in acclimatising, with inspections by the Inspector General of Cavalry in India, and others, who were much pleased.

1907

On 4th January the Officer in charge of the Family Hospital at Bangalore and the 14th Hussars Commanding Officer registered the birth of the Goddards' second child, another girl. At the time of registration next day, the names Ethel Louisa were written into the column 'Baptismal Name if added after Registration of Birth'. She sadly died of meningitis 39 days later on 11th February, with again officers registering the death. It was noted that the father was still Sergeant Goddard. One wonders whether there is any residual marker in Bangalore.

From 13th January to 3rd February the Regiment were on manoeuvres in an area some 50 miles east of Bangalore.

On 15th March a Regimental swimming test was introduced by the commanding officer, as the cavalry had often to negotiate rivers by swimming as has been shown, with sometimes loss of life - both human and equine. All ranks had to pass, and was a practice to be continued.

As well as Generals' Inspections, and its own Regimental Sports and Meetings, there was to be Regimental participation in the local Horse Show, and the Central Assault-at-Arms. In the *Historical Record* of the Regiment is now found John Goddard's first mention. At the Central Assault-at-Arms at Bangalore, on 24th

September, Sergeant Goddard was second in the 'Sword v Lance, Other Ranks'. He was thus maintaining a certain degree of soldiering ability.

1908

Perhaps the army's earlier deficiencies among the cavalry had been the most glaring, since all their previous training had been based on the idea of the knee-to-knee charge at full speed, and hardly any attention had been paid to musketry and dismounted tactics. The next few years were to be devoted to a complete revision of training. But even then, between 1902 and 1914 it was still based primarily on shock tactics and the 'Cavalry Spirit'. There was also a lively continuing debate between use of either lance or sword, and between point and edge of the sword. A new pattern of cavalry sword - the last to ever be produced - was introduced in 1908, which showed that point had won over edge. It was to be described as the 'finest thrusting sword ever invented', though just a little late. The new sword, optimised for thrusting, had a thin blade, a large bowl guard and pistol-grip hilt which enabled the user to align the blade perfectly.

The year was to be spent on manoeuvres, General Inspections, official parades, field days, as well as various Competitions - when winners' and runners-up names have not always been recorded.

At the Bangalore Horse Show on 18th August, Sergeant Goddard came 2nd in 'Best Turn-Out (Mounted)'.

On 13th September the Goddards were to have their third child, this time a son, Graham Elliott. The birth appears in the Army Returns of 1908, Bangalore.

On 1st November, at the Central Assault-at-Arms at Bangalore, amongst the Regiment's successes was:

'Sergeant Goddard, 1st, Jumping; and came out best swordsman in the Regiment.'

At the 10th November Regimental Mounted Sports:

'Sergeant Goddard was 2nd Best Man-at-Arms for Other Ranks.'

1909

Again the year was to be spent in training and manoeuvres, but these were to be restricted sometimes by lack of water. There were also official Parades, and General Inspections with the Regiment receiving very good reports, when one such read:

'Warrant and Non-Commissioned Officers are a smart and well-educated class of men, with professional ability above the average.'

There were also the usual competitions, when again not all named results are known. It is known however, that in April, Sergeant Goddard won the Three Furlong N.C.O.'s Purse at the Bangalore Gymkana Races.

Then on 15th July at the Central Assault-at-Arms, also at Bangalore, when this time:

'Sergeant J. Goddard was Best Man-at-Arms of N.C.O.'s and men.'

On 24th July, the Regiment's Commanding Officer, Lt.Colonel Browne-Synge-Hutchinson VC instituted the Regimental Medal, intended as

'a reward to any Officer, Warrant Officer, N.C.O., or Man of the 14th (King's) Hussars who shall contribute in some conspicuous manner to the Military Efficiency, or Military Honour, of the Regiment.'

The Medal was to be of silver, $3/16$th of an inch thick, and $1\,7/8$ inch in diameter. On the obverse in high relief the Prussian Eagle and Battle Honours. The reverse plain on which would be inscribed the recipient's name. The Medal to be attached to a silk ribbon $2\,1/8$ inches broad of the Regimental Colours of a central wide vertical yellow stripe on a black background. The medal was to be worn on the recipient's right breast. In the *Historical Record*, five names are given for the 1909 first recipients, including:

'No. 3796 Sergt. J. Goddard'

Presumably John Goddard earned it through his abilities to earn relatively quick promotion, as well as his horsemanship and prowess with cavalry weaponry.

1910

During the year, as well as the introduction of a new Mark III rifle, there was the usual routine of Parades, Inspections, musketry training, with over half the men being 1st Class shots, and a very large number of N.C.O.s and men achieving 1st Class certificates of education. Warrant Officers and N.C.O.s were again complimented at Inspections. The Regiment also did well in Competitions, but again no names were given for this year.

1911

Again there was to be the usual training, manoeuvers, inspections, and competition, and again winners of the many competitions were not recorded in the *Historical Record*. On 1st November the 14th Hussars began a move from Bangalore to Mhow in central India, arriving on the 16th.

1912

The Goddards were to have their fourth child, a third daughter, Audrey, on 4th January, appearing in the Army Returns for 1912, Mhow.

The year passed with again the usual round of training and Inspections, and competitions, with continued success.

1913

This year passed with again the usual round of training, and Inspections of men and horses, and competitions, with continued success.

There was usually between 15% to 25% turnover of regimental manpower due to discharge, illness, death, etc. Remaining long service men may well therefore hopefully have anticipated being rewarded with some form of promotion. Thus by this time it could be safely assumed that John Goddard had been promoted to Staff Sergeant, or even to Squadron Sergeant Major. He would doubtless have now worn an embroidered Eagle without an oval backing on his sleeve.

If he was still in Squadron 'B', then he would have been in the Squadron team that won the Napier Memorial Shield, which was open to Southern India.

Around this time Mrs Hilda Goddard and the three surviving children came back to the U.K. because the eldest child, Eleanor, aged about 7 years, was ill. They were to stay with Hilda's mother ('Granny Elliott') at Redan Hill, Aldershot, who had a shop possibly on the corner of Mount Pleasant as has been previously surmised.

1914

The year started with again the usual round of training, exercises, Inspections, Competitions, etc. According to the *Historical Record* the 14th Hussars achieved the

'reputation of being the best-drilled Regiment in India.'

It was also noted that some 80% of the men in the Regiment were teetotallers. John Goddard was presumably not one of them, as a descendant recalls that certainly in later years he only drank in moderation.

At the outbreak of war in Europe on 4th August 1914 the 14th Hussars were still at Mhow, in India. Hilda Goddard and the children, still at Aldershot, had been about to return to India, but could not now do so.

The Regiment was then to form part of the newly formed 5th Cavalry Brigade, with expectations of quickly leaving India - but this did not happen. It was not until Turkey made an official Declaration of War against the Allies, and commenced hostilities at the end of October, that preparations began.

During the second week in November the Regiment was moved to Meerut to join the 4th Cavalry Brigade. The Regiment at this time comprised 512 officers and men. The 40 wives and 77 children may well now have been sent home to England at this stage. For the remainder of the year Regimental training was carried out.

THE GREAT WAR

1915

To quote the *Historical Record*:

'On January 1st the usual full-dress parade of the Garrison, in memory of the Proclamation of the Queen-Empress, was held on the Maidan. This was the last occasion on which any British Cavalry Regiment paraded in full dress as worn previous to the Great War. It is probable that the 14th (King's) Hussars never made a finer display than on this occasion: they were magnificently mounted at this time and the horses looking beautiful; the men were all of long service and perfectly trained; the Regiment moved with the precision and accuracy of a machine; while the brilliant sunshine of a crisp Indian winter day on the gold lace, white helmets and steel of the troops, and on the burnished coats of their big blood walers, produced an effect never to be forgotten by those who were present on that occasion.'

The only discordant note was the fact that the Regiment was still being held back and not allowed to take part as yet in the war. Again the *Historical Record*:

'At an Officers' Mess Meeting held in Meerut in May, it was decided to discontinue wearing the Eagle Badge and to adopt instead the second crest of the Regiment, the Royal Crest within the Garter.
A short time later an intimation was received from the Army Council that His Majesty the King desired that the wearing of the Eagle Badge should be discontinued for the present.'

The Eagle cap and collar badges were replaced by the Royal Crest of England in a Garter, above a title scroll.

An embroidered 14th (King's) Hussars banneret, or whatever it is called, could only have at some time come into the possession of the Weymouth British Legion through its connection with John Goddard. It measures some 1 foot 10½ inches x 1 foot 7 inches, and has a marked similarity to the covering on the mounted band's kettle-drums. The author hazards a guess of its date as sometime just before the Great War, for three reasons:
1. Amongst the Battle Honours individually listed on the leaves, the latest (and last) is that of the Relief of Ladysmith, so it would have been after the Boer War.
2. The banneret shows the Prussian Eagle, which the 14th Hussars adopted as its badge after 1791, following the marriage of the Duke of York (2nd son of King

George III) to Princess Frederica of Prussia, who was to become the Regiment's 'Royal Patroness'. The Prussian Eagle badge was to be dropped in 1915 for obvious reasons as noted above, and was not to reappear until 1926 - after John Goddard had been discharged the year prior.

3. And finally, the brackets around the word King's were to be dropped in 1921.

For these reasons the banneret could well have been discontinued following the introduction of an updated version. By virtue of his position John Goddard could have been able to acquire one of the old ones. It is not known for certain what particular purpose this banneret was used, but the curator of the Museum of Lancashire considers it was used on a trumpet.

Early in January the Brigade camped at Ghaziabad, near Delhi, for training. But heavy rain and flood curtailed this, and everyone returned to Meerhut, where the 14th Hussars were inspected by the Brigade Commander, who gave a good report, which included "The N.C.O.'s are a smart, intelligent and well-trained lot, who know their work and do it well."

The long exceptionally hot summer was to be spent in continued frustration at still not being able to participate in the war.

At last on 27th October came the long awaited order to mobilize the Regiment for active service, with all ranks being medically examined - none of whom had less than five years service. The men were each armed with the short Lee-Enfield Mark VI rifle and 90 rounds of ammunition in a personal bandolier, and 90 rounds in a horse bandolier, plus the latest pattern cavalry thrusting sword. Instead of a rifle, Warrant Officers and Staff Sergeants carried a revolver and 24 rounds of ammunition.

On 5th November the Regiment left Meerhut in three trains for Karachi, via Lahore.

En route it was learned that the then Regimental Sergeant Major had been promoted to officer rank. Thus it was that on 6th November, John Goddard was promoted to Regimental Sergeant Major - a position he was to hold for the next ten years, until his retirement in 1925. He was then aged just over 36 years, and having some 17 years service. Considering his initial limited formal education, his was literally an example of someone pulling himself up by his bootstraps. To have reached this position within a prestigeous cavalry regiment reflects on what an exceptional man, soldier, and character he was.

The Regiment embarked and sailed from Karachi on 8th November, to join the India Expeditionary Force in Mesopotamia. Headquarters staff (which presumably would have included newly-promoted R.S.M. Goddard) sailed in the s.s. *Elephanta*. This 5,292 tons ship had only been built in 1915, was capable of 16½ knots, and belonged to the British India Steam Navigation Co. Ltd., and was to be used both as a troop-ship and for carrying wounded soldiers. Another soldier in another unit, who was also to sail at some time on this vessel, described it as "a small boat . . . a shallow draught ship". The rest of the Regiment travelled in the 5,237 ton s.s. *Islanda,* and 3,035 ton s.s. *Chakdara.* The *Elephanta* arrived at Basra in Mesopotamia on the 13th, with disembarkation on the 14th. Both men and horses were to immediately sail up the River Tigris on board four river steamers. After 220 miles they arrived at Kut-el-Amara during 20th-22nd November.

As with the Boer War, some indication of the number of engagements the Regiment was to undertake against the Turkish enemy, as well as the conditions endured by the men and horses is recorded in their official *Historical Record.* Only by reading this and other records can the full story be understood and appreciated.

Kut was described at the time as being a ramshackle, dirty town, situated on a peninsula. It is a name that has come down with some notoriety in military history. The subsequent disastrous siege of Kut during 1915-1916 is another story to itself, with amongst books being published about it was one by Major E. W. C. Sandes (see BIBLIOGRAPHY), a copy of which is in a locked glass cabinet in the Weymouth Reference Library.

Briefly, the British force under General Townshend had earlier thought they could advance from Kut and capture Baghdad without too much difficulty. But the occupying Turks (assisted by Arab irregulars) pushed a superior force against them, with the result that the British had to retreat back to Kut, where they were to be besieged by the Turks.

Without delay, on the 25th the 14th Hussars marched to take its part in this war sector, in a country suited to cavalry, unlike on the Western Front in Europe. Thus the Regiment was to be one of the last to be used as such. It was now to meet up after 60 miles with the tired retreating British force at Aziziyeh, joining the 6th Cavalry Brigade on the 28th as reinforcements. And on the way, quickly realising 'the horrors of the Mesopotamia climate' at this time of year of rains and thick mud. General Townshend (who had earlier visited the 14th Hussars when at Bangalore) was later to record about Kut:

'There I was glad to find the 14th Hussars and half a Battalion of West Kents, sent up to reinforce me.'

The Cavalry Brigade was in action the next day at El Kutunie, with a degree of success, but this time hampered by blinding dust. News travelled fast, and these energetic first actions of the 14th Hussars particularly were to deter or restrict further Arab assistance to the Turks. As General Townshend was to record:

'The advent of the 14th Hussars had put new spirit and dash into the Indian Cavalry.'

On 30th November, at 11 a.m., the 6th Division under General Townshend retreated from Aziziyeh, with the cavalry leaving behind surplus supplies and equipment which had to be burned. They then went the short distance of seven miles to Umm-al-Tabul, with the 14th Hussars forming a guard on one of the column's flanks. All arrived by 3 p.m. where the Division, the 6th Cavalry Brigade, and transport, bivouacked and parked. At 9·00 p.m. that evening, the bivouac camp was shelled for quarter-an-hour by enemy guns, with a large Turkish force camped only about a mile away.

The next morning the retreat continued with the 6th Cavalry assisting in the rearguard by holding off the Arab cavalry. There was a fiercely fought action in Umm-Al-Tubal against a large Arab force, when it was found that the dismounted firepower of the Regiment had a turning effect on the action. According the *Historical Record* the 14th Hussars was a 'Regiment of Marksmen', though it did suffer some casualties of both men and horses. At 10 p.m. the troops arrived at Shaidie, (known as Monkey Village), some 24 miles from Umm-al-Tabul. Every one was dead tired, the night was bitterly cold, and no food, and with horses only able to get a rare drink of water. During the night the Cavalry Brigade was again called out to form a forward guard. Each man laid down where he was, and tried to get what sleep he could.

The next morning, 2nd December, the British force left Monkey Village and proceeded on its way along the Tigris River towards Kut. On its way it was being sniped at by Arabs on the other side of the river. At 10 p.m., after travelling 26 miles that day, the 6th Cavalry Brigade reached and bivouacked near Kut. During the night they were again to suffer heavy sniping from across the Tigris.

General Townshend's retreat from Baghdad had both nature and the native Arabs against it. The winter rains caused rivers to flood, and the land become a quagmire. Across the flat, dreary plain of mud which was Mesopotamia, exhausted by forced marches, to drop out of the column was to risk murder and mutilation.

On 3rd December, the 6th Cavalry Brigade moved into the town. As it was soon to be noticed that the Cavalry could be a hindrance rather than an advantage during the forthcoming siege, it was then ordered to leave and move the 60 miles to Ali-al-Gharbi to join General Aylmer's relieving force from Basra.

Thus on 5th December, Major Sandes of the Royal Engineers was ordered to hurriedly build a bridge across the River Tigris to allow the 6th Cavalry to escape before the Turks arrived. Using a mixture of boats, and an enormous stack of large beams, and planking of all sorts, after eight hours they were within ten yards of a large sandbank close to the other bank. Then in the cold of night, men got down into four feet of chilly water to place trestles and complete the bridge as far as the sandbank. Brigadier-General Roberts, commanding the 6th Cavalry Brigade decided not to attempt to cross that night, although the sandbank seemed hard and firm, with a further twenty yards of three feet deep water separating it from the further shore.

At 9 a.m. the next morning, the 6th December, the mass of the 6th Cavalry Brigade arrived to start the crossing. It was not long, however, before both the sandbank and sandy shore became something of a quagmire and quicksand, with one man and his horse almost lost. Further crossing ceased until Major Sandes had erected a makeshift trestle bridge across the sandbank and ford. After an hour and a half's delay the Cavalry Brigade continued its successful crossing. Luckily the Turkish force had not yet arrived to fire upon the troops while they were crossing the bridge, which could easily have turned this exercise into a massacre. As Major Sandes later wrote in his book:

'A marvellous stroke of luck indeed, was the escape of the 6th Cavalry Brigade from Kut. The rearguard troops of the cavalry waved their *adieux* and disappeared about noon *en route* for Ali-al-Gharbi and freedom.'

During the Mesopotamia Campaign Private Moses Baggot of the 14th Hussars made a series of some fifty well executed sketches showing episodes and aspects of life at the time in the Regiment. One such shows the cavalry leaving the doomed fortress of Kut. The bridge then had to be hurriedly destroyed before the Turks and Arabs arrived.

Again the cavalry had to leave tents and other heavy baggage behind, none of which was to be replaced until well into the following year. Therefore the Regiment had to endure an exceptionally cold and wet winter, clothed in thin drill uniform; without tents, waterproof sheets, or a second blanket; and in many cases without even a greatcoat. The cavalry's chief role in this particular campaign was to cover the open flank of the British Army against Arab attacks.

The Cavalry arrived Ali-al-Gharbi on 8th December, getting together with the Kut relief force, and setting up camp. Except for some light guard duties and reconnaissance, both men and horses of the 14th were able to recuperate with rest and food. Luckily there was relatively fine weather. The welfare and morale of the 14th was helped by charitable donations from Regimental ladies in India, plus the Regimental Comforts Fund organised by Regimental ladies in England. Unfortunately, extra comforts for Christmas failed to arrive in time. Similar help was sent to 14th Hussars prisoners of war. As the wife of the Regiment's R.S.M., one wonders whether Mrs Goddard at Aldershot participated in this welfare work.

Troops leaving India for Mesopotamia at about this time could obtain from the Army Y.M.C.A. of India a small 20-page booklet (plus a map) for two annas, entitled *The Land of the Two Rivers*. It included a potted history of the region; a short history of the current campaign up until the beginning of December 1915; some useful Arab words and phrases; and Health Hints. Was there an earlier edition available for the 14th Hussars to take with them in the November?

1916

By 4th January the haphazard and rushed preparation of a relief force for Kut was more or less made. It was however a hotch-potch of units arbitarily joined together, and thus no coherent chains of command from top to bottom had time to be established, which was to be responsible for some fatal results. The force - under-equiped and supplied - optimistically started to move along both sides of the River Tigris, with supply boats travelling along between. The cavalry was part of the force on the south bank. The enemy was soon encountered, on the 5th. The strength and ability of the Turk and Arab troops was under-estimated by the British Command, who thought they would be something of a push-over. There were to be three days' heavy fighting starting on the 6th, at Sheikh Saad, when the 14th Hussars advance-guard came upon enemy trenches, from which the enemy eventually withdrew upstream with heavy losses. The British suffered at times from heavy rain, with resultant mud. There were also the cold nights. But subsequent advances by the British again met stiff Turkish and Arab resistance. From mid-January this British relief force was to be held up for some three months in the area of Sheikh Saad, still some 30 miles or so from Kut.

This area was unsuitable for the cavalry, and the campaign was to turn into trench warfare. The cavalry could only be really used for observation and reconnaisance duties, or protective forays, at all hours of the day and night. Whatever the British did, the Turks could not be moved. Continuous rain and mud; deficiences in food, clothing, and equipment, and wood for fires, made conditions terrible for both men and horses, somewhat similar to those suffered on the Western Front. Several men had a fever, sometimes being a recurrence of malaria caught in India.

Early in March a determined 'push' was finally made, which almost came within sight of Kut, but again indecisive command was to be its downfall on 10th March. There were now to be floods and wind storms, necessitating the 6th Cavalry Brigade - including the 14th Hussars - being returned to Sheikh Saad. Meanwhile, the beseiged garrison at Kut under General Townshend was still fighting for its existence.

It was then, in early April, that 27-year old Captain T. E. Lawrence of the General Staff (Intelligence) in Cairo, (not yet the legendary 'Lawrence of Arabia'), was one of a small party sent to Mesopotamia and Kut. Part of this mission's aim was to try to bribe the Turkish commander with much gold to allow release of the besiged British force. The idea apparently came from Townshend, being approved by the War Office and Lord Kitchener. The other Mesopotamian officers were, however, appalled, considering it bad for British prestige. Lawrence's party arrived at Kut mid-April. On the 29th Lawrence and his party met the Turkish commander, who refused the initial £1,000,000 and also the final £2,000,000. It was really a pointless exercise as the final British relief force had recently been defeated, and General Townshend was about to surrender, and had already negotiated the conditional release of some 1,000 wounded British. Whilst in the region Lawrence was also to look into the feasibility of instigating an Arab revolt in Mesopotamia.

During his return journey back to Cairo, Lawrence wrote a letter on 18th May to his mother, describing his mission. He said that when he had landed at Basra on 5th April, 'it was pouring with rain & dark.' It also rained on his way up the Tigris. At Kut

'The weather cleared up and breeded myriads of flies. At sundown the awning over the deck used to change swiftly from grey to brown as the swarms alit on it to roost. The cavalry sometimes had to ride at foot pace, being blinded.'

Also on his return journey Lawrence prepared a devastating report on military, political, and intelligence operations in Mesopotamia. His evidence was to be later used in a submission to the Mesopotamia Commission set up by Parliament at the instigation of Lloyd George, whose critical Report was published in May 1917. Its damning findings were that the Campaign had been mismanaged and over-confident from the start, with inadequate preparation, lack of knowledge of the countryside, and the abundance of red-tape coupled with under-funding. Lloyd George regenerated the chaotic Mesopotamia Campaign, with a new command structure, supplies and reinforcements. If Lawrence's observations and suggestions had been subsequently better acted upon immediately the outcome of the Mesopotamia Campaign, and therefore the operations and conditions of such as the 14th Hussars may well have been different.

Meanwhile, in April a draft of 87 men for the 14th Hussars arrived from England. This was comprised of Reservists, and others who had been wounded and gassed in France, so that many were not able to stand the rigours of campaigning in the climate of Mesopotamia for very long. Trench warfare with its further attack and counter-attack - with little for the cavalry to do - failed to change the situation. The weather was now starting to get hot, on top of the already bad conditions. Then came news on 29th April that Kut had surrendered after 145 days siege.

The British, including the 14th Hussars at Gomorrah, remained in the general area of Sheikh Saad. During April and May some cases of cholera and typhoid arose, plus other diseases attributable to the climate and other adverse conditions. Adding to their already painful conditions, the sick (including delirious cholera sufferers) and wounded were brought by whatever transport was possible to the

River Tigris. Here they were transferred to British Red Cross motor launches to be taken either to the Tanooma military hospital at Shatt al Arab, south of Basra, or to field hospitals set up on the riverbanks, or the numerous steamers converted into hospital ships. One such launch was *The Wessex*, the first one on the Red Cross register of launches in Mesopotamia.

Meanwhile, the 14th Hussars were still undertaking observation duties, amidst plagues of flies (some biting), mosquitoes and sand-flies. Temperatures could reach 130°F in the shade. There were also desert sand storms. Long distance operations detected that the Turks had somewhat consolidated their situation by the withdrawal from some of their positions near Kut. The cavalry was detailed to follow them, in terrible desert heat, and under Turkish fire.

At the end of May the British went into summer camp at 'Arab Village' in a relatively cooler spot (average 112°F) alongside the River Tigris. It was still too hot for much military activity by either side, except against the marauding Arabs, and employment on convoy escort duties. This was an opportunity for the force General to inspect the 14th Hussars, and to thank them for their fine efforts as a flank guard. However, men and horses still suffered from bad conditions, illness and disease, and lack of food and other supplies. There were still swarms of mosquitos, sand-flies, ants, and large spiders and scorpions. Many officers and men were sick or invalided, plus some deaths.

In August weather conditions began to improve, it becoming cooler. Sports matches, Competitions and boxing-matches were now being organised by Corps, Division, Brigade and Regiment. Training continued in October, with new drafts of reinforcements and replacements from England. Hotchkiss guns newly invented, and Mark VII rifles were also issued.

In the *Supplement to the London Gazette*, 17th October 1916, page 10047, was printed the Despatch of 24th August 1916 from Lieutenant General Sir Percy Lake, KCB. He referred to his despatch of 12th August and attached a list of Officers, Warrant Officers, Non-Commissioned Officers and Men whom he desired to bring to special notice. At page 10049, from the 14th King's Hussars there were listed one Major, one Captain, two Lieutenants, the R.S.M (3796 J. Goddard) and one Sgt.

In mid-December the British force again began to make a determined offensive - with some success - against both Turkish and Arab resistance, despite heavy rain. The British were able to move along the Tigris, getting closer to Kut, despite casualties - including in the 14th who were carrying out their usual screening and flank protection actions. Some morale boosting mail with gifts arrived on Christmas evening.

1917

The waterlogged state of the ground was to restrict Cavalry movements during January. At the end of the month the total strength of the Regiment when it left Arab Village was 508 men of all ranks, but it was to suffer further loss through death and wounding - as were the horses - as it fought its way to Kut.

24th February finally saw the recapture of Kut by the British, some ten months after its surrender to the Turks. There then began a Turkish retreat, with the 14th Hussars leading the pursuit. The retreat turned into a rout, with resultant capture of much equipment, river vessels, and prisoners. The Arabs now typically were harrassing and looting their beaten ally. The next goal was Baghdad, 100 miles north-west of Kut. During the first week of March a 3-day stop had to be made halfway, at Aziziyeh, to allow supplies to catch-up.

Despite being a defeated force the Turkish rear-guard could still put up a stiff resistance, including inflicting casualties on the 14th Hussars.

After sixteen exhausting, sleepless, hungry days and nights, and fighting since leaving Kut, - now with dust-storms and lack of water - on 11th March the British eventually entered and captured Baghdad. According to the despatch by General Maude, the British force commander:

'About midnight [10th] patrols reported the enemy to be retiring. The dust-storm was still raging, but following the Decauville Railway as a guide our troops occupied the Baghdad Railway Station at 5·55 a.m. and ascertained that the enemy on the right bank [of the Tigris - full of bends and sandbanks] had retired upstream of Baghdad. Troops detailed in advance occupied the city, and the Cavalry moved on Khazimain, some four miles north-west of Baghdad, where they secured some prisoners.'

According to the *Historical Record*:

'On the morning of March 11th the 6th Cavalry Brigade left bivouac at 6·30 a.m. and moving on the left flank of the 7th Brigade were directed to advance on Khazimain and take the surrender of the inhabitants. The hot dusty march was accomplished at a slow pace owing to the complete exhaustion of the horses, many of which dropped out of the ranks during the day.

'At 3·30 p.m. the leading Squadron of the 14th Hussars crossed the Baghdad Railway and approached the outskirts of Khazimain. Lieut.-Colonel R. W. Hewitt [commanding officer] with a party from the Regiment proceeded into the town to receive its surrender and returned shortly afterwards with some half-dozen of the leading inhabitants, one hundred Turkish prisoners and several British prisoners whom they had released.

'The Brigade concentrated along the embankment of the Railway and with mixed feelings contemplated "the gilt twin domes and graceful minarets of Khazimain, mystic and wondrous, beautiful in the evening light and reflecting the setting sun." ...

'Perhaps somewhat of an anticlimax this comparatively peaceful ending to the struggle for the possession of the seat of Ottoman power in the East. . .'

Then, to quote from a soldier's letter written at Khazimain:

'As we gathered and sat down in groups on the bank [of the railway], with Baghdad on the right and Khazimain with its beautiful mosque in front, there was much to think over for those of us who had been toiling and striving out here for the past eighteen months. Baghdad, the goal towards which we have been looking for so long, sometimes with hope, very often with some doubt. But here we were, and we realized that with our presence one Pan-German dream was shattered and that the Union Jack and not the German Eagle soared over the City of the Caliphs. And we felt that at least one very definite success had been gained.'

A painting of this event by G. W. Lambert - 'The Surrender of Khazimain' - was subscribed to in 1920 by past and present Officers and friends of the Regiment, and hung in the Officers' Mess. R.S.M. Goddard is purported by his descendant family to be the lead horseman in the picture.

As far as John Goddard was concerned, this victory was to be somewhat tarnished by the knowledge that his brother, '18749 Private Moses Goddard of the 2nd Battalion, South Staffordshire Regiment' had been killed on the Somme, on Thursday, 8th March. His is one of the Commonwealth War Graves at the Pozieres British Cemetery, Ovillers-La-Boiselle, Somme, France.

The British, excluding the 6th Cavalry Brigade, were then soon involved in a further gruelling progress northwards up the Tigris, chasing and fighting the defeated retreating Turks, who nevertheless put up some resistance. Meanwhile, the 6th Cavalry Brigade remained at Khazimain; but on 23rd March, after a short reconnaissance, the 6th Cavalry Brigade were suddenly mobilised to overcome part of this stiff resistance. This resulted in a decisive defeat of a large Turkish force on the 27th March,

'in which the 14th Hussars played a very gallant part, and indeed took the main share in holding up the determined attack of two enemy divisions. . .'

For a while afterwards the Cavalry carried out reconnaissance and "spirited" defensive missions. During this period, on the 22nd and 27th April, parties each of 32 officers and men left the 14th Hussars for hot-weather leave in India. On the 29th the Regiment was ordered back to GHQ at Baghdad, reaching there on the evening of the 30th, after marching about 48 miles in 24 hours, in great heat and with a shortage of water. Half the Regiment was to be part of a small mobile column, to proceed westwards to the River Euphrates to punish certain Arab villages for the murder of a Colonel. Theses actions were carried out on 4th and 5th May, with the burning and destroying of certain crops and villages, and collecting a number of sheep and cattle. A scrap with Arabs on the 6th was severely punished by rifle and gun-fire. The column then returned to Baghdad.

The hot weather season had now begun, and was to be "the hottest season there in the memory of man" according to local arabs. The temperature inside tents could reach 133^OF, and there were many admissions to the Field Hospital. Many men were to suffer from heat-stroke in this great heat-wave, together with sand-fly fever, and intestinal troubles caused by having at times to drink brackish and muddy water. Operations came to an end for a while, with the 14th Hussars leaving on 9th/10th May and arrivinf on the 18th to set up a tented Summer Camp at Chaldari, 7 miles north of Baghdad, alongside the Tigris. Further batches of officers and men proceeded to India for furlough and a well earned rest, whilst others returned. Summer conditions here were a little better than in 1916 due to more and better supplies and comforts. Training however continued - including with new equipment and weaponry. There were also Inspections, boxing shows, plus a Race Meeting in the cooler September. There was during all this an abortive sortie against the Turks at Ramadi in mid-July, in abnormal heat and a dust storm.

With much of the country being flat, and without any landmarks of any description, directions had to be found by compass.

Meanwhile, in the UK, it was recorded in the *Supplement to the London Gazette* of 15 May 1917, page 4725:

'The following formed part of the Russian Decorations awarded in July 1916 to the British Forces for distinguished services rendered during the course of the Campaign. H.M. the King has given unrestricted permission in all cases to wear the Decorations and medals in question.

General Headquarters

Indian Expeditionary Force 'D'

22 December 1916

page 4727:-

Russian Cross of St. George, 4th class.

H/3796 Regimental Serjeant Major John Goddard, M.C. (Hussars).'

   This Order was founded in 1769 by the Empress Catherine, and was awarded only for conspicuous bravery in action against the enemy. Getting on for two million Crosses were distributed during the Great War, before the abolition of the Monarchy in December 1917. The black and orange ribbon of this Order meant 'through Darkness to Light', the black representing darkness and the orange light.

   (N.B. One recipient on this occasion was awarded the 1st class, having got the British V.C.; four were awarded the 2nd class; 18 were awarded the 3rd class; 36 were awarded the 4th class.) It is not known what the circumstances were for such awards. The various allied countries often gave one another a number of such awards, presumably to be distributed as the receiving country thought appropriate.

   On eventually marching out of Chaldari on 18th September, the Regiment now numbering 26 officers, 445 other ranks, and 557 horses, was part of a force to proceed up the Euphrates to capture Ramadi from a strong force of Turks, and Arabs. This was successfully accomplished, after stiff fighting, on 28th and 29th September, for which the 14th Hussars again received fulsome thanks for their part.

   By 4·30 p.m. of the 28th September three Squadrons of the 14th Hussars were blocking the Aleppo Road, and during the moonlit night were to be under sporadic light and heavy fire from the mixed Turkish and Arab force. At 7 a.m. next morning the Regiment set off to follow in support of the 21st Cavalry who were in pursuit of the Turks, but had to give up as the Turks were too far ahead, and returned to bivouac on the Aziziyeh Canal.

   It is noted that not until Order of the Day No. 108, dated 1st June 1918, was R.S.M. Goddard announced as having been awarded the Military Cross.

   It is the opinion of Patrick Dwyer of 'Hussars Research' that it could well have been in this engagement at Ramadi that R.S.M. Goddard's deeds were to be eventually rewarded with the Military Cross, and the report of the battle in the *Historical Record* seems to bear this out; though an alternative suggested engagement for R.S.M. Goddard's Military Cross was that on 5th November 1917 - see below. The citation was unfortunately not specific in the subsequent *London Gazette*, number 31119, of 10/11th January 1919:

Page 577: 'His Majesty the KING has been graciously pleased to approve of the following awards to the undermentioned officers and warrant officers in recognition of their gallantry and devotion to duty in the Field:-'
Page 603: 'AWARDED THE MILITARY CROSS.'
Page 621: 'No. 47438 S.M. John Goddard, 14th Hussars. (MESPOTAMIA)

'For conspicuous gallantry and devotion to duty. He was in charge of the led horses of three squadrons who came under heavy fire. He showed great coolness and resource in making arrangements for safeguarding them. Later, when relieved by an officer, he assisted, under heavy fire, with the evacuation of casualties from the firing line and the replenishment of ammunitions from the led horses.'

The MILITARY CROSS had only been instituted by George V in December 1914, 'in recognition of distinguished and meritorious services in time of war.' It being an Army decoration, no person was eligible to receive it unless he was a commissioned officer up to the rank of captain, or a warrant officer - which of course R.S.M. Goddard was. (In this particular list of about 170 recipients, only three were not officers, with Goddard being one of them.) Recipients are entitled to use the letters M.C. after their name.

The Cavalry Brigade marched back into the village of Falujah on 1st October. The Regiment's commanding officer, Lieutenant Colonel R. W. Hewitt D.S.O. had been wounded early in the morning of the 29th September, and the Regiment arrived to hear that he had died in hospital there the previous day. He was buried that same evening in the little cemetery outside the village, alongside the Euphrates. The funeral was attended by all of the Regiment who could be spared, plus representatives from other units in the area.

The Cavalry Brigade then returned back at Chaldari alongside the Tigris on the 6th October, where the 14th Hussars were to be thoroughly overhauled, and Inspected.

On the 23rd October the Cavalry started to proceed northwards along the Tigris, often at night, and caught up with the retreating Turks on 2nd November, who could still put up a spirited rear-guard defence. The British reached the Turks' strongly entrenched position at Tekrit, who also had flanking reinforcements arriving close at hand. The 14th Hussars thus had to defensively entrench against their approach. The 'Battle of Tekrit' took place on 4th/5th November, when British infantry and other cavalry units over-ran the Turkish positions; and with the Turkish reinforcements not materialising the 14th Hussars joined the subsequent clearance of the battle area. The British force eventually dispersed, with the weary Cavalry Division going to a congenial camp-site at Sadiyeh, reached on 11th November. Whilst here the 14th Hussars heavy baggage was brought up from Chaldari.

As the *Historical Record* was to say regarding 22nd November:

'While the Cavalry Division were at Sadiyeh the 14th Hussars had the opportunity of celebrating the anniversary of "Ramnuggur". In the afternoon an Inter-Squadron Football Tournament was successfully held. . . In the evening a splendid smoking concert was given by the Sergeants' Mess. Six E.P. tents were erected and joined up, making a large hall on the front of the camp. All Officers and Sergeants of the Division, together with many from neighbouring units, were invited. A very large supply of drinks and cigars and cigarettes were collected, and a most merry evening was spent. Four General Officers graced the proceedings. The most noticeable event of the evening was an excellent and most humourous speech by R.S.M. J. Goddard. The merriment was continued, according to time-honoured custom, until the small hours of the morning.'

Then on the 30th November the 6th Cavalry Brigade moved across the Tigris to Sindiyeh to stop any strong Turkish reinforcements coming to assist their retreating forces. The 14th Hussars were still part of this Cavalry Brigade, and at the time was comprised of 19 Officers, 445 other ranks, and 525 horses. Turkish defences were encountered on 1st December, which were overcome on the 6th following stiff resistance, during which the 14th Hussars at one time operated dismounted. After which the 6th Cavalry Brigade returned to Sadiyeh camp on the 9th. It was now the cold weather season again, with as much as 20 degrees of frost at night.

However, sports and football matches were subsequently held. The *Historical Record* reads:

'Christmas Day was spent very cheerily. The men of the Regiment had an excellent dinner, helped out by liberal gifts from home and extras purchased with Regimental funds and Officers' subscriptions. Church Parade was held in the morning.

'At midday the Officers, together with Brig.-General Holland-Pryor and his Staff, visited the Sergeants' Mess, and speeches were made and toasts drunk in the time-honoured fashion.'

1918

Early in January, after a very wild wet night, during which the whole of the Sadiyeh Camp was flooded out, the Regiment was ordered to leave the 6th Cavalry Brigade and to proceed into Persia, as the major part of a small column. This was to support the Russians who were suffering a large number of desertions following their 1917 Revolution. Persia, what is now Iran, was then a mountainous largely roadless country, as against the somewhat flat plains of Mesopotamia. The column marched out on 13th January, arriving at Qasr-i-Shirin - six days and 102 miles later - where it set up camp. Not only were some Turks in Persia, but reinforcements had to be stopped entering. Also some Germans were actively stirring up the native population. This necessitated punitive action against certain tribes and villages, as well as individuals who were caught doing such things as cutting telephone wires.

The 14th Hussars were often to be scattered, with Squadrons sometimes apart from Regimental Headquarters by as much as 400 miles or so. It also carried out escort, reconnaissance, and flanking duties. There were in turn to be adverse conditions similar to those in Mesopotamia - with prolonged pouring rain (which necessitated moving camp), heat, mosquitoes, midges, and sand flies by the swarm. Parties of Regiment officers and men were thus glad to go for well-earned leave in India in April. At the same time the Regiment was often visited by travelling Generals and Staff Officers, plus a Russian Cossack detachment.

R.S.M. John Goddard was to again receive bad news, by hearing of the loss of a second brother, '58995 Private Charles Goddard, of the 59th Battalion, Machine Gun Corps', who died on Monday, 15th April 1918. He is commemorated on the Commonwealth War Graves Commission's Ploegsteert Memorial, Comines-Warneton, Hainaut, Belgium. This Memorial commemorates more than 11,000 U.K. and South African servicemen who died in this sector and have no known grave. Neither Moses nor Charles Goddard are recorded on the War Memorial inside the Wednesday parish church of St. Bartholomew. Probably because they had moved to adjoining Tipton following the death of their parents in 1896.

According to the *Historical Record* the news of John Goddard's award of the Military Cross arrived at Regimental Headquarters on 5th July, which had only just arrived at Hamadan Camp in north-west Persia, to be joined by much of the Regiment. Here the mountainous altitude reached some 6,280 feet, with its own natural difficulties.

This part of the Regiment had been ordered here to take over places previously occupied by the Russians, who were evacuating Persia back to the Caspian Sea. The Russians and the 14th Hussars were to sometimes have friendly encounters. The Turks meanwhile, with help, were still putting up a spirited resistance, and at times would also be offensive. The British troops suffered privations and resultant sickness, including cholera.

Regimental HQ and part of the Regiment on 15th July marched 99 miles to Bijar, and then 59 miles to Sain Kaleh by 23rd July. Supplies were difficult as rations had to be transported at the same time as none could be purchased along the way. The situation meant that HQ returned to Bijar, having covered 480 miles since 21st June. Refugees were now a problem, who were being attacked by both the Turks, and Kurdish raiders. On 10th August the Regimental HQ had now to start a move to reinforec the Squadron at Taken Tappeh who were going down sick - including with cholera.

'On August 25th two Troops "B" Squadron under Lieutenant Whidborne left [Takan Tappeh] for Bijar as escort to a sick convoy and spare transport. Seven mule stretchers constructed under R.S.M. Goddard's design from poplar-trees and blankets proved a satisfactory method of carrying the worst cases. Each stretcher was carried between two mules, one in front and one behind with one lying, or two sitting, patients between. The Medical Officer accompanied the party, which was attacked by Kurds near Kizil Bulagh, but they were driven off with loss.'

As a Turkish force was approaching Taken Tappeh, defensive measures were taken. At the same time it was reported that a German Division had landed in the Black Sea, which resulted in the 14th Hussars entrenching and sending out regular patrols, plus the arrival of other units as part of the North Persia Force. Regimental HQ and part of the Regiment left for Bijar on 8th September.

Takan Tappeh was evacuated on 20th September, soon to be occupied by the Turks who approached within 10 miles or less of Bijar where the 14th Hussars were billetted. The latter were to suffer from a deal of sickness during August and September, chiefly as a result of contact with Armenian refugees. During October it was influenza which was to cause medical problems, causing some deaths. Some British units were to be on half rations for three weeks as the flooded rivers between them and their supply base at Baghdad had prevented the food vans from bringing up rations. In some instances this meant one mug of tea, two biscuits and half a tin of bully beef each day. Influenza and pneumonia were rife amongst the British Force.

With the capture of Damascus from the Turks on 2nd October, over in Palestine, the situation in north-west Persia dramatically changed. Here the Turks started to withdraw from Persia and the Caucasus.

On 28th October an Armistice was signed with Turkey, with a cessation of hostilities. Evacuation of Bijar was thus to take place on 7th November. Whilst dressed only in summer clothing this took place in bitterly cold, windy, snow conditions. The Regiment finally arrived in an exhausted condition at Hamadan on the 13th. On the 12th news was received of the Armistice with Germany the day previous.

Although patrols still had to go out to watch for Kurdish raiders, the troops could now relax, such that they could visit a local bazaar to buy carpets. There was a race meeting organised by one of the Units, but none of the 14th's horses were in a fit enough condition to take part. Preparations were also being made to leave Persia and return to Mesopotamia.

On 1st December the majority of the 14th Hussars started the march away, but later heavy rain soon caused the column to become bogged down in a morass of mud. The men had to do as much as, or even more than the animals to move the waggons, etc. Eventually they reached a metalled road which took them to the Camp at Qasr-i-Shirin on 16th December. Then half the Regiment went to the Camp at Shahraban back in Mesopotamia, for rest, re-organisation, re-equipment, and the start of demobilization. It was a quiet Christmas, followed by the the greeting of the remainder of the Regiment who arrived on the 28th December and the following 6th January.

The *Historical Record* was to say:

'To celebrate the reunion of the Regiment and to see out the end of the Old Year, a great Smoking Concert in the Sergeants' Mess was organized. It was pleasant to see all the well-known faces gathered together again, though it was felt that it would probably be for the last time.'

For certain actions during the War the Regiment was to be awarded further Battle Honours: **Tigris 1916, Kut-al-Amara 1917, Baghdad**.

R.S.M. John Goddard seems to have again come through this War unscathed, as his name does not appear in the Regimental casualty list.

The names of the two Goddard brothers killed in action have yet to be located on any U.K. war memorials.

POST-GREAT WAR

1919

At the beginning of the New Year the Regiment received orders that they would form part of the Post-War Garrison of Mesopotamia. However, large-scale demobilisation was to be carried out during January, February, and March.

As well as his Military Cross, R.S.M. John Goddard was also qualified for what were called the 'Pip, Squeak and Wilfred' medals - named after three contemporary newspaper cartoon characters. These were the 1914 STAR, the BRITISH WAR MEDAL, and the VICTORY MEDAL. Having been mentioned in despatches R.S.M. Goddard would also have been qualified to have an oak leaf on his Victory Medal, but it is noticed that one is not so displayed amongst his medals.

By 1919 R.S.M. Goddard would seemingly have qualified for the Army's LONG SERVICE AND GOOD CONDUCT MEDAL. This was instituted by King William IV in 1830, to be granted to soldiers of irreproachable character who had served 21 years in the infantry, or twenty in the cavalry. During the Great War, its ribbon, because of its similarity with that of the Victoria Cross, was changed to crimson with white edges.

Further orders were received that a Cadre of the Regiment consisting of 7 Officers and 107 Rank and File including

'47438 R.S.M. J. Goddard, M.C.'

should proceed to the U.K., and the remainder of the Regiment to remain in Mesopotamia until relieved by a Regiment from Home. To facilitate this the Regiment left Shahraban on 11th February, and arrived at Iron Bridge Camp on the 15th. The Cadre embarked on the "*P.58*" on 10th March, arriving at Basra on the 15th and sailing from there in s.s. *Ekma* on 25th March. This ship was of 5108 tons, capable of 16½ knots, and built in 1911 for British India. The ship arrived in Bombay on 31st March, and the Cadre having then to be transhipped onto the crowded s.s. *City of Sparta*, sailing for England on 3rd April. This latter ship was of 5,415 tons, capable of 13 knots, and built in 1897 for the City Line.

After a severe gale in the Bay of Biscay the 14th Hussars Cadre disembarked two days overdue at Liverpool on 30th April. Owing to an earlier case of bubonic plague amongst the crew, the 14th Hussars were put in quarantine at Knotty Ash Camp. They eventually left Liverpool by train for Tidworth Garrison in Hampshire on 5th May, where they were to be greeted by the Regimental Band. This was followed by two month's Overseas leave.

The 14th's Cadre reassembled at Tidworth on 15th July, being augmented by the now ceased 5th Reserve Cavalry Regiment. This made the Regiment's total strength 36 Officers, 1,067 Other Ranks who included 438 reservists who needed training, and 308 Horses.

During September a detachment was sent out to Monmouth for about ten days, on duty connected with the then Railway Strike.

In November, seven 14th Hussars' officers and R.S.M. Goddard (Military Cross) were summoned to Buckingham Palace to be presented with their respective decorations by the King George V.

1920

One result of R.S.M. Goddard's return from the Middle East was the subsequent arrival during February of a fifth child (a third surviving daughter), Jessie Beryl.

After demobilisations, discharges and transfers the Regiment's strength was now down to 36 Officers and 557 Other Ranks, plus 413 horses. As most of the men now left were Recruits, as many as possible were undergoing appropriate training. The G.O.C. 2nd Cavalry Brigade, after Inspection in September, was to report the Regiment 'fit for War up to a limited strength'.

Sometime in June, at Tidworth, a group photograph was taken of all W.O.s, Staff Sergeants and Sergeants, with R.S.M. J. Goddard in the middle of the front row.

There was to be the resumed round of Sports, etc. R.S.M. Goddard, after qualifying in the Southern Command Bronze Medal Tournament, took part in the Military Tournament at Olympia. He was second in 'Sword v Sword', and third in 'Sword v Lance'. In the Military Meeting at Milton Lisbourne, R.S.M. Goddard won the 'Tent-Pegging' and 'Dummy-Thrusting'. In the 2nd Cavalry Brigade Sports on 10th August, the 14th Hussars won the Cup for the Best Regiment, and R.S.M. Goddard won the G.O.C.'s Individual Cup. Then in the Southern Command Rifle Meeting the Regimental Team was third, and R.S.M. Goddard was first in Class "B".

In the A.R.A. matches the Regiment's team of sixteen (which probably included R.S.M. Goddard) won the Duke of Connaught's Cup. This competition was actually between teams of six, with each man firing 12 shots for a maximum score of 120.

Ramnuggur was celebrated on 10th September instead of in November, as the Regiment was about to be moved from Tidworth to the Rhine in Germany. The move to the out-of-date Deutz Cavalry Barracks in Cologne was completed on 3rd December.

Almost immediately there began a social round of entertainment. The Members of B.A.O.R. G.H.Q. Sergeants Mess at Cologne invited the sergeants of the 14th

Hussars to a Whist Drive and Dance, held at the Bürgergesellschaft, Cologne, on Tuesday, 11th November, as part of the Armistice Anniversary Celebration. There was a similar invitation for New Year's Eve, Friday, 31st December.

1921

The author, amongst his 14th Hussars memorabilia, has a New Year's Day B.A.O.R. H.Q. Sergeants Mess printed *Menu*, signed by many attendees, but R.S.M. Goddard's name does not appear. The same Sergeants Mess invited other Warrant Officers, Staff Sergeants and Sergeants to a Smoking Concert in the Mess on Tuesday, 25th January.

Wives were issued with pink Identity Cards, issued by the Military Permit Office, G.H.Q., countersigned by the Provost Marshall's Office. It contained a photograph of the person concerned, and authorised 2nd Class travel in the Occupied Area.

The Regiment was again to be renamed - this time to the 14th King's Hussars, i.e. dropping the brackets around the word '(King's)'.

A subsequent contemporary recruiting poster for the 14th King's Hussars gave the following rates of pay:

'Recruit on joining: 19s. 3d per week all found.
Recruit after 2 years' service: £1 4s. 6d. etc.
Lance-Corporal: £1 9s. 9d. etc.
Corporal: £1 15s. 0d. etc.
Lance-Sergeant: £1 18s. 6d. etc.
Sergeant: £2 9s. 0. etc.
Sqdn. Quartermaster-Sergt.: £3 6s. 6d. etc.
Sqdn. Sergt.-Major: £3 10s. 0d. etc.
Regt. Quartermaster-Sergt.: £4 4s. 0d. etc.
Regt. Sergt.-Major: £4 15s. 0d. etc.'

There were also allowances for a wife and family.

Early in March, in consequence of the London Conference and the German Government's holding out on the question of Reparations, the Regiment was ordered to take part in the occupation of Dusseldorf as part of the British Army of Occupation on the Rhine. This exercise did not end until 29th May when the Germans had given in, and all the Regiment were then back in Cologne.

In Cologne, on 10th March, an officer and R.S.M. J. Goddard M.C., with seventeen Rank and File attended a Ceremonial Parade at the Nordfreidhof for the laying of wreaths by General Gaucher (Commander of the Allied Army of

14th Hussars Medal of which John Goddard was one of its first recipients

R.S.M. John Goddard

Private Moses Baggott's sketch of 14th Hussars driving back two regiments of
Turkish cavalry at the battle of Umm-al-Tabal on 1st December 1915

Private Moses Baggott's sketch of the withdrawal of the cavalry from
Kut-al-Amara on 6th December 1915

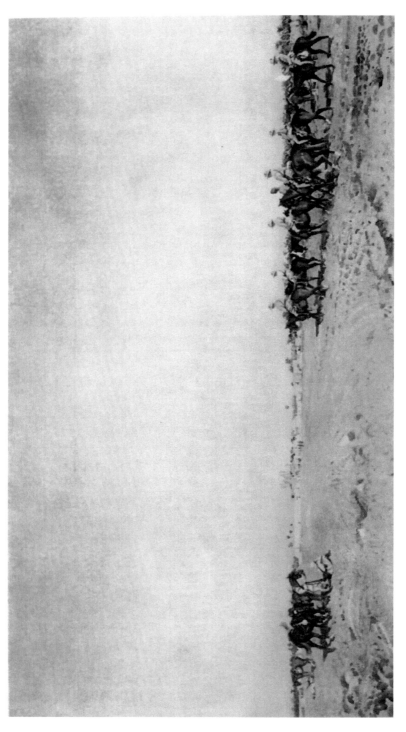

The surrender of Khazimain, 11th March, 1917. From an Oil Painting by G. W. Lambert. The leading horseman said by family to be R.S.M. John Goddard.

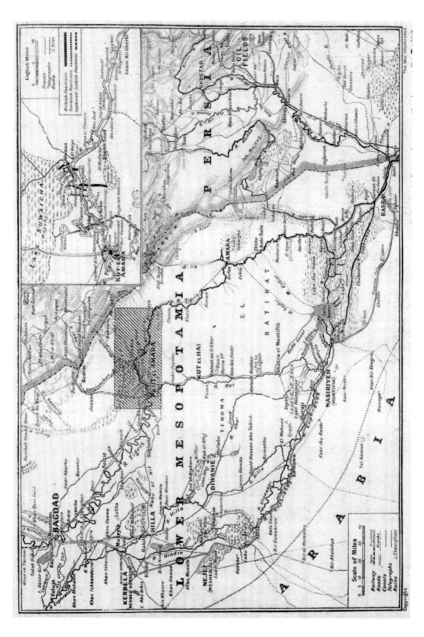

Map of Mesopotamia and Persia in Great War showing locations of 14th Hussars engagements.

R.S.M. John Goddard on his horse possibly "Ramnuggur"

R.S.M. John Goddard standing proud with his medals,
including the Military Cross

14th/20th Hussars Revolver Team at what could be Tidworth Camp, 1925. R.S.M. John Goddard seated far left.

Occupation) on the graves of French soldiers killed in 1871 (Franco-Prussian War) and in the Great War.

The rest of the year was spent on training, Ceremonial Parades, Inspections, and Sports and Competitions when again the Regiment did well. In an Inter-Allied Jumping Competition at Mainz, R.S.M. Goddard won a prize, riding a horse appropriately named *Ramnuggur*. This may have been the occasion when on 8th October he won a medal in the B.A.O.R. Open Jumping. He also represented the B.A.O.R. in the Allied Shooting Meeting at Aachen. Some of his prize-winning medals - including one inscribed 'Inter Troop 1921' - were subsequently made into brooches for the female members of the family.

During this period some members of the Regiment went to assist in Silesia, where the Germans and Poles were fighting one another.

Also at some time during the year R.S.M. Goddard was again a member of the 14th Hussars Team that won the Duke of Connaught Cup. A photograph was subsequently taken of the team with the Cup, with each member holding his revolver.

In the *Dorset Evening Echo* of 21st November 1931, it was mentioned that

'One year he won the coveted silver jewel awarded for rifle shooting at Bisley. A special journey from abroad had to be made in this case because his regiment at the time was serving in Germany'

The Warrant Officers, Staff-Sergeants, and Sergeants held their annual Ramnugger Ball and Supper on the usual date, 22nd November, with a mixed Programme of twenty-four dances, held at the Bürgergesellschaft, Cologne.

1922

The 14th Hussars, still in Cologne, continued with training and courses, Guards-of-Honour, Parades; and with some still assisting in Silesia at Lublinitz until 24th June. Social life in Germany was good; and with the 'crash' of the German mark during 1921-1923 everything became extremely cheap to the Army of Occupation who were paid in sterling.

At the Army Rifle Association Competitions, R.S.M. Goddard was 7th for the Individual Revolver Medal. The 14th Hussars came 2nd in the Duke of Connaught's Cup competition. In addition, R.S.M. Goddard possibly competed in Horse Shows.

On 1st October the 14th King's Hussars were amalgamated with the disbanded 20th Hussars, to form the 14th/20th Hussars, with John Goddard remaining as the R.S.M. The two Regiments had long been exchanging drafts of both officers and other ranks, so that their eventual amalgamation was an inevitable result of changing times. A distinction between the Regiments were maintained as regards Dress, Marches and Calls. The 14th Hussars Prussian Eagle was to be re-introduced in 1926. Along with other similar amalgamations this was part of the reduction in the number of cavalry regiments.

1923

It has been said by the family that it was whilst in Germany that R.S.M. Goddard began to appreciate the music of Richard Wagner, and consequently began going to the Opera House in Cologne to listen to Wagner concerts. Here seats were reserved at very low prices for the personnel of the Army of Occupation. The annual outing for the Married Families took the form of a trip up the Rhine in a tourist steamer. The Goddards became friends with a German family there, in spite of the general natural reserve of the Germans, and before WW2 some family members used to go over and visit them.

The 14th/20th Hussars returned home from Germany in October, with much of the regimental baggage which was stored on deck being lost overboard during a gale off Dover. On eventual disembarkation the Regiment went on to Tidworth, to become part of the 2nd Cavalry Brigade. The horses had been left behind in Germany, and thus new ones had to be obtained.

There was to follow a reappraisal of the role of Cavalry Regiments, which arose from the belated realisation that such were becoming outmoded with the introduction of tanks and armoured cars, and the increased use of machine guns against which mounted cavalry had no defence. This resulted in the gradual disappearance of the horse, except for show-jumping and steeplechasing. For the time being, however, the

'cavalry training during this period was largely devoted to inclusive encounters or co-operation with tanks, but the old skills were still practised regimentally and every cavalryman had to be an expert swordsman, capable of galloping over a series of obstacles while making the correct thrusts at dummies on either side.'

The published Regiment's *Historical Record* finishes at this date, to be supplemented by the subsequent history of the 14th/20th Hussars - the published *Emperor's Chambermaids*.

1924

When the Chief of the Imperial General Staff (C.I.G.S.) visited the Cavalry

Brigade at Tidworth in 1924, the first signs of this reappraisal were made clear. There were also changes in nomenclature of certain Regimental ranks, with privates now officially being designated Troopers - something they had been called unofficially for many years.

In competitions the Regiment continued its successes, though in the *Emperor's Chambermaids* the names of winners and runners-up are almost invariably conspicuously absent, unlike in the *Historical Record*. However, a photograph exists of the winning 14th/20th Hussars Team in The Duke of Connaught Cup, showing R.S.M. Goddard as a member of the team.

PUBLICAN

1925

John Goddard retired from the 14th/20th Hussars sometime in 1925, after 27 years distinguished service, with the rank of Regimental Sergeant Major which he had held for ten years. The previous four R.S.M.s had held this rank for six, three, five, and two years respectively back in time. Thereafter he used to attend the annual Regimental Dinner for past and present officers, n.c.o.'s, and men.

One wonders why he had never applied for a commission, e.g. as a Quartermaster, when he might have expected an automatic rank of captain, or even major, albeit in another regiment.

It had been said by a member of the descendant family that one or other of the then Devenish and Groves breweries in Weymouth were somehow connected with the 14th/20th Hussars. And that John Goddard, supposedly along with three fellow sergeants - Ilott, Northam, and Spring (said to be a saddler) - came down to Weymouth, to become landlords of local public houses. Subsequent research has confirmed much of this.

According to the Weymouth Museum archives, just before October 1925 John Goddard became landlord of the *Prince of Wales Inn*, Park Street, Weymouth. This was owned by Dorchester brewers, Eldridge Pope & Co. Ltd. This tenancy is corroborated by *Kelly's Directory 1927* which shows him in the *Prince of Wales* at 11/12 Park Street, Weymouth.

In the Weymouth Royal British Legion's archives there is a contemporary *Prince of Wales* advertising artifact - a dark green metal match-box holder, kindly donated by the family. The front is marked:

With Compliments from
J. GODDARD, M.C.
================================
Prince of Wales
================================
PARK STREET,
WEYMOUTH.

On the back is printed:

When you lie, let it be by a pretty woman,
When you steal, steal away from bad company,
When you swear, swear by your country.

When you drink, drink at the
'Prince of Wales' and smile like old
JOE GODDARD.

James A. Ilott at the same date was in the *Terminus* public house at 2 Queen Street, Weymouth, opposite the town's end-of-the-line railway station, and barely a hundred yards from the *Prince of Wales*. According to the Weymouth Museum this public house was owned by the Hurdle family, but leased to Devenish's. The *Terminus* is now (2007) called *The Giant Pot*. Nothing so far has been found of a Northam at a Weymouth public house.

It was the same wounded John Spring who John Goddard helped carry from the field of battle in 1900. According to the *Southern Times* of 10th September 1943, after his discharge in 1910 Spring later became licensee of Eldridge Pope's *Lamb and Flag* in Lower Bond Street, and later the *Rodwell Hotel* from where he retired in 1931. Weymouth Museum's records show him as landlord at the *Rodwell Hotel* in Rodwell Road, Weymouth, by April 1926. This was another Eldridge Pope public house.

Thus it would seem that John Spring was the first to come to Weymouth, and would have recommended Goddard and Ilott for Weymouth public houses.

From the *Historical Record* and other sources it is possible to ascertain the Goddard-Dorchester and Weymouth brewers connection. A 2nd Lieutenant A. V. ('Darky') Pope joined the 14th (Kings) Hussars in 1908, being of the Dorchester brewing firm Eldridge Pope. He was eventually in 1936 to become Lieutenant-Colonel and commanding officer of the 14th/20th Hussars, which was by this time a Tank Regiment. A Lieutenant Leslie H. S. Groves was transferred to the 14th Hussars from the 20th Hussars in 1921, at about the time of their amalgamation. He was son of Alderman Herbert John Groves, of the Weymouth brewing firm John Groves & Son, who at one time had been Mayor of Weymouth. In 1940 he was to become Lieutenant-Colonel commanding the 14th/20th Hussars.

The same newspaper also said that John Spring had been a founder and Past Master of the United Services Freemasons Lodge No. 3473, Portland. This Lodge had been formed in September/October 1910, and used the premises of its sponsors the Portland Lodge No. 1037 in Victoria Square, Portland. According to the Library and Museum of Freemasonry, Sergeant John Goddard had been initiated into Hope Lodge No. 413, Meerut, on 7th October 1924, aged 35; and Resigned 31st March 1926. He then joined United Service Lodge No. 3473, Portland, on 21st December 1925. This latter event could naturally have only been on the recommendation of John Spring.

There is, however, an anomaly. John Goddard had left Meerut in India in November 1915, after only a year's stay - as an R.S.M.; and in 1924 he was in Tidworth. In addition, to tie in with his declared age of 35, it would seem that his initiation at Meerut should have been recorded as 1914. The author has queried this with the Freemasons, but without a satisfactory explanation.

1926

22nd April saw the death of Mrs Hilda Goddard's mother, Eleanor Elliott, aged 77. This took place at her home, 5 Mount Pleasant, Redan Hill, Aldershot, with her married daughter Ethel Gerrard being present. Cause of death was given on the Death Certificate as: "1. Carcinoma of liver. 2. Icterus. Cardiac Failure." Her late husband William was described as a "Furniture Remover". Eleanor was to be buried in her husband's grave in the Redan Road Cemetery, still in "Unconsecrated ground". Their son, Hector, purchased the grave on 1st July. Although the position of the plot is known there is nothing on the ground to denote it. However, a few old memorial stones are still *in situ* in 'B' section, most of it being flat grassed ground.

1927

During the year, after only two years in the licensed trade John Goddard was made Chairman of the South Dorset Licensed Victuallers Association (*Dorset Daily Echo* 21st November).

1930

According to the Weymouth Museum, in the May of 1930 John Goddard moved from the *Prince of Wales* public house in Park Street, to the *Royal Adelaide Hotel*, 180-182 Abbotsbury Road, Westham, Weymouth, about a mile across town. The *Royal Adelaide* was owned by Weymouth brewers John Groves Ltd. This move is confirmed in the *Kelly's Directory 1930-1931*.

The Weymouth British Legion's archives are fortunate to contain a copy of John Goddard's 'Tariff Souvenir' brochure for the *Royal Adelaide*, containing photographs of the exterior and of the Coffee Room. The Tariff quoted is:

'APARTMENTS
Single Bedroom 4/-. Bed and Breakfast 6/-. Bath (Hot) 6d.
MEALS: Plain Tea 1/6. Lunch 3/-. Dinner 3/6.
Special Terms by the week'

According to a member of the family, John Goddard had apparently hoped to transfer to the larger *Spa Hotel*, situated on the corner of Dorchester Road and Spa Road, Radipole, Weymouth. But seemingly the owners, Dorchester brewers Eldridge Pope strangely did not consider him suitable.

POLITICIAN

1931

The *Dorset Daily Echo* of Wednesday, 8th April, carried the following report:

'NAVAL WEDDING AT WEYMOUTH
WOODFORD - GODDARD

'The wedding took place at St. Paul's Church, Weymouth, today, of Eleanor Goddard, daughter of Mr. and Mrs. J. Goddard of the Royal Adelaide Hotel, Westham, Weymouth, and Mr. Reginald Woodford, gunner, Royal Navy, son of Mr. and the late Mrs. W. Woodford of Letchmore, Cliff Road, Hythe.

'Both the bridegroom and the best man, Mr. Donald Cull, gunner, Royal Navy, wore their naval uniform.

'The bride, who was given away by her father, wore an ankle length dress of cream georgette, with veil and coronet of orange blossom, and carried a bouquet of white heather. Audrey Goddard, her sister, who was bridesmaid, wore an ankle length dress of yellow georgette with black picture hat. She carried a bouquet of daffodils.

'The wedding service was conducted by the Rev. A. F. G. Christie.

'A reception was afterwards held at the bride's home, after which the couple left for London, where the honeymoon is being spent. The bride's travelling attire consisted of a Chinese blue silk dress with hat to match, and a musquash fur coat, the gift of the bridegroom.

'The couple received numerous presents, including a dinner service from the customers of the Royal Adelaide Hotel.'

It will be noted that 'Joe' Goddard seems not yet to have made a name for himself in the local community, with for example no mention of his M.C., or anything that would make this wedding something out of the ordinary. But that was soon to change.

November 1931 saw John Goddard's entry into local politics, when he was elected unopposed for Wyke Regis Ward onto Weymouth Town Council, subsequently making his Declaration of Office on 6th November. He was then to be placed onto the Council Committees of: Estates and Housing; Health and Maternity and Child Welfare; Local Pension; Publicity; Selection.

The *Dorset Daily Echo* of 21st November was to feature him as No. 35 in its regular 'Our Portrait Gallery' column. It naturally concentrated on his 'romantic career' in the 14th Hussars, being a 'crack' shot, and 'also excellent at tent-pegging.' One detail not elsewhere seen mentioned was that he had 'something like 40 shooting trophies and medals'.

'Mr Goddard is still keenly interested in his old regiment and only at the beginning of this year he went to Southampton to bid "bon voyage" to those now serving with the 14th/20th Hussars when they left for the East [Egypt].' (According to the *Ramnuggur Boys* this could actually have been the previous September.)

'For the past four years he has been chairman of the South Dorset Licensed Victuallers Association, and his efforts on the Association's behalf have received the appreciation of all members. During his term of office the Association succeeded in securing alteration of hours for the licensees.'

1933

In the *Southern Times* of 30th September he was one of a depiction of a group of 'Weymouth Celebrities in Caricature' by "Matt", which had originally been published in the *Sunday Graphic*. Amongst those depicted was 'Mr. J.T.Goddard, Chairman of S. Dorset Licensed Victuallers'. It is noticed that John Goddard had not been credited with his Military Cross, unlike others in the group whose decorations were mentioned.

At that time tobacco smoking was not generally known for the medical danger it was later acknowledged to be. So the depiction of John Goddard with a cigarette dangling from his mouth, was not quite so foolhardy as might at first be supposed. According to the family, at some stage John Goddard had one lung removed.

1934

On the evening of 5th April, at the quarterly meeting of Weymouth's Honorary Court Highclere No. 7634 of The Ancient Order of Foresters, No. 1 of the Honorary Courts, John Goddard was proposed a member by Brother George G. Smith, and seconded by Brother P. J. A'Court (Past Chief Ranger). The ceremonial induction then took place. He would have been invested with his Member's V-shaped Neck Collar of Lincoln green (the Foresters' colour), with the emblem of the Order on one side. The Collar being specified as 2½ inches wide and 1½ yards long with a dark green tassel. As usual with such charitable organisations, the Member's Certificate was a large ornate affair with much symbolic pictorial content. For further details of the Order see Appendix IV.

During August the Goddards' son Graham, (presumably by now in the London Police), was married at Holborn, London, to Margaret Clark.

Early in November 'Joe' Goddard was to be re-elected onto Weymouth Town Council, this time for his home Westham West Ward, and making his Declaration of Office on the 9th.

1937

At the Weymouth British Legion's General Committee meeting of 9th February, it was

'Resolved that Mr Munroe [manager of the *Clinton Restaurant*] be asked to permit Mr Goddard of the R.Adelaide to run the bar'

at the forthcoming Annual Dinner. This was confirmed at the subsequent House Committee meeting of 17th February - though minuted this time as being the 'Adelaide Arms'.

Ethel Gerrard (neé Elliott), niece of Hilda Goddard, is said to have now come to live at the *Royal Adelaide*. She was to stay there until her marriage some years later in 1944 (*q.v.*).

In November John Goddard was to be re-elected for a third term onto Weymouth Town Council, again for Westham West Ward, and subsequently making his Declaration of Office.

1938

In January, 'Joe' Goddard, as Chairman, was a host at the annual banquet of the South Dorset Licensed Victuallers Association at the Sidney Hall, Weymouth. According to the report in the *Southern Times* of 22nd January, at the end of his Presidential speech, Sir Herbert Morgan, K.B.E., chairman of Smith's Potato Crisps Ltd:

'He coupled with the toast the name of the association's chairman, whom he believed to be sincere, who had rallied the forces of the trade together in that great town [Weymouth]. [He] knew of Councillor Goddard's earnestness and of his ability.'

In his response, Chairman Goddard expressed a hope that the Government would treat the licensing trade well, and he expected similarly the favourable report at the forthcoming licensing sessions.

'After all, they were servants of the public, and the last thing a licensee wanted to see was a land worse for drink. (Hear, hear.)'

On 17th October, 'Joe' Goddard paid £2 to the Weymouth British Legion's New Premises Fund, plus being also a guarantor for the sum of £25. Although the list opened in May 1933, this seems to have been the first of his recorded contributions.

Described in the local Press as 'Mayor-elect', 'Joe' Goddard was present at the funeral on 2nd November of Colonel R. F. Williamson C.B., the President of the Weymouth Branch of the British Legion.

MAYOR

1938 continued

On the 9th November, Councillor John Goddard was unanimously elected as Mayor of Weymouth Town Council, after being only seven years a Councillor. At the time he was Chairman of the Watch and Fire Brigade Committee, whilst also still being Chairman of the South Dorset Licensed Victuallers Association.

The Mayor-Choosing Ceremony was not without some incident, as recorded in the local Press:

'The Guildhall had been beautifully decorated with flowers and plants from the corporation greenhouses, and aldermen and councillors attended wearing their robes of office.

'The court-room, in which the ceremony was held, was so crowded that "Echo" representatives who arrived five minutes before the commencement of the proceedings were unable to gain admission to the Press box, which was occupied mainly by officials and ladies.

'An official of the corporation informed representatives of the "Echo" that they "could do what they liked." The reporters were unable to find accommodation in the court-room and the "Echo" regrets as a consequence it is unable to give an adequate report of the proceedings. This is the first time "Echo" reporters have been unable to find accommodation in the Press-box at the Mayor-choosing ceremony.'

Another newspaper had previously said that the new Mayor was

'(more familiarly known as "Joe") . . . a good speaker, and hail fellow well met with everybody.'

During the ceremony he was invested with the Mayor's gold chain and rich scarlet robe of office; whilst the official chain of Mayoress was similarly placed round the shoulders of his wife, who it was believed would "uphold the traditions of the office.".

Another Press report however was able to be quite euphoric in glowing terms about the proceedings, where reference was made that of John Goddard's 27 years Army service some 22 years had been spent abroad. As his Deputy-Mayor and Mayoress the new Mayor chose Councillor and Mrs Bert Biles, who had been Mayor and Mayoress for the previous three years.

Mayor 'Joe' Goddard and his Mayoress wife would now both have to embark on a usual round of formal and informal civic duties and social events connected with his new post, such as the opening of fetes and bazaars, attending meetings of local clubs and associations, etc. And on becoming Mayor he assumed the *ex-officio* position of Chief Magistrate in the borough. It would not be possible, or even desirable, to chronicle each and every one of the hundreds of such mayoral engagements, but a few have been chosen to give something of a flavour of the busy time the Mayor and Mayoress would now be enjoying.

It was not long before the new Mayor was to start his year's round of such engagements. On Friday morning, 11th November, he, with his chaplain the Rev. T. W. Graham, headed the procession from the *Hotel Burdon* to the Armistice service at the Weymouth Cenotaph on the sea-front opposite. In the afternoon, being now Chairman of the Weymouth Bench, he took his seat at the first police court held since his election, when he was welcomed by his predecessor, Councillor Biles. As the *Dorset Daily Echo* of the same date recorded:

'Mr Kenneth Kusel, on behalf of the legal profession, congratulated Councillor Goddard, saying that the town had conferred upon him the highest honour it was possible for them to do . . . The Mayor, replying, warmly thanked the bench, the legal profession and the officials for the welcome they had extended to him. He too hoped he would have a happy term of office, but that he would not have to spend too much of it there (laughter).'

As regards the remark about the town's 'highest honour', he was to be granted a superior municipal honour, albeit posthumously, in 1946 (*q.v.*).

On Saturday, 10th, he attended his first social function as a guest of honour at the Royal Engineers Old Comrades Association Dinner at the *Clinton Restaurant*. In the *Dorset Daily Echo* of 15th November, amongst those pictured standing wearing their medals at the top table were not only the Mayor but Lieut.Col. E. W. C. Sandes D.S.O. who had both been at Kut during the Great War. Chairman of the Weymouth branch, R.S.M. D. E. Hammond, when proposing the toast of the visitors, recalled the days when he and Mayor Goddard were together on the Rhine. He felt all present would join with him in wishing the Mayor a successful term of office. Replying briefly for the visitors, the Mayor said he was proud to think that their dinner was the first gathering attended by him since taking office.

"I have come among what I might call my own kind. I am an old soldier and so are you and as long as we keep that spirit of *esprit-de-corps* we have nothing to be afraid of."

Was he noting the storm clouds gathering over Europe?

The first Sunday after the Mayor Choosing at Weymouth was traditionally known as Mayor's Sunday, when he, the Mayoress, and the Town Corporation attended church service. This year was no exception, and thus on Sunday, 13th November, such a service was held in the parish church of St. Mary, fully reported in the *Dorset Daily Echo* the next day. The Mayor read one of the lessons.

The Mayor then attended the Weymouth Chamber of Commerce Dinner, on Wednesday evening, 17th November. According to the *Southern Times* of 19th November, in his humorous reply to the main speaker

'he disclosed to the company some of the embarrassing "offers" which reached him when he took on the office - from gowns to a guinea offer to prepare a 200 words speech to a Chamber of Commerce. (Laughter).

'"First of all," he said, "I did not know what the 200 words would consist of and I didn't actually know what they would say about a Chamber of Commerce. It might not have been exactly what I might say to the Chamber, so I struck that out. But it did include a humorous tale."'

'In a more serious vein the Mayor pleaded for co-operation between the Chamber of Commerce and the Town Council, which, he said, was bound to mean progress.

'[He] spoke of the progress of the last ten years and admitted that there had been criticism. He promised to do his [twelve months'] duty to the satisfaction of the Council and of the Chamber of Commerce, . . .

'"and I hope at the end I shall be told, 'Joe, you did your job very well.'" (Applause)'

The Mayoress, Mrs Hilda Goddard, was also to soon assume her own civic social duties. On the afternoon of 21st November she opened the Continental gas cookery demonstration and exhibition at the *Burdon Hall*. She was to also perform the opening ceremony at the two-day sale of work by disabled ex-servicemen, held at *George's Restaurant*, Weymouth. This was organised by the Women's Section of Weymouth British Legion. On this latter occasion she was accompanied by her youngest daughter - 18-year old Jessie (Beryl). The Mayoress was to say:

'"I felt very proud when I was asked to declare the sale open. After 21 years with my husband in the service I feel I am an old soldier myself, and I know the deep understanding, fellowship and comradeship which exist between servicemen. In declaring the sale of work open I hope it will be a bumper success and that you will realise more than you ever expected.'"

She also presented the prizes at a whist drive at the *Rock Hotel* assembly rooms, organised by the gentlemen's committee of the Westham District Nursing Association.

The *Dorset Daily Echo* of 30th November contained the following appeal from the Mayor:

'It has been an excellent custom for some years past for a fund to be raised at Christmas-time for the relief of necessitous cases in the borough, and the Mayoress and I have decided to appeal for subscriptions to provide a little Christmas fare for those of our less fortunate townspeople.

'Remembering the success which has attended similar efforts in past years, it is with a feeling of confidence that I launch this appeal, and I very much hope that through your generosity it will be possible to relieve every deserving case.

'It has given me great pleasure to learn that I may rely upon the ready help of a strong committee in the administration of the fund, and in carrying out the immense amount of work entailed.

'I am sure you will appreciate how anxious I am that an amount should be subscribed sufficient to enable the work to be carried out in as satisfactory a manner as the object deserves, and so ensure that no home in Weymouth during the coming festive season shall lack a sufficiency of food and warmth.

'Any amount, therefore, sent to me will be gratefully received. All subscriptions will be acknowledged in the local Press, and should be sent to me at the Mayor's Parlour, Municipal Offices, Weymouth.'

This appeal followed a meeting the previous day, under the chairmanship of the Mayor, which consisted of the Mayoress, several Aldermen and Councillors, Council Officers, and other appropriate prominent people of the borough. This meeting decided the necessary bureaucratic logistics as to the efficient running of the appeal.

Following this meeting the Mayoress in the afternoon had an "At Home" at the *Gloucester Hotel*. In attendance were the Mayor and the majority of the members of the corporation among the representative company. Supporting the Mayor and Mayoress were Mr. and Mrs. R. Woodford (their son-in-law and daughter), and Misses Audrey and Beryl Goddard (daughters) and Miss E. Gerrard (niece).

This had been reported in the *Dorset Daily Echo* of 1st December, as was that of Mayor Goddard being a guest the previous evening of the Poole and District

Licensed Victuallers' Association, held at Sandbanks. He proposed the toast of "the Borough and County of the Town of Poole." He also commented that he was the only Mayor in Dorset who was a licensed victualler. Presumably Mayor Goddard had been invited as being again chairman of the South Dorset Licensed Victuallers Association. But according to the *Dorset Daily Echo* of 9th December, this position he seemingly relinquished (possibly as a result of becoming Mayor and chief magistrate) in December to Mr G. F. Paget of the *Phoenix Hotel*, Dorchester (who was to die 1941/1942).

At the Weymouth British Legion's General Committee meeting on 5th December, a letter was read from the Mayor, 'Joe' Goddard. He thanked the Branch for supporting him at the Mayoral Service, and the Armistice Day Service at the Cenotaph.

The *Dorset Daily Echo* of 9th December was also to carry a fine photograph of both the Mayor and Mayoress, together with their daughter Mrs Eleanor Woodford, taken when the Mayoress had recently opened the Hope Congregational Church Yuletide Fayre.

Along with the local M.P. and other Mayors, Mayor Goddard had his Christmas goodwill greeting (by far the shortest one) published on the front page of the *Dorset Evening Echo* of Saturday, 24th December:

'It is with very great pleasure that the Mayoress and I convey to all readers of this paper our Christmas greetings, with the hope that happiness may prevail in every home this festive season, and that the New Year may bring to all of us security, happiness and prosperity.'

As the *Dorset Daily Echo* of 27th December was to report:

'The Mayor and Mayoress . . . were among the visitors yesterday at Portwey House, Wyke Road, Weymouth, where special Christmas festivities had been arranged. The party, numbering over 120, with ages ranging from 70 to 90, was one of the jolliest in the town and the happy faces on all sides paid tribute to the work of the Area Guardians Committee, the staff and others, in giving the old people the best possible time. . .

'In the morning the Mayor and Mayoress made a tour of the wards, afterwards assisting to serve the dinner in the dining hall. Short speeches were given by Councillor and Mrs. Goddard and others present, who expressed satisfaction and pleasure with all they had seen, at the same time thanking the staff for all they had done to make the day so happy for the inmates. . .

'The following gifts were gratefully received: Decorated Christmas cake, Mayor and Mayoress; . . .'

At some time during the year one of several Mobile First Aid Parties was to be stationed at the *Royal Adelaide Hotel*, consisting of 1 N.C.O., 3 Privates and 1 Auxiliary, with a car and driver.

According to *Kelly's Directory 1938-1939* the *Terminus* public house was now being run by Mrs Margaret Ilott, with Weymouth Museum saying that she took over as landlady some time between September 1939 and March 1940. Why is not known, as a James Ilott (ex-14th Hussars) was seemingly alive in 1946. There was still no sign of anyone named Northam running licensed premises in the town.

1939

One of Mayor and Mayoress Goddards' first engagement of the year was on the 4th January, when they attended the Edward's Charity Dinner for old people at the Sidney Hall. The *Southern Times* of 7th January photographed them as they were helping to serve the Christmas pudding.

The A.G.M. of the Weymouth Angling Society was held at the Guildhall on the evening of 10th January. The Mayor was a guest, and said that the Society was a great asset to the town, as 100s of people came solely for the fishing.

On 11th January, the Chief Ranger of Weymouth's Honorary Court Highclere of the Ancient Order of Foresters congratulated 'Joe' Goddard on becoming Mayor. This was presumably expressed at the Court's quarterly meeting. The *Dorset Daily Echo* of 12th January reported that on the afternoon of the same day the Mayor and Mayoress attended a party and entertainment for blind people of the area and their friends at the Sidney Hall, when 'the Mayor cut a magnificent iced cake.'

During discussion at a Weymouth Town Council committee meeting, concerning the merits of building a new club-house on Weymouth golf-course, Mayor Goddard expressed a considered positive view of the scheme.

At the Weymouth British Legion's Special General meeting on 23rd February, for the election of the Branch President, Mayor 'Joe' Goddard (who was not present) had nominated one of two candidates - Lt.Col. W. Puxley Pearce - who was to be the successful candidate. He too had been a cavalryman in the Boer War (the South African Light Horse), and later an R.A.S.C. officer in Mesopotamia, though their paths are not believed to have crossed at either time. When the meeting discussed the proposed new Legion premises to be built in Westwey Road, Weymouth, amongst the mentioned donors of items was Mayor Goddard who promised an excellent bagatelle board. It was proposed the Mayor be asked to lay the foundation-stone, and at the same time to launch an appeal for the remaining £400 to make up the £1,200 cost - which the Mayor had promised to support. This meeting was to be subsequently fully reported in both the *Southern Times* and *Dorset Daily Echo*.

The President of Weymouth's British Legion wrote a letter to the *Dorset Daily Echo* on 2nd March, about the plans for the new building, saying that

'The Mayor, himself an enthusiastic member of the Legion, authorises me to say that he whole-heartedly endorses this appeal and, what is very much to the point, wishes it to be known that he will personally receive donations at the Mayor's Parlour, Munichial Offices, between 10.30 a.m. and 1 p.m. and 2.30 p.m. and 5 p.m. on Monday, Tuesday and Wednesday next. I can only add, in offering him the most grateful thanks of the Legion, that his comradely spirit will meet with the bumper success it deserves.'

On 4th/5th March were mentions of a Mayor's Fund of a total of £25-6-0, which possibly was increased.

The Legion in fact further inserted a large display advertisment in the *Dorset Daily Echo* of 6th March, announcing the Mayor's vigils on 6th/7th/8th March. According to the minutes of the Weymouth Legion's General Committee meeting of 6th March, regarding the laying of the foundation stone for the new premises:

'TROWEL - After discussion as to whether or no a trowel should be presented to the Mayor as a momento of the Ceremony it was agreed that, on the score of economy, the matter should not be pursued. The Voting against being 13-5. Capt. Hamblin offered to present a trowel and was suitably thanked.'

At 3 p.m. on Saturday, 11th March, was the official ceremony of the laying of the Foundation Stone by the Mayor, Councillor Joe Goddard, of the new Weymouth British Legion headquarters in Westwey Road. This occasion was extensively reported in both the *Dorset Daily Echo* of 14th March, and the *Southern Times* of 18th March. Despite the heavy rain there was a good attendance. Members of the Legion and Branches' standards had previously assembled at the King's Statue, to march to the site behind the Weymouth Military Band. After an inspiring address by the Chaplain, the Rev. E. V. Tanner M.C., the Mayor then walked over to the corner of the foundations with the builder, and laid the foundation stone, saying as he did so "I declare this stone well and truly laid." The Mayor then addressed the gathering

'with medals adorning their dripping macs and overcoats . . . The Mayor had a string of them, too, including the Military Cross.'
'He said he was reminded that after the Great War, as after every war, something was created to remind them of that particular war. In London the Union Jack Club, which was visited by young soldiers from all parts of the world, was a memorial and reminder of the South African War. In the same way the British Legion, inspired by Earl Haig, was a reminder of the Great War. Since its formation in 1921 the Legion had been a source of comfort to many old sailors and soldiers. The Earl Haig Fund had raised something like £10,000,000 toward the alleviation of those who suffered in the war. The Legion now stood on greater foundations than ever; he hoped that this would long continue.
'When the club was open they would be able to go there and not only fight their battles over again but talk of things which were necessary in war if it came again. The occasion ended with three cheers for the Mayor, and then the band played the National Anthem.'

As well as copies of the official *Order of Procedure* and several press cuttings in the Weymouth Royal British Legion Branch's archives, there are Press photographs. There is even the trowel used on that occasion, appropriately inscribed. There is also an anonymous contemporary handwritten pencilled manuscript of a diary of jobs done and to do, with the first notation being that the writer had seen the Mayor on 27th February to arrange for the laying of the foundation stone, and that the 'Mayor will lend Bunting for decorations.' On 7th March it was noted: 'Mayor's effort only raised 30/- the first day!!' - presumably relating to his money collecting vigil the previous day.
    The *Southern Times* report also mentioned that 'Subscriptions were still urgently needed and they can be sent to Councillor J. T. Goddard at the Mayor's Parlour or to the *Royal Adelaide Hotel.*
    At Weymouth British Legion's 10th Annual Dinner on Friday, 17th March, at the Clinton Restaurant, amongst mentioned recent donations for the new premises was £30 from the Mayor from his fund. In proposing the toast of 'Our Visitors and Good Friends', the Branch Chairman, Captain A. F. Jolly mentioned the Mayor who had done great work for the Legion and would not rest until they were able to open the headquarters free of debt. The Mayor, in his 'Visitors Reply', said he felt the Legion would play a very important part in any crisis which might occur. Gathered round that night were people all of whom had gone through the mill in defence of their country; in National Service there were 101 things to put their hands to.
    On the afternoon of Wednesday, 12th April, the Mayor and Mayoress were present at the Opening by the Earl of Shaftesbury of the new St. John Ambulance

Hall in Westwey Road, adjoining the new British Legion building.

In the *Dorset Daily Echo* of 4th May, was a report of the Mayor and Mayoress's attendance the previous day at the presentation of awards won by pupils of the Weymouth centre of the London College of Music, at Bank Buildings Hall, Weymouth.

'The Mayor said he thought there was much joy to be derived from appreciation of good music. He had seen and enjoyed many operas and he was sorry to say that England did not support the opera in the way it should. The Mayor commented upon the remarkable way in which opera was patronised in Germany. The awards were distributed by the Mayoress.'

The occasion and comments were most apt when it is remembered that the Mayoress had been a music teacher before her marriage, and the Mayor had been introduced to opera when his regiment had been posted to Germany after WW1.

WAR-TIME MAYOR

1939 continued

The duties of a Mayor of any town or city, whilst being varied and of uncertain frequency, are generally of a somewhat ceremonial and social nature. But with the increasing possibility of war the official duties could naturally become more prominent, and onerous. Councillor 'Joe' Goddard's were no exception. His (and naturally also his wife's) increased engagements would as a result now be even more too many to enumerate in detail. A family source says that whilst Joe and Hilda Goddard were attending to their mayoral duties, their daughter Eleanor (Nell) used to be in charge of the *Royal Adelaide Hotel*.

In the 13th and 20th May editions of the *Southern Times* there were identical full-page advertisments, paid for by a large number of named Weymouth businesses, featuring a photograph of Mayor Goddard in his robes of office, and the following letter:

'TO THE PEOPLE OF WEYMOUTH & PORTLAND

Mayor's Parlour,
Weymouth.

In my position as Chairman of the National Service Committee for Weymouth and Portland I am desirous that the whole of the inhabitants of this area should fully realise the vital need for a greater effort to bring our defence forces up to strength.

The present unsettled condition of international relationship carries with it the possible danger of war. I want you all to realise that if such catastrophe should come, the horrors of modern warfare would be brought to your very door. These horrors can be combated, but only if everybody knows what to do. The only way in which you can learn what to do is to enrol in some department of National Service, so that in an emergency you would have a duty for which you were trained. My appeal, therefore, is to your common sense to safeguard your home and your family.

Weymouth and Portland are in need of volunteers for the following branches of National Service:-

MEN

TERRITORIALS (4th Dorsets; 94th Field R.A.)
WARDENS
AUXILIARY FIRE SERVICE
MOTOR DRIVERS

NATIONAL DEFENCE COMPANY (4th Dorsets)
NAVY
ARMY
AIR FORCE

WOMEN

WARDENS
MOTOR DRIVERS
NURSING AND FIRST-AID
AUXILIARY TERRITORIAL SERVICE

Don't depend on your neighbours for YOUR National Service.

There is a job for YOU and only YOU can do it. Enrol to-day by filling up a National Service form which can be obtained at any Post Office.

If you want information or advice as to the job for which you are best suited call at or write to:-

The National Service Offices at 88, St. Thomas-street, Weymouth, and 6, Fortuneswell, Portland.

Do it now. There is safety in service. The need is urgent. I appeal confidently for your help.

J. T.GODDARD, M.C., J.P.
Mayor.'

The *Dorset Daily Echo* of Thursday, 25th May, carried a full article and two photographs of Mayor Goddard performing the opening ceremony of Weymouth's new pier bandstand that afternoon.

'To the roll of the drums [and fanfare, by drummers and trumpeters of the 2nd Battalion Lincolnshire Regiment] gleaming brilliantly in the sunlight the Mayor pressed a button which threw open the gates at the entrance to the new pier and bandstand...

'In doing so the Mayor declared that it was the proudest moment of his life... "I regard it as a great honour to be able to press the button which will open the gates of the bandstand."

'The Mayor then walked over to the button set on the pedestal and pressed it.'

On Saturday, 27th May, 'Joe' Goddard paid a further £1-5-0 to the Weymouth British Legion's New Premises Fund, presumably at the same time as he officially opened the almost completed new premises in Westwey Road at 3·30 p.m. The Mayor said that on 11th March the Branch had done him the signal honour of asking him to lay the foundation stone of the premises, and today they had further honoured him by inviting him to open the new headquarters. He knew of nothing that should please Weymouth people more than the opening of this building for the British Legion of which he was proud to be a member. Such buildings as the new Headquarters furthered the spirit of comradeship with which the Legion was inspired. Mr Sidney Tewson, the architect, then presented the key to the Mayor, who unlocked the main door. At the same time the Mayoress, Mrs Goddard, became a collector for the local Branch of the Legion, when she stood on the steps of the new headquarters receiving gifts from the large number of people who had taken part in the opening-ceremony. She had earlier been presented with a bouquet by her grand-daughter, three-year old Ann. (The Mayor's presentation silver-gilt key is also preserved in the Weymouth's Legion Branch archives, as well as newspaper reports and photograph of the event.)

Whether he knew it or not at the time, the Mayor had not been the first choice to do the honours. At the Weymouth British Legion's Committee meeting on 1st May it was agreed that Lady Peter be invited to undertake the opening. But through a bereavement she was unable to be present. Lady Alice Hope Peter was the daughter of the late Captain W. Chimmo RN, of Weymouth. She was the wife of Sir John Charles Peter (Knight Bachelor), late of the Hong Kong & Shanghai Banking Corporation. They had married in 1900, and according to *Kelly's Directory 1938/9* lived at 319 Chickerell Road, Weymouth. Why Lady Peter had initially been chosen has not been ascertained.

The *Dorset Daily Echo* of 29th May carried a report that

'The Mayor of Weymouth . . . is indignant because a rumour to the effect that he has asked the Commander-in-Chief of the Home Fleet to cancel all leave, is in circulation. During the week-end the rumour has gained great currency. . .

"'In fact, we welcome the Navy in Weymouth. It is true to say that we do not see nearly enough of them. No one in the town would wish for their leave to be cancelled."'

Also at the end of May, Mayor Goddard was one of the Dorset Mayors who attended the Dorset County Police Sports at Dorchester.

In plans for the deployment of suggested First Aid Posts around the town during emergencies, one was to be at the *Royal Adelaide Hotel*. This wouldconsist of one N.C.O., three Privates, and one Auxiliary. But at the beginning of August it was heard that the Regional Officer was against such Posts being at Hotels.

On Friday, 2nd June, Mayor Goddard was in attendance at the official opening by Lord Horder of Weymouth's new crematorium - said to be the most modern in the country. Lord Horder, as chairman of the Council of the Cremation Society, was invited by the Mayor to open the door, and declare the crematorium and

Garden of Remembrance open. He took away with him a momento of his visit, a clock presented to him by the Mayor, who, after tea served in a marquee near the crematorium, thanked Lord Horder for coming to Weymouth. Editions of the *Dorset Daily Echo* of 2nd, 3rd and 6th of June carried extensive reports of the proceedings, with a photograph of dignatories (including the Mayor and Lord Horder) in that for 6th June. In the 8th June edition questions were reported as to whether invitations had been received by the Mayoress (Mrs Goddard) and the deputy-Mayoress. The reply was that invitations were not sent to wives of councillors, etc. as there was very limited seating space in the crematorium chapel, though the Mayoress had been informed that if she desired to go, accommodation would, of course, be reserved for her.

After several days disabled at the bottom of the ocean some 14 miles north-west of the North Wales coast, H.M. Submarine *Thetis* was declared lost on 3rd June, having sunk on Thursday afternoon, 1st June, whilst on acceptance trials. 80 plus men lost their lives. Subsequently, Mayor Goddard had the following letter published in the *Dorset Daily Echo* of 6th June:

'I have been informed by the Lord Mayor of London that he has, in response to nation-wide requests, launched a national appeal for the dependants of the men lost in H.M. Submarine *Thetis*, and I am opening a supporting fund in Weymouth.

'Few disasters in our history have been so tragic, and though there is little any of us can do to comfort the bereaved of those who gave their lives in the submarine in the service of their country, we can at least ensure that the dependants of those brave men shall not suffer financially.

'Weymouth has a long and valued association with the British Navy and will, I feel sure, wish to contribute as a town to the Lord Mayor's appeal. I therefore ask that donations may be sent to me at the Mayor's Parlour, Municipal Offices, Weymouth. I will acknowledge individual contributions in the Press, and will forward the gift from the town to the Lord Mayor of London.

J. T. GODDARD, Mayor'

It was reported that the Mayor himself had already contributed £5.5s.0d to the fund.

On a somewhat lighter note, the Mayor was warmly welcomed at the Sidney Hall, Weymouth, on 7th June, when attending the prize-giving of the Devenish Darts League. He took advantage of the occasion to make an appeal on behalf of his *Thetis* fund, with a collection being made.

In his column in the *Southern Times* of 17th June, "Mr. Weymouth" wrote:

'WHEN THE MAYOR SHAVED-
An Idea Came!

'All great minds are agreed that all great thoughts come to all great men either-

(1) When they are shaving or

(2) When they are in their bath.

'The Mayor of Weymouth, Councillor J. T. Goddard ("Joe" to you, Sir), was half-way through a shave when a Great Thought struck him.

'Fortunately he uses a safety or the Big Idea might have marked him for the rest of the week.

'Why he should suddenly have thought of local newspapermen is one of those inscrutable workings of the human mind, or shall we say of Providence, which will always baffle the psychonumerologists.

'But the fact remains that his Worship, thinking to himself that the local Press had been very useful at times, decided he would like to get them all together to see what they looked like, from the junior cub upwards.

'To get a 100 per cent. attendance of Pressmen at a social "do" is possible only on a Sunday or a Good Friday.

'So Sunday it was when the editorial staffs of the three papers, *"Southern Times"*, *"Dorset Daily Echo"*, and *"Western Gazette"*, found themselves the guests of his Worship (Good Old "Joe") at lunch in the pier-bandstand cafe, pleasantly conscious that they could enjoy their grape fruit, soup, salmon mayonaise, duck and green peas, and a peach of a Melba, with copious libations as each appetising edition went to press, and not have to get out a notebook afterwards. . .

'After lunch glowing tributes to the Mayor came in turn from Messrs. P. H. Thompson, E. E. House, W. H. Hill, and J. A. Pellow, representatives of their respective newspapers.'

A more formal report had earlier been published in the *Dorset Daily Echo* of 12th June, when it was commented that it had been 'one of the happiest functions attended by Weymouth newspapermen for many years.' Several there expressed thanks to the Mayor, referring 'to the sterling qualities of the Mayor as a host, not only in Weymouth but all over Dorset and even further afield . . . it was quite a unique gathering. . . . many Mayors of Weymouth [were remembered], but never an occasion like that one.'

The *Dorset Daily Echo* on 15th June encouraged all Weymouth British Legion members to attend at the new Legion headquarters the following evening, as Mayor Goddard would be showing his prowess at billiards when the new donated table is opened. He would be having a match with the Branch's president, Lt.Col. Puxley Pearse. It was later to be reported in the *Dorset Daily Echo* of the 17th that the Mayor had been defeated by 23 points, after catching his opponent several times. There was also a photograph of the Mayor about to take a shot.

Earlier that day the Mayor had fulfilled his first official duty in the Weymouth district of Wyke Regis. He had presented the trophies at the annual Wyke Regis school athletic sports, saying he particularly liked to see sports amongst boys and girls, and sorry he was not able to witness more of the events.

On Sunday evening, 18th June, there was a concert in the Alexandra Gardens Theatre, in aid of the *Thetis* Fund. The massed bands from four warships of the Home Fleet played music of all descriptions. Mayor Goddard caused some alarm during an interval when he stepped onto the stage to say a few words on behalf of the Fund,

'. . . the audience, numbering over 1000, were alarmed to see him lose his balance and fall over the edge into the empty orchestra pit.

'For a moment there was silence and then many rushed forward to help. Fortunately, the Mayor appeared none the worse for his fall of several feet and a moment later, smiling and treating the incident lightly, he again mounted the stage. . .

'The Mayor today [19th] told an *Echo* reporter that apart from some bruises there were no ill effects from his fall. He explained that he mistook a canvas covering over the orchestra pit for the actual stage and stepped on to it. The canvas gave way, but to some extent it broke the force of the Mayor's fall.'

Mayor Goddard was to send a letter to the Admiral Commander-in-Chief on 22nd June, to express pleasure of the recent visit of the Home Fleet to Weymouth. This had been gathered in Weymouth Bay for the reception of the King, but which had to be put off on account of the weather.

On Saturday, 22nd July, Mayor and Mayoress Goddard welcomed King George VI, Queen Elizabeth and the two Princesses to Weymouth, with photographs published in *The Illustrated London News* of Saturday, 29th July. The Royal Family came to Weymouth by train. During the mayoral welcome Mayoress Goddard presented the Queen with a bouquet. The Royal party then drove to Weymouth Pier along a route packed with spectators, where they were taken by the Royal Barge to the Royal Yacht *Victoria and Albert*. This was to take them round to Dartmouth where they were to visit the Royal Naval College there.

It is noticed that medals were not worn on this occasion, unlike nearly three weeks later, when the King, this time on his own paid another visit to Weymouth. This was on Wednesday, 9th August, when he came to Review the Reserve Fleet Assembly of 121 ships out in Weymouth Bay. Mayor Goddard was photographed then proudly wearing his medals, as he escorted the King on the drive to

Bincleaves Pier mid-morning. The King returned late afternoon, when again the Mayor was present to bid farewell. Many of the ships inspected were subsequently to be lost in the coming war.

In the *Southern Times* of 12th August, the regular column 'Talk of the Town (By "Mr. Weymouth")' was largely devoted to this second visit, which took place in thin, misty rain, with clouds hanging low over a grey choppy sea.

'Much to be envied man on Wednesday was the Mayor of Weymouth (Councillor J. T. Goddard) - still "Joe" to his friends - who met His Majesty at the station in the morning and saw him off in the evening. Unfortunately His Majesty had to apologise for the weather in the morning, but King George VI was light-heartedly indifferent to the rain, and made the philosophic comment that it appeared to be the same everywhere.

'When the Mayor greeted him in the evening the King was still in the highest spirits and, so the Mayor informs me, jokingly referred to the figure of his ancestor George the Third cut in the chalk on Osmington Hill. The point of the joke was that the rider is represented riding away from Weymouth, and the King's humorous comment was "it looked as if Weymouth did not want him."

'Standing near the Mayor during this conversation was Mr. Frank Potter, superintendent of the line, and, turning to him "Joe" said to the King, "Mr. Potter is now going to build us a new station." "That will be very nice," was his Majesty's reply. So the Great Western Railway Company's directors can hardly escape this very important commitment, and all we hope is that no more excuses will be put up.'

The Mayor eventually was able to write to the *Dorset Daily Echo* on 2nd August:

'Sir,--May I be permitted to express through your columns my gratitude for the magnificent sum of £363 3s. 6d. contributed to my fund for the dependants and relatives of the officers, ratings and civilians who lost their lives in the submarine *Thetis*.

'I have today forwarded a cheque for this amount to the Lord Mayor of London, who is anxious to close the fund, and he informs me that the money which has been collected at London and throughout the country will provide a sum which will substantially augment the incomes of the bereaved.

'I am deeply grateful to all who have responded so readily to my appeal and whose generosity has made it possible for me to raise such a splendid contribution and who have thus helped to ameliorate the hardships which follow such a tragic happening. . .

J. T. GODDARD,
Mayor.
Weymouth.'

Mayor's Parlour,
August 2, 1939.

As a further part of the contingency planning for the approaching war, Mayor Goddard was to make this appeal:

'BILLETING

I APPEAL

'To motorcar owners to Volunteer Their Services in connection with Billeting of Transferred Population who would be allocated to Weymouth in the event of hostilities.

'The Council have been informed that 9,000 persons will be allocated to Weymouth and it is essential that arrangements should be made for transporting the women and children from the Railway Station to the houses to which they will be billeted.

'I feel that there will be no lack of volunteers amongst our townspeople who own motorcars to place themselves and their cars at my disposal for this purpose.

'Please send your name and address and if you are on the telephone, your telephone number, to me at the Mayor's Parlour so that a register may be made of those who are willing to co-operate in this work.

J. T. GODDARD M.C., J.P., Mayor'

This referred to the thousands of evacuee schoolchildren and their teachers from London, who subsequently descended on Weymouth and surrounding areas at the beginning of September. (This biography author came privately in the vanguard, from his home in Portsmouth, to relatives in the northern suburb village of Upwey).

It was probably during a week-end at the height of Weymouth's hectic holiday season that Mayor Goddard welcomed a party of 250 Welsh ex-servicemen on holiday from Carmarthen, who were to hold a 'heart-stirring' tribute at Weymouth's Cenotaph before marching to the new headquarters of the Weymouth British Legion, in Westwey Road.

War against Germany was to be officially delared by Britain on Sunday, 3rd September.

At the end of September, King George was to make a third visit to Weymouth, as a morale-boost "to troops in the south-west of England", but this time it was cloaked in secrecy due to war-time censorship restrictions.

On 9th November Councillor 'Joe' Goddard was re-elected to a second term as Mayor of Weymouth & Melcombe Regis. In proposing him Alderman Moggeridge made mention of the Mayor's service with the 14th King's Hussars, which was currently

'commanded by [Lieut.-] Colonel Leslie Groves, son of the late Alderman Herbert John Groves, a past Mayor, and previously by [Lieut.-] Colonel Pope, a member of the well-known Dorchester [brewing] family of that name . . . and expressed to the Mayoress the Council's appreciation of her energetic co-operation with the Mayor in all charitable and social movements in the borough. He spoke, too, of the enormous amount of work that fell on the Mayor in connection with the Royal visits and then came to his present war-time activities.' 'To the Mayor also fell the privilege of opening the £35,000 pier bandstand on the Esplanade . . . Another happy occasion for the Mayor was when he opened the 1,000th council house erected by the corporation . . . Other imposing public buildings erected and opened included the £45,000 South Dorset Technical College at Westham . . .; the headquarters of Weymouth Division of the St. John Ambulance Brigade and the British Legion headquarters, both in Westwey Road; and the £18,000 fire station . . .'

Amongst those projects delayed 'for the duration' were the promised alterations to the railway station.

Nobody of course knew what lay ahead during Mayor Goddard's second term of office, though it was obviously not a task for the faint-hearted or weak in body. One can only suppose, therefore, that he was fitted for the task, despite having now turned 60 years of age.

There was a smaller gathering than previously when Mayor Goddard led the annual Remembrance Service at Weymouth Cenotaph on the 11th November. Understandably, notable absentees were detachments from the armed services.

Published, for instance in the *Southern Times* of 8th December, was a letter from the Mayor to launch his Christmas Appeal. This year it was anticipated it would not only provide some Christmas cheer to the old, infirm, and other needy people, but because of the war there may be many more applications to the Christmas Fund. Heading the list of early donations was £10. 10s. from himself.

On Tuesday, 12th December, the Mayor was at a meeting in the Guildhall to launch a local Savings Movement as part of the National effort. This was to encourage every person possible to help the war-effort by monetary savings, when "even the honest penny must not be despised in these days."

A 'highly successful' social and dance organised by Weymouth A.R.P. services took place at the *Clinton Restaurant* on Wednesday evening, 13th December. The Mayor, as guest, praised the working of the voluntary A.R.P. system, and thanked the local A.R.P. members for their hard work in this essential service. He then presented awards of certificates and badges, 'after which he was handed a bouquet of carnations for the Mayoress.'

1940

In the *Dorset Daily Echo* of 2nd January was a short report concerning the £378 19s. 8d. (plus six joints of meat) subscribed to the Mayor's Christmas Relief Fund.

Three days later the *Dorset Daily Echo* reported:

'Instead of the annual banquet, which had to be cancelled shortly after the outbreak of war, Honorary Court Highclere No. 1, Ancient Order of Foresters, last night held a supper at the *Hotel Burdon*, Weymouth.

'Numbers, of course, were smaller than usual and the company wore lounge suits or uniform instead of conventional evening dress. In every other respect, however, the supper compared favourably with the successful banquets held in peace time.'

Amongst those Forester Brothers seated at the top table was Mayor Goddard. In his toast "Our Civic Authorities", the proposer

'described the Mayor's year of office as memorable, a year of great anxiety and honour to Weymouth . . .'

'Responding, the Mayor said he was convinced that no town was better served so far as the administrative staff was concerned. "I, perhaps, did not hold that opinion before I came in possession of the true facts," he commented . . . [He] said the authorities had the welfare of the evacuees in mind and accommodation had been provided for the British Legion. But for the war [several projects could not now be started].'

Wartime conditions were also to affect John Goddard's membership of the Freemasons' United Service Lodge No. 3473 at Portland, who were still using the premises of the Portland Lodge No. 1037 in Victoria Square, Portland. Apart from any difficulty of access because of Portland now being a restricted area, there were to be some ten occasions when Lodge meetings were disrupted because of air raids, and several members had to leave for civil defence purposes, which presumably would have included John Goddard. He was eventually to reach the 3rd Degree of Masonry (out of 33) - that of Master Mason.

The *Dorset Daily Echo* of 12th January carried an article:

'Plans are now going well ahead at the Weymouth Palladium, which is to become the Services Club for men and women of the forces . . . apart from the requisitioning of the premises, has to be supported entirely by public funds, and it is sincerely hoped that the Mayor's appeal will receive a generous response . . .

'Members of the General Committee [and the House, or Working Comittee] include the Mayor and Mayoress . . .

'At a meeting of the House Committee an excellent example was set when . . . the Mayoress undertook to provide two armchairs . . .

'The club will include canteens, reading and card rooms, billiards and table tennis facilities. It is hoped that the official opening will take place in late January or early February.'

The same newspaper also carried a large block advert 'Appeal from the Mayor' who was Chairman of the above House Committee. His request was not only for money for this project, but for appropriate furniture, indoor sports items, pictures, furnishings, flags bunting, etc. The Services Club was subsequently opened by Mayor Goddard in the February, in the requisitioned ex-Palladium Cinema building on the north-western corner of the Town Bridge, now occupied by a night-club.

In the middle of March a local newspaper carried the following item:

'"Joey's" Stage Debut
Missing from its usual place in the home of the Mayor and Mayoress of Weymouth is "Joey" one of Councillor J. T. Goddard's pet canaries. The reason is that "Joey" is making his stage debut, and has moved to the *Hotel Burden* for three days.

'"Joey" makes several appearances on the stage during the course of the presentation of "Lot's Wife" by Weymouth Drama Club and plays his part extremely well singing merrily - and at the appropriate moments.

'"Joey's" presence gave the Mayor and Miss Goddard an added interest at last night's performance.'

There were three performances, on Thursday/Saturday, 14th/16th March. In another report it was stated the Mayor and his daughter Audrey had attended the first night, at which there was apparently a disappointingly-size audience.

According to the local Press, during April the Mayor led a Town Council team in a darts match against the British Legion, organised by the Legion. The match was won by the latter.

That ever faithful chronicler of local events, the *Dorset Daily Echo*, on Monday, 20th May reported:

'For over an hour on Saturday the Mayor carried out an inspection of Portwey Hospital, Weymouth.

'It was an eye-opener to the Mayor for it was difficult for him to realise it was the same place he visited 12 months ago last Christmas when it was entirely a Public Assistance Institution.

'Many of the old people are still in residence and occupy the best wards. One could not help feeling that it would be a wise policy to move them to another institution elsewhere in the county and allow the entire buildings to be used for the soldiers. . .

'The Mayor's inspection was complete in every sense of the word, for he toured in company with Dr. Gerard Pearse not only the wards occupied by soldiers, but also those in which the old people are accommodated.

'He took a peep into the operating theatre - where the 14th operation of the week was being carried out - walked round the kitchens, laundry house, boiler house and storerooms.

'A friendly word was exchanged with patients and staff, and an order was sent out by the Mayor for a dozen packs of playing cards as soon as he learnt they were wanted. The Mayor was concerned at the shortage of wireless apparatus and promised to do what he could. . .

'Another urgent need of which the Mayor was acquainted was easy chairs for convalescent patients to use in the grounds.'

Many, if not all, of the wounded soldiers were presumably from France.

Sunday, 27th May was a National Day of Prayer. Weymouth's observances were reported by the *Dorset Daily Echo* next day:

'The Mayor and Corporation walked from the Guildhall to the parish church [St. Mary's] for morning prayer [with a congregation of about 1,500].

'The Mayor read the second lesson and a special form of prayer was followed.

'"No matter what success the enemy may have temporarily, no matter what trials we may be called upon to bear, 'God is on the Throne' and as sure as He is on the Throne, so sure will Hitler and all he stands for be 'broken without hand'."

'With these words the Rector of Weymouth (Rev. E. L. Langston) concluded his sermon, the theme of which was a Bible prophecy of the war . . .

'Five thousand people prayed for victory and peace on Weymouth sands [that same] evening at one of the most remarkable open-air services the town has ever seen. All the Allies in the Christian Crusade in Weymouth took part in it. The unity of the churches in this stirring response to the King's call to the nation was complete and inspiring.

'Before he read the Scripture, the Mayor spoke of the King's call to prayer, and said he was quite certain that the response was one of the factors which would lead to victory.

"'There is no question of the ultimate result of this war," he said, "because I feel, as you do, that there can only be one winner - and Christianity will win. That will be the feeling of everyone who has taken part in these services. I, as your representative of the King in Weymouth, today feel proud of you. It is a day which has been well spent. I have reports from the churches that they have all been packed today."
'Then he read a comforting psalm.'

On 31st May several boats arrived at Weymouth carrying over 4,000 Dutch and Belgian refugees, who were sent on to London by train. They were followed on 1st June by some 15,000 French soldiers by train, as part of the great Dunkirk evacuation, many of whom were billetted for a few days in and around Weymouth. Then on 20th June came over some 23,000 refugees from the Channel Isles, who were trained directly to North England.

On 4th July, German aeroplanes started bombing ships in Portland harbour. The first of many air raids over the years on Weymouth came in the late evening of 11th July, though the first bombs were not dropped until the night of 26th/27th July. All of these incidents would have taxed the local war-time Civil Defence contingency plans overseen by the Mayor.

'Joe' Goddard was apparently to be among the early enrolments in the L.D.V. (Local Defence Volunteers) formed nationally in May, to be renamed as the Home Guard in the July. This force was firest brought into action on 11th August incontrolling the traffic and crowds of sightseers after a bombing air-raid. Presumably because of his increasing official mayoral duties he would have had to soon relinquish his service in the L.D.V. The Emergency Committee would now have to prepare for a possible invasion by the Germans.

Day and night air-raids continued on Weymouth throughout the year, causing damage and loss of life. After a heavy raid on Sunday, 11th August, the Mayor subsequently received a letter from the Civil Defence Regional Commissioner, in which he congratulated all organisations that had coped well on that occasion. A similar letter was received from the Earl of Shaftesbury at the end of the month, following a series of air-raids.

At the annual Changeover Meeting, on 3rd October, of the Honorary Court Highclere of The Ancient Order of Foresters in Weymouth, 'Joe' Goddard was elected Senior Beadle. Presumably he could have been presented with his (axe and) bugle horn of office, to be worn slung over the left shoulder; and also have placed the initial letters of the office on his collar, now green with a red edging stripe and red tassel, on the opposite side to that of the emblem.

The Mayoress this time presided at the official opening on Saturday, 5th October, by Viscountess Cranborne, wife of the local M.P., of a new Club for servicemen in the St. John's Mission Hall, Chelmsford Street, Weymouth. This was to be known as the B.W. Social Club, organised by the British Women's T.A. Union. Mayoress Goddard said she was sure the Club would be a boon to all Servicemen, and that they would use it often, and hoped that the Union would receive more money with which to continue their work. She was thanked by Lady Cranborne for her kind wishes.

On the 9th November 'Joe' Goddard was re-elected to a third term as Mayor of Weymouth. The ceremony was memorable firstly because it did not take place by custom in the Guildhall, but in the *Burdon Hotel*; and also because of the record number of townspeople present. Glowing praise on his unstinting work on behalf of Weymouth during those trying times was lavished on him by fellow Councillors, and similarly to the Mayoress, Mrs Goddard. As the *Dorset Daily Echo* of 11th November commented:

'It was a notably proud day in the life of the chief citizen who enjoys an immense measure of popularity among all sections of the community. His re-election has caused great satisfaction . . .
'[His proposer said:] The duties of the Mayor had substantially increased, but Councillor Goddard had never been found wanting. He was always at his post and he had carried out the duties to the satisfaction of everyone. At council meetings the Mayor was firm yet kindly. It would not have been possible for the Mayor to have carried out the duties had he not had the support of Mrs. Goddard, who had done wonderful work.
'He spoke of Councillor Goddard's close connection with A.R.P., A.F.S. and first-aid matters . . . "We cannot take the captain off the bridge." he declared. He hoped the Mayor would be given good health to carry out the duties.'

There was a touch of over-optimism in that this proposer, and the Mayor himself in his stirring speech of acceptance, hoped that the war would end during his year's term of office. He also paid tribute to the work done by the various sections of the community.

According to a member of his family, Mayor Goddard during the war often broke or circumvented rules and regulations, and stood up to officialdom, in order to get things done.

On Sunday morning, 10th November, the Mayor and Mayoress attended at St. Mary's Church the usual Civic Service on the Sunday following Mayor-choosing. The Mayor read one of the lessons. The subject of the sermon was that on this same day they remembered all those who had fallen in the Great War, "the war to end all wars", and yet the nation was already in another major war.

The *Dorset Daily Echo* of 11th November reported the attendance of the Mayor and Mayoress at the Remembrance Service, the previous afternoon, in Holy Trinity Church (the first time it had not been held at the Pavilion Theatre). As usual, however, it was organised by the Weymouth British Legion. Nearly 1,000 people were present, most being in some form of uniform.

The same newspaper reported:

'The absence of a service at Weymouth Cenotaph made the observance of Remembrance Day less impressive, but the spirit of the hour was not altogether lost. The Mayor, accompanied by the Town Clerk and the Mayor's Chaplain, visited the shrine and together with representatives of other bodies, an Army captain, and an Army chaplain, observed the Two Minutes' Silence while buses and lorries rumbled by. The Mayor then laid the Town's wreath.'

1941

Air-raids continued into the New Year.

The following item occurred in the *Dorset Daily Echo* of 6th January, but even allowing for the degree of Press censorship of the time, who else could it refer to but Mayor 'Joe' Goddard?

'A Mayor's Good Turn

The "Alert" had sounded when the Mayor of a south coast town went out into the black-out the other night to attend a function connected with a troop of Scouts. He felt certain, however, that the parade would be held - just as certain as the boys knew that the Mayor would turn up.

'There was a full muster, marred only by the appearance of two small lads without uniform. The Mayor was informed that one of the boys was an evacuee. Both, despite the absence of uniform, were attending parades regularly and pulling their weight. They could not afford a proper rig-out and no funds were available from any source. The Mayor's instructions were: "Order a couple of uniforms, and tell them to send the bill to me."'

In the same newspaper there was a report about a house-warming party on 4th January, staged by the personnel of a first-aid depot who had recently moved into a new home. This was at Dorchester House ('Nine Elms') in Chickerell Road, Weymouth. The Mayor was one of the guests. However with all being on duty they were ready to leave at a moment's notice in the event of an emergency arising, but luckily there were no interruptions. In replying to the toast to the Emergency Committee of the Town Council, the Mayor said that the Committee was committed to a great deal of responsibility, but little money to carry it out. Reliance was dependent upon volunteers, though it was characteristic of the average Englishman to be apathetic towards the subject of voluntary service until a real and serious crisis arose. He then rushed to perform his duty, but it was a pity that he waited so long. According to Acutt:

'He congratulated the unit upon the organisation of the dinner, and acknowledged the importance of developing the social side of the A.R.P. activities.'

An undated newspaper cutting reported the Mayoress, Mrs Goddard, as having sent a box of toys to a New Year party for members' children at the British Legion Headquarters. This probably refers to that advertised in the *Dorset Evening Echo* of 13th January, to be held on Saturday, 18th January.

According to the *Dorset Daily Echo* of Tuesday, 4th March, the day previous the Mayor had received from Weymouth in Massachusetts the following cable:

"Mr. Mayor, Advise what you need most - mobile kitchen, ambulance or surgical supplies, or money. Cable answer to Jack Thorpe, 866, Washington Street, Weymouth, Mass."

'In reply, Councillor Goddard immediately sent off this cable:

"'Hearty greetings and thanks. Money most acceptable for use in directions most necessary from time to time. Everybody in good heart. Mayor, Weymouth, England.'"

The following day the Mayor sent the following letter to Mr. Thorpe:

"I think my reply telegram calls for some explanation of the reason why I suggested that money would be more useful than the other things which you mentioned in your cable, but first of all let me say how very pleased we all were to receive your telegram from Weymouth, Mass. Immediately it arrived I, of course, showed it to the Town Clerk, Mr. Smallman - who with Alderman Percy A'Court, the Mayor at the time, and two other members of the council, visited your town in 1926 - and we discussed how best we could take advantage of your generous and spontaneous offer of help.

"I would like to say at once that there is no pressing need which is not reasonably provided for either by the Government or by the local authority; for example, we have just put into use a new mobile canteen and we are already supplied with ambulances and surgical supplies, which up to the present have proved adequate and which we hope will continue to do so.

"The people in this country are, in fact, being well looked after having regard to existing conditions and the confidence and morale is stronger and higher now than it has ever been. We did feel, however, that we would like to accept your kindness in the form of money, because when people encounter difficulties owing to air raids, it is very useful indeed to have a fund from which we can supplement the grants made by the Government and so provide a little more than bare necessities for people who have lost their homes or their furniture or in any other way suffered injury. As a matter of fact there is a local fund raised from amongst our own people for doing exactly this class of work and if the people of Weymouth, Mass. would like to identify themselves with that fund we should not only accept the contribution gratefully for the good it would enable us to do, but we would also accept it in the more spiritual sense of an indication of the good wishes which prompted you to make the offer.

"We all feel that with the continued and increasing assistance of the United States of America the conflict in which we are engaged will result in a complete victory for Democracy and the right not only for the English-speaking people themselves to live their own lives but for other nations also decide for themselves the lines upon which their Government shall proceed. In this atmosphere of co-operation between the English-speaking peoples we remember with pride and great pleasure the incidents which have happened in the past, including an interchange of visits, which indicate the indissoluble ties which bind the people of America with the people of Great Britain.

"With heartfelt gratitude for your kindness and your generous gesture."

The mobile canteen mentioned by the Mayor may well have been that shown illustrated. The photograph appears to have been taken on the occasion of the canteen's official 'opening' on the Esplanade at Weymouth. The canteen, or 'mobile kitchen' as it is designated on its side, is also marked as having been 'Presented by the ATLANTIC WAR FUND CLUB, HALIFAX, NOVA SCOTIA, CANADA, to the people of WEYMOUTH'. The photograph taken on the Esplanade at the time shows the Mayor, the Mayoress (second from the left of the caravan, and who seems to be wearing a W.V.S. badge in her hat) and others enjoying a cup of tea on what looks to be a somewhat cold day.

The American Red Cross had already sent two ambulances to Weymouth.

In his capacity as President of the Weymouth War Savings Committee, Mayor Goddard sent a duplicated letter to every household and business in the Borough. To give a flavour of war-time feelings at the time it is reproduced here in full:

'War Weapons Week Appeal
April 12th to 19th, 1941

March, 1941

Dear Sir or Madam

You will, no doubt, have heard of the great effort to be made in Weymouth during its WAR WEAPONS WEEK which is arranged for the 12th to 19th April inclusive. During that week we aim to raise £125,000 (one hundred and twenty five thousand pounds) in War Savings Certificates and the Government Investments which have been brought out since the War campaign started.

This Committee is particularly anxious, in order to ensure the success of the campaign, that all business houses as well as every individual in the town should be invited to lend to their utmost by purchasing Government Securities in one or more of the following forms or by deposits as shewn below:

1. 3% Savings Bonds (maturing 1955-65)

2. 2½% National War Bonds (maturing in 1946-48)
3. 3% Defence Bonds (redeemable at 101% in seven years, limited to a
   maximum of £1000 per person).
4. National Savings Certificates (limited to 500 Certificates per person, including
   those already purchased).
5. Post Office Savings Bank Deposits.

Our Navy, Army and Air Force require, and must have unlimited supplies of materials, equipment and munitions. The maintenance of such forces needs a continuous flow of savings from our civilian populations. It is, therefore, not necessary to stress the urgency of providing the money which is vital for the successful prosecution of the War and indeed for our very existence, and it is hoped that every person and firm will do their utmost to invest to the limit of their means and make our War Weapons Week an unprecedented success.

So far Weymouth has done well, but when we think of the husbands, sons and brothers who are ready to give their lives for each of us on sea and land and in the air, CAN WE DO OTHER THAN OUR VERY BEST?

Yours faithfully.

J.T.Goddard

Mayor.

Francis B.Johnson

Chairman of

Bonds Committee.

P.S.--Investments may be made in any of the securities mentioned above at any of the Banks in the town, who will be pleased to give advice if required. Advice will be given by your Solicitor or Accountants who will also be pleased to help you.'

By specifying redemption dates the authorities were either confident that the War would be ended by that time, or recklessly encouraging the populace on the basis that if the War was lost then there would not be any repayments. It is noticed that there is no specific mention of Forces women serving home and abroad.

The Mayor was also President of this Weymouth War Weapons Week, for which was published a 9-page Official Programme for 2d - sub-titled *'Show Weymouth's will to Win'*. This gave details of all the money-raising events taking place during the Week, which coincided with Easter Week.

The Official Opening Ceremony by the Mayor took place at 11 a.m. on Saturday, 12th, on "Weapons Island" adjoining the King's Statue, detailed in the *Dorset Daily Echo* of the same date. He drove there in a Bren gun carrier, and made a speech from the top of a tank. Pointing to the indicator lashed to the

King's Statue (and which hid half of it), the Mayor said to the large crowd (which included his wife the Mayoress):

'"Let us dip into our pockets, get right to the top and give old King George a shock. . . Money for all sorts of weapons was vitally needed - money for the cost of a ·303 bullet to a battleship worth eight or nine million pounds. We have no right to sit on the fence. We must realise that there is something everyone can do. This is our war - the civilians' war - just as much as it is the war of the Army, Navy and Air Force . . ." He then read out a letter of good wishes from the Chancellor of the Exchequer.'

The *Dorset Daily Echo* on Easter Monday, 14th April, reported:

'Today, the little Spitfire on the Weymouth War Weapons Week indicator soared towards the £50,000 mark. At noon the Mayor visited "Weapons Island" on the Esplanade to adjust the indicator in accordance with the result of the effort on Saturday. He said to the large crowd, "We have done very well for one day, and I hope to give you some more good news tomorrow."'

One notable event during the Week took place at 3 p.m. this same day, when there was an advertised meeting in the Alexandra Gardens:

'The Chair will be taken by His Worship the Mayor, and addresses will be given by Mr. Jan Masaryk, C.B.E., the Czecho-Slovak Minister [in exile?], and Viscount Hinchingbrooke, M.P.'

The event was covered by a detailed report in the *Dorset Daily Echo* of 15th April. Amongst those on the stage with Mayor and Mayoress Goddard were the local Member of Parliament, Viscount Hinchingbrooke, and representatives of the armed services and the National Savings movement. There were a few brief words of welcome for the Czech Foreign Minister from the Mayor, who thanked him warmly for coming down to Weymouth. Jan Masaryk was to conclude his stirring speech:

"This country of yours is the last lighthouse and you are the lighthouse keepers. It is a terrific responsibility, but it is a glorious one, and I know the lighthouse will be alright during and after the war."

It is known the 55-year old Masaryk signed at least one autograph book on that occasion, that of the Goddards' young grandson Anthony Woodford.

There were further tit-bits in the *Dorset Daily Echo* of 16th April:

'M. Masaryk's "Fiver"
'When the Mayor of Weymouth (Councillor J. T. Goddard) visited the concert at Wyke Women's Institute Hall yesterday he had a story to tell about M. Jan Masaryk, the Czechoslovak Foreign Minister, who has been in Weymouth in connection with War Weapons Week.
'M. Masaryk responded cordially to an invitation from the Mayor to subscribe £5. When the "fiver" was produced, he not only backed it with his signature, in accordance with the usual practice, but wrote his name on the front of the note as well.
'Somewhat puzzled, the Mayor said to M. Masaryk "Why have you signed it on the front?" The distinguished visitor replied that the banknote would now look very interesting in a frame!
'The Mayor regretted that he was not sufficiently wealthy to have a "fiver" framed. He "purchased" the banknote, however, and is retaining it for the time being in the hope that he may be able to devise some scheme by which this expensive autograph can be made to earn some interest for the War Weapons Week funds.

* * *

'Valuable Pieces Of Paper
'Both the £5 note bearing M. Masaryk's signature and the cheque for over £100,000 from Messrs. Cosens and Co., representing that firm's War Weapons Week investments, were handed for inspection to members of the audience at Wyke upon payment of a penny.
'The showing of these two valuable pieces of paper brought in 10s. in pennies.'

On Wednesday the 16th, from 9 p.m. up to 1 a.m. there was a Ball at the Gloucester Hotel, tickets 5s each, under the patronage of the Mayor and Mayoress.

The Week's Official Programme had announced that on every day of the week (Sunday excluded) at noon, the Mayor would announce the total money subscribed up to the close of the previous day. In fact, according to a circular from the Mayor's Parlour, dated 29th April, he was pleased to announce that instead of the aimed £125,000, what was actually achieved was £467,682. 'A truly splendid result.'

Those same British Legion wooden structure premises in Westwey Road, which had only been opened by Mayor John Goddard on the 27th May 1939, were burned down by incendiary bombs on the night of Saturday, 3rd May. According to Acutt's book, this 'was the date of the most serious effort by enemy fire-raisers . . . The British Legion Headquarters, built a few years previously was burnt out. The debt on the building had only just been cleared. Soldiers and members of a decontamination squad in the Corporation Yard nearby helped to extinguish the blaze.'

On 14th September the Mayor was an invited spectator at a First Aid Party Inter-Depot Competition, held in Weymouth. It took the form of a realisitic air raid incident with casualties at a house in Rodwell Road, with four teams taking part.

At the annual Changeover meeting on 2nd October of Weymouth's Honorary Court Highclere of The Ancient Order of Foresters, Brother John Goddard was elected as Senior Woodward. This would have meant relinquishing his bugle horn of office as Senior Beadle, and the changing of the gold initials on his Collar.

The *Dorset Daily Echo* of 7th October reported on Mayor Goddard's formal re-opening of the Welcome Club in the former Christ Church on the corner of King Street and Park Street (since demolished for shops and apartments). Apparently the Club had at one time been in danger of having to close, but by the firm intervention of the Mayor the Club had been saved. 'A warm vote of thanks was accorded to the Mayor', who was accompanied by the Mayoress.

In the *Dorset Daily Echo* of Monday, 3rd November, there was the following front page headline and article:

'MAYOR INJURED IN RAID ON SOUTH COAST TOWN
Three People Killed And Others Taken To Hospital

'Among the casualties at a south coast town on Saturday night after a lone raider had dropped bombs in a residential area was the Mayor, who was trapped in a wrecked bedroom in a hotel.

'The Mayor was imprisoned in the debris, and it took three quarters of an hour to get him out, a beam having to be cut away to release him. Providentially he escaped with shock and some cuts and bruises.

'There were three fatal casualties in houses near by. A few injured people were taken to hospital.

'When the Mayor was lifted out of the wreckage he was attended to at once by a doctor and first-aid workers and was then rushed to hospital, the Mayoress accompanying him. The Mayor was later transferred to a nursing home.

'One of his daughters said to a reporter: "I had wished Daddy 'Good-night' and my mother and the rest of us were in the other part of the hotel when the bombs fell. We were all preparing to go to bed. Then came an explosion and it seemed as if the whole place had caved in. My father had gone to the end bedroom, which had collapsed and took him with it. Workmen helped to get him out. He was terribly shaken and the doctor gave him some morphia, but he seemed quite cheerful with it all. My mother went with him to the hospital.

'The Mayor is recovering satisfactorily . . .
'The rescue squad which helped to get the Mayor out was headed by one of the Mayor's own mace bearers.
'"We were able to recover the Mayoral medallion," said one of the rescue squad, '"and also the Mayor's war decorations." . . .'

Although this was wartime, when 'Careless Talk Costs Lives', this was perhaps carrying secrecy a bit too far. Local residents would have soon realised where and who was involved, that is Mayor 'Joe' Goddard at the *Royal Adelaide Hotel*; and any enemy spy or agent could likewise have soon found out about any lone bomber plane and the consequences. Even some days later in the *Southern Times* of 7th November, the incognito pretence was still being maintained almost word-for-word. There were, however, a few additional details, such as that the bomb fell in the roadway outside, demolishing the front part of the building (actually the end part), trapping him lying face down on his bed; but able to direct the rescue squad in their work of extricating him, he was to suffer from shock; he was expected out of the nursing home by the Monday.

'When a *Southern Times* representative called at the hotel on Sunday morning it was "business as usual". In the lounge a Morrison indoor shelter was being used as a bar, and in another room was Polly, the Mayor's 14-year-old parrot, who received the noise of the falling bomb with "Hallo!"
'A daughter of the Mayor said both her parents had gone to bed, and she was about to follow when the bombs fell. The Mayoress, who was in another room at the time, was unhurt, and another daughter, though her room was badly damaged, sustained only scratches.'

Another report said that on the morning following the bombing, a Union Jack was defiantly raised, albeit limply, above the debris of the *Royal Adelaide*.
Further details of this event are found in Acutt's book, where a photograph taken at the time shows the damage to the *Royal Adelaide* being at the west end, right on a road junction. According to Acutt's account:

'The next notable date for an air raid was November 1st, 1941, when three people were killed.
'The Red was sounded at 20.31 hours, and the First Aid Depots were soon fully manned.
'At 23.20 hours, four H.Es. were dropped in the vicinity of the Adelaide Hotel, Abbotsbury Road, at the following points:-
1.-West end of Southview Road.

2.-Junction of Abbotsbury Road and Perth Street.

3.-Junction of Abbotsbury Road and Longcroft Road.

4.-West side of Sussex Road.

'Gas mains were damaged and Abbotsbury Road blocked to traffic.

'The casualties were three killed and 11 injured, including four persons admitted to Hospital, one of whom was the Mayor, Councillor J. T. Goddard.

'Cromwell Road Rest Centre was opened, and the Rock Hotel Cookery Nook was used to provide meals for those without cooking apparatus. Westham had 171 houses damaged. Five First Aid Parties were called into action.

'The Mayor, who was trapped in a bedroom of his hotel was imprisoned in the debris and it took three quarters of an hour to get him out, a beam having to be cut away to release him. Providentially he escaped with shock and some cuts and bruises. There were three fatal casualties in houses nearby, all females.

'When the Mayor was lifted out of the wreckage he was attended to at once by Dr. [E. J. Gordon] Wallace, who was standing by with a First Aid Party, then rushed to Hospital, the Mayoress accompanying him, and he was later transferred to a Nursing Home.

[There then follows an almost *verbatim* repeat of the above newspaper report of the Mayor's daughter's comments.]

'The Rescue Squad which helped to get the Mayor out was headed by one of the Mayor's own mace bearers, Bill Docksey. "We were able to recover the Mayoral Medallion" said one of the Rescue Squad, "also the Mayor's war decorations.". . .

'On November 5th, a copy of a letter issued by the Mayor on behalf the Emergency Committee, was sent to all branches of the Civil Defence. It read as follows:-

Mayor's Parlour,
Weymouth.

5th November, 1941

'*To All the Civil Defence Services.*

'On behalf of the Emergency Committee and indeed of the Borough as a whole I desire to express to all members of the Civil Defence Services grateful appreciation of the work which they performed in connection with the air raid last week-end.

'It was reported to the Emergency Committee by the Controller that the whole organisation, including the Gas Company who were also heavily involved, worked extremely well and smoothly, and as always on these occasions every member of the service engaged in the work pulled his or her full weight and it is a splendidly encouraging characteristic of our people that when occasion arises everything else is subordinated to "get on with the job."

'The best thanks of the townspeople are once again due to all of you and on their behalf I extend to you their sincere gratitude.

'On this occasion a more personal note is called for. I now have my own experience of the effects of bombing, and the work of our Civil Defence Services. I realise I had a very narrow escape but I realise too that had it not been for the efficiency of our various services the damage which I sustained would have been much worse and might have been fatal. You will realise that I cannot adequately express my own feelings towards you but I take this, the earliest opportunity, of letting you know that my family and myself are quite unable to put into words the gratitude that we feel for the personal service you rendered to us and our admiration at the efficiency of your work. It confirms me in the opinion I had always held with regard to the Civil Defence Services and gives me the greatest confidence for the future.

Yours sincerely,

(Signed) J. T. GODDARD, Mayor

'*Note.* The Mayor insisted upon signing the original of this letter himself, but he regrets very much that the injury to his right hand has not permitted him to sign each individual copy.'

On a slightly lighter note, Des Fry in his book was to say:

'There was a tendency at the time, for people to over or underestimate *the skills* of the luftwaffe pilots, after some incidents people would apply fanciful reasons for the attack, i.e. when the home of the Mayor was demolished, lady on bus, remarks, "of course they knew the Mayor lived there, that's why they bombed it!"'

'Joe' Goddard apparently came out of the nursing home *in time to* be re-elected on 10th November for a fourth term as Mayor. He had to speak at the mayor-choosing ceremony seated in a chair, having previously been 'accorded a hearty welcome'. This again took place at the *Burdon Hall* instead of the Guildhall. In the photograph believed to have been taken at the ceremony Mayor 'Joe' Goddard appears to be wearing a narrow white arm sling. And one of the mace-bearers in the photograph would have been the one who assisted in the Mayor's rescue. In the *Dorset Daily Echo* of the same day, reporting the words of the proposer:

'He sometimes wondered how Councillor Goddard was able to carry on as he had done.

'The Mayor and his deputy seemed to thrive on their years of office. They continued year after year without taking much holiday.

'Another reason for re-electing Councillor Goddard was because of his knowledge of civil defence requirements, as chairman of the Emergency Committee.'

As well as glowing tributes to the Mayor, they were also paid to his wife, the Mayoress, for her help and support, and to their children (three daughters and a son).

In his acceptance speech, the Mayor was to praise the Defence Services, for obvious reasons, and also the children of Weymouth who were playing their part in the war effort:

'" We must keep smiling," he added, "do what we can for each other, and prepare ourselves for any eventuality, and we shall win through. . . the ways in which the children are doing their bit to help destroy the monster who deprive them of their freedom. When young, middle-aged, and old are all united in this one endeavour, then surely we shall achieve victory."'

'Joe' Goddard was to subsequently receive from Viscount Hinchingbrooke, the local Member of Parliament, a letter of warmest congratulations:

St John's College
Cambridge
13th November 1941

'Dear Mr. Mayor,
'I have heard from Mrs. Daw and have read details in the Press of your very fortunate escape from the bombing which took place in Weymouth the other night. I write to offer my warmest congratulations on that but, at the same time, to say how sorry I am to hear that there were a number of deaths, that you yourself were hurt and that your hotel suffered damage.
'I saw that you attended the ceremony for the election of Mayor for the ensuing year, which must have been a great effort for you in the circumstances, but may I say how pleased I am that the town should have had the good sense to elect you again as Mayor to enable you to carry on with the great work which you are doing in Weymouth.

With kind regards to you and your wife,
Yours sincerely,
Hinchingbrooke'

The *Dorset Daily Echo* of 31st October reported on a goodwill wireless broadcast that had been beamed to Weymouth the evening previous from

Weymouth in Massachusetts, U.S.A. It had apparently been heard loud and clear by local listeners.

'Within 10 minutes of the broadcast ending the Town Clerk (Mr Percy Smallman), on behalf of the Mayor (Councillor J.T.Goddard), sent the following cable through the Post Office to "Daniel O'Donnell, Weymouth, Mass - Broadcast received splendidly. Mayor, Weymouth, England."'

As a further reply back to Massachusetts, on 12th November, Mayor 'Joe' Goddard made a 7-minute recording in *Gloucester Lodge*, along the Esplanade, Weymouth, back to Massachusetts. With him were the Town Clerk (Mr Percy Smallman), and Alderman Percy John A'Court who had made a visit to Weymouth, Massachusetts in 1926, during his own Mayoralty, at the tercentenary celebrations of the founding of that State. A transcript of this recording can be found in APPENDIX I.

During the first week in December the Japanese attacked the United States Naval Base at Pearl Harbour, in the Philipines, and this quickly brought America into the war on the side of the Allies.

There was again the Mayor's Christmas Fund for the sick, aged and needy of Weymouth, with the Mayor himself donating £5.

1942

There were still to be fairly frequent siren alerts during the early part of the year, but no actual air-raids as such.

The *Southern Times* of 2nd January reported that in the New Year's Honours List, Mayor 'Joe' Goddard was one of three Weymouth citizens awarded an O.B.E. (Civil Division). More precisely it was called 'The Most Excellent Order of the British Empire, Fourth Class. He would now have been entitled to use the letters 'O.B.E.' as well as 'M.C., J.P.' after his name. This newspaper also said that at the St. Mary's church service the previous day, in conection with the day of prayer, the rector (Rev. E. L. Langston) congratulated the Mayor on the honour, and said they thanked him for his self-denying services.

The *Southern Times* of Friday, 13th February, carried the item:

'The Mayor of Weymouth, Coun. J. T. Goddard M.C., was decorated with the O.B.E. by the King at a recent Buckingham Palace investiture.
'He was accompanied by the Mayoress and their son Graham, a detective-sergeant [later a Superintendent] in the Metropolitan Police.
'The Mayor told the *Southern Times* he was deeply impressed by the ceremony.'

This was of course his second visit to Buckingham Palace, and his third meeting with the King.

In the same edition of this newspaper was a further item:

'There was an interesting prelude to the business at Weymouth Town Council yesterday, when by means of a loud speaker members listened to a record of the recent broadcast to Weymouth, Mass., by the Mayor (Coun. J. T. Goddard), Ald. P. J. A'Court, and the Town Clerk (Mr. Percy Smallman).'

For full details of this broadcast see APPENDIX III.

At the quarterly meeting in January, of the Honorary Court Highclere of the Ancient Order of Foresters in Weymouth, it was moved by Chief Ranger Brother W. J. Whittle, duly seconded and resolved unanimously: That the congratulations of the Court be extended to His Worship the Mayor, Brother J. T. Goddard, Senior Woodward, and Brother A. E. Reddell, Senior Beadle, on their being awarded the Order of the British Empire in H.M.'s New Year Honours list.

The *Southern Times* of 23rd January had carried details of a meeting attended by the Mayor to plan Weymouth's Warship Week 7th-14th February, with a target of £350,000, to entitle it to 'adopt' H.M. Submarine *Rorqual*. This vessel was launched in 1936, and the target sum would pay for the hull and main and auxiliary machinery. Mayor Goddard was naturally involved with some of the events. On the first day (Saturday) he accompanied Vice-Admiral L. D. I. MacKinnin C.B., C.V.O. on the saluting base outside the *Gloucester Hotel*, for a march past of Service and Civil Defence personnel. According to the *Southern Times* of 13th February:

'The Mayor reminded the borough that when, a year ago, he appealed for £175,000 the response was £465,000 . . . and [in aiming for £350,000 this time] he was confident they would not let him and the town down.'

He also read out telegrams of good wishes from the First Lord of the Admiralty, and the Chancellor of the Exchequer.

In February the minds of Weymouth's Civil Defence chiefs were still considering the impact of a possible German invasion, though such threat was now thought to be dwindling.

On the following Wednesday afternoon, according to the *Southern Times* of 13th and 20th February, the Mayor and Mayoress were among the players at a fund-raising whist drive. In the evening the Mayor and Mayoress lent their patronage to a ball, cabaret, and gala dance at the *Burdon Hotel*, with the Mayoress distributing the prizes and gifts. On the final Saturday afternoon, 14th, the Mayor kicked-off at a football match between an RAF XI and an Army & Home Guard XI on the Recreation Ground. In the morning he had been at Estelle's, a local dress-shop, to receive a cheque for £55, being the proceeds from a raffle for a silver fox fur. At the Week's final event that same evening, a concert by the Black Berets (Royal Tank Corps) at the Alexandra Gardens, the Mayor announced that the figure raised at 7 p.m. was £425,000 - enough to pay for the complete submarine. The final total was to be £434,018 18s 2d.

'NOT THE TIME FOR ILL-FEELING
Mayor Condemns Speeches Which
Harm Morale'

was a headline in the *Southern Times* of 13th March. These sentiments were expressed at the 18th annual meeting of the South Dorset Ladies Auxiliary League of the Licensed Trade, at the New Bridge Hotel, Weymouth. In proposing a vote of thanks to the guest speaker, the Mayor recalled that at the last annual meeting he (the Mayor) spoke the truth and upset one or two people, but he did not propose to tread on anybody's corns this year.

'I think really there is an excuse. The war has upset people's nerves. They have got panicky, and are not responsible for what they say.'

He did not believe in the alleged incident reported by a temperance speaker of drunken sailors, because if he did he would have lost faith in the conduct and manner of the gallant fellows who brought over tea, which the people drank who criticised them, and also the food they ate. He appreciated the way the brewers were looking after licensees' interests, and endeavouring to keep up as high as they possibly could the supplies of the commodities they sold. He thought remarkable the way the League had raised money during the year, and he asked the ladies to associate themselves with HM Submarine *Rorqual* which the town had adopted. The crew had asked for comforts.

March saw the resumption of occasional air-raids on Weymouth, with a large-scale dive-bomber attack on 2nd April.

The next big event was the Weymouth Medical Aid For Russia Week, 14th-18th April, organised by the Weymouth Labour Party, Trades Council, and Co-operative Society. This event was covered in the *Southern Times* of 17th and 24th April. The culminating highlight of the Week, during which there had been special events to raise funds for medical aid for Russia, was a meeting at the Alexandra Gardens Theatre, on the Saturday afternoon of 18th April, chaired by His Worship, Mayor Goddard. Under the meeting's title of 'RUSSIA AND THE WAR', the guest speaker was Mr. D. N. Pritt, KC, MP. He showed good reasons for the opening of a Second Front in the West, to enable the Russia allies "to finish off" Germany.

'The Mayor said the audience was unanimous on one point - their admiration of and gratitude for the magnificent resistance the Russians were making. He personally knew little about Russia, but added that during the Great War he rode 100 miles with a Cossack regiment, and was fully aware of their admirable physique and horsemanship. Admiration, however, was not enough. We should give Russia all the help we could in munitions, tanks, aeroplanes, and advice.'

On a lighter note, the Mayor and Mayoress attended a dance at the *Hotel Burdon*, on Friday, 5th June, organised by the manager in aid of the Red Cross Supply Depot.

The *Southern Times* of 19th June reported:

'With the echo of a fanfare played by the band of the Royal Tank Regiment still in their ears, a large crowd assembled on the Weymouth Esplanade on Sunday afternoon [14th June] saw the flags of the United Nations hoisted on the flagstaffs of the *Gloucester Hotel*.

'This impressive ceremony inaugurated the open-air service on United Nations Day, initiated by President Roosevelt.

'A message from the Prime Minister was read by the Mayor from the hotel balcony. He was accompanied by the Mayoress (in W.V.S. uniform), . . .'

It was also reported that the amongst the assembly were members of military units, plus ex-service, auxiliary and youth organisations.

There were further occasional air-raids during June, with one on the night of the 28th. Next morning the local M.P., the Mayor and Controller of Civil Defence visited the damaged sites, and witnessed a rescue. Then they went on to a British Restaurant and saw work being done for the homeless by Rest Centre workers. During a raid on 29th, several hundred incendiary bombs fell in the Abbotsbury Road and Westham area, with (according to Acutt) one penetrating the roof of the Mayor's residence. But any fires were very quickly got under control.

Air-raids on Weymouth continued in July, and then discontinued for almost two years, though nearby Portland still suffered for a while.

According to the *Southern Times* of 10th July, the previous Sunday (5th) was observed throughout the country as A.T.C. Day. This was at the request of the Air Ministry, 'in order to give this great R.A.F. youth movement the widest publicity. Nearly 100 smart boys of Weymouth's 249 Squadron paraded to a service at St Mary's Church; after which they marched round the town to the saluting base at the *Royal Hotel*. Amongst the V.I.P. guests was Mayor Goddard.

A joint letter from the Mayor of Weymouth and the Chairman of Portland U.D. was published in the *Southern Times* of 24th July. This was an appeal to all householders to make a special effort to leave out as bagged salvage for the dustmen any unwanted worn-out woollen, cotton and linen clothing and rags, etc., rope or string. This would be another important way in which the public could help the war effort.

The Mayor presided at a mass meeting in the Alexandra Gardens Theatre, on Friday, 7th August, in connection with the Dorset County Salvage Drive which was to run 15th-29th August. He was supported by his wife, the Mayoress, and members of the Town Council. Speakers impressed the need for the salvaging of all waste materials to enable the war effort to continue successfully. Old flat irons could be converted into steel helmets. Broken garden forks could be made into tommy guns. Bones could be turned into glue for high explosives, paper for cartridges, rags to make the uniforms, and rubber to make the dinghies or 'Mae Wests'. According to the *Southern Times* of 14th August:

'The Mayor said he thought it remarkable that after three years of war it was necessary to call a meeting to encourage the collection of salvage. The reason must either be that all the salvage had been collected, or that people did not realise the value of it, or perhaps the machinery which existed was not functioning properly.

"There was no doubt about it," he went on, "we have got to sit up and take a great deal more interest in salvage."'

The Mayor also chaired a meeting of Weymouth traders, to discuss mutual aid in the salvaging of stock and damage being caused to businesses from air raids.

The *Southern Times* of 14th August reported:

'Weymouth and District Hospital is in need of money, and on Wednesday [12th] the Mayor called an informal meeting of supporters and hospital workers to "iron out" plans for a Hospital Week from September 19 to 26 . . . The Mayor said a flag day would be held on the 19th, but a big effort was needed to wipe off the overdraft.' Several money-raising events were suggested and planned.

According to the same newspaper the Mayoress, Mrs Hilda Goddard, presided over a meeting of the W.V.S. in the Alexandra Gardens Theatre, Weymouth, on Wednesday, 12th August. Those present heard an outline of the work and achievements of the W.V.S. which had only been formed in 1938 to help in the Government's evacuation plans. There were now 1,500,000 members, many of whom had done gallant work during the blitz; and that the threat of invasion was still a possibility, as well as renewed bombing. The Mayoress was undoubtedly also involved in the W.V.S. flag-day in Weymouth, on Saturday 8th August, for the Dorset Comforts Committee, mentioned in the same newspaper.

At 2·15 p.m. on Saturday, 15th August, Weymouth's start to the Salvage Drive took place with the opening of an Exhibition at Marks & Spencers by Viscount Hinchinbrooke, South Dorset's M.P. He was welcomed by Mayor Goddard. Amongst the exhibits was a torpedo, and munitions were shown being manufactured. There were also loudspeaker vans and films.

The *Southern Times* of 21st August declared the challenge by Dorchester to Weymouth to collect more salvage per 1,000 of the population during August. Mayor Goddard had accepted the challenge at the opening of Salvage Week. He said on that occasion:

'During the past fortnight he had received 20 contributions from children for various organisations, by selling lavender bags, iron holders and the like. He saw no reason why the children of Weymouth should not carry out a salvage campaign of their own, and it would be a fine effort on their part.'

It was subsequently announced in the *Southern Times* of 28th August that Dorchester had won the Salvage Week wager, and Mayor Goddard accordingly handed over a cheque for £5 to the victor, the Mayor of Dorchester, at the Weymouth Municipal Offices. The latter thanked Weymouth for the friendly and sporting spirit that the townsfolk had shown in the competition. For his part Mayor Goddard thanked all the local organisers, etc. It was noted that 196 tons of cut-down railings were not included in Weymouth's total.

The *Southern Times* of 21st August noted that the Queen was to send a gift with all possible success to the 'H.M.S. Dorsetshire Market' at 5 St Mary Street, Weymouth, and all good fortune to the organisers. It was opened by Viscount Hinchinbrooke M.P. on Thursday afternoon, 27th August. Again he was supported by Mayor Goddard.

The same newspaper also reported on a recent meeting at Weymouth, Portland and District Trades Council meeting. During some discussion it was commented that there seemed to be some distinction made regarding the rebuilding of the *Royal Adelaide Hotel*. It was felt that attention was given to the building at a greater cost, while other business premises and dwelling houses were left unrepaired. The Westham branch of the A.E.U. proposed the following resolution:

'The members emphatically protest against the cost of rebuilding the *Adelaide Hotel* while bombed houses in the district are not being made habitable.
'Has the sanction of a Ministry been obtained for the repair of this hotel?'

The meeting's chairman said the question had been raised in the House of Commons, and that the Ministry of Supply had given permission for the necessary material to be available for partly rebuilding the premises. Although it was suggested the matter be left in the hands of Lord Hinchingbrooke M.P., it was carried that the matter go to the Executive Committee with power to act. What the outcome was has not been determined.

On Thursday afternoon, 27th August, the Borough Surveyor took the Mayor and other officials on a tour of the town. They visited all depots, and salvage collectors in the streets, and thanks were expressed to 'salvage drivers'.

The Mayor presided at a sub-committee meeting of the Citizens' Advice Bureau at Weymouth Guildhall on Friday, 21st August, when it was proposed to open the first such Bureau in Weymouth on Monday, 7th September. He appealed for more volunteers to help at the Bureau. The *Southern Times* of 11th September reported his subsequent performance of the official opening ceremony at 3 Johnstone Row, Esplanade, when he said that it was regretted the bureau had been so long coming. He was sure Weymouth citizens would make good use of it. It would be of tremendous help to the townspeople, and to local Servicemen as well. He heartily thanked those whose persistent efforts had made it possible. It was not just a war-time temporary institution, but (and here he was obviously now being optimistic of the outcome) would continue to be of great service to the public after the war.

The *Southern Times* of 2nd October, in a front page article, mentioned that Mayor Goddard had made a bet with the managing director of the local Whiteheads (torpedo) factory that the latter would not contribute as much during the current Weymouth Hospital Week as the Borough. On the latest figures available it looked as if the Mayor's money was safe, though Whiteheads were making a final effort. In the event it was Whiteheads who finally won the £1 bet with the Mayor, having raised £1,540 compared with the town's £1,111.

On another front, Weymouth had sent a gift of £250 to Lady Cripp's Aid to China Fund, forwarded through the Mayor and W.V.S.

It was leaked at about the same time that Weymouth Town Council's Selection Committee had invited 'Joe' Goddard to be Mayor for yet another year, and it being likely that he would accept.

At the annual Changeover meeting in October of the Honorary Court Highclere of the Ancient Order of Foresters in Weymouth, Brother Goddard was elevated another rung by being elected as Sub Chief Ranger. This would have meant another change of gold initials on the Collar.

Mayor and Mayoress Goddard, on Saturday, 24th October, were in a welcoming party which greeted Lady Louis Mountbatten to Weymouth. She had come to open later that day the Y.W.C.A. at the Sidney Hall, where Mayoress Hilda Goddard was amongst the VIPs on the platform. Lady Mountbatten stated how fortunate the people of Weymouth were to have the active support of the Mayor and Mayoress. According to the *Southern Times* of 30th October, Lady Mountbatten was later escorted to a civic reception at the Mayor's Parlour; and afterwards the Mayor and Mayoress accompanied her when, as Lady Superintendent-in-Chief of the St John's Ambulance Brigade, she inspected the local Brigade at their Westwey Road headquarters. Here the Mayor said that this was the first unit of the S.J.A.B. Lady Louis had inspected since she accepted the position of Lady-Superintendent-in-Chief. He stressed that it was a source of pleasure to have such an efficient organisation in the town, and he was thankful for the women's section at first-aid posts, rest centres, etc., and for the help of the cadets in the new nursery started in Weymouth. One speaker spoke of the practical interest of the Mayor as president of the ambulance division. The Mayor and Mayoress also accompanied Lady Mountbatten on her inspection of the First Aid Post at the Weymouth Health Centre.

On Monday, 9th November, 'Joe' Goddard was re-elected for an unprecedented fifth term as Mayor of Weymouth. One proposer, as part of the high tributes and praise to be paid to Councillor Goddard, the Mayoress and family

'"We Councillors who for four years have worked under the chairmanship of the Mayor, fully realise what a large amount of time, work, and energy he has put into the office."

'He recalled how 12 months earlier, in a blitz, they nearly had the misfortune of losing Councillor Goddard. They thanked God that today he was with them, full of vigour and vitality.'

'During the eight years Councillor Goddard had been a member of the corporation he had given unstinted service to the town generally.

'Mention of the service rendered by the Mayoress brought forth renewed applause. Socially, Mrs Goddard had served the town as well as any Mayoress could possibly have done. [She was] a busy lady with a home of her own to run. Yet she always found time to do anything asked of her.'

Another proposer drew the analogy of 'not changing horses in mid-stream', describing the Mayor

'as a good mixer, a man who was always accessible for all manner of things, in spite of the calls on his time, and "a Mayor who is always on tap."'

In his acceptance speech Mayor 'Joe' Goddard was also to compliment his wife, saying that

'in his opinion [her] chief qualification was that she was a good cook. He felt that if the Mayoress had carried out her duties to the satisfaction of the council, she had been a good Mayoress.'

Still somewhat optimistic, Mayor Goddard was to end:

"If, during my year of office, this war finishes, it will be the crowning success to whatever I have tried to do."

There was not to be an Armistice Service on 11th November this year, but just a civic wreath-laying ceremony at the Cenotaph.

The Christmas Season brought the usual round of goodwill visits by the Mayor and Mayoress. For example, on Christmas morning they headed the singing of carols in the wards of Weymouth & District Hospital. They also visited Portwey Hospital. Later the same day the Mayor was amongst visitors at the 'Christmas party for mothers and children in Weymouth whose enjoyment was restricted'.

The *Southern Times* of 1st January 1943 also reported that both were again present later in the week at a party for friends and helpers of the W.V.S., at the *Clinton Restaurant*.

1943

According to the *Southern Times* of 12th February, the Mayoress presided at the February monthly meeting of the relatives of prisoners of war, held at the *Victoria Hotel* on Sunday, 7th. The Mayor at the same time was able to hand the county secretary of the Red Cross a cheque for £130 from the Weymouth branch. The same newspaper reported the formation of a Garden Produce Association for Weymouth, when at a meeting held at the *Waverley Hotel*, the Mayor was elected its President.

The front page of the *Southern Times* on 26th February reported:

'The Mayor of Weymouth, Coun. J. T. Goddard O.B.E. announced at a meeting at the Guildhall on [the 24th], organised by the local branch of the Russia Today Society as part of the town's celebrations to commemorate the Red Army's 25th anniversary, that at the next meeting of the Town Council he would ask the Authority to sanction a Flag Day for Mrs Churchill's Medical Aid for Russia Fund.

'Coun. Goddard also asked the Russia Today Society to organise a special Aid for Russia Week, which he hoped would be more successfull than last year's effort, in itself a credit to the town. . .

'The Mayor, who presided at the well-attended gathering, said everyone was amazed at what our Ally had achieved in the East, and he hoped the great successes would go on. The British workers had done much to contribute to Russia's victories, and whether we agreed with their politics or not, they certainly had a wonderful system. Ninety per cent of the Russian people today had attained a high standard of education or they could not have achieved what they had. We now saw things from a different viewpoint. "Wise men change their minds," he said, "but fools never do!" He hoped the mutual good relationship between Russia and ourselves would grow stronger.'

It was also decided that Weymouth would have a collection of books to either send to the Forces, stock a local reference library, or for paper salvage. The former would have stamped inside them:

'This book was given during the borough Book Appeal, and is sent with the best wishes of the Mayor and Mayoress (Coun. J. T. Goddard, O.B.E., M.C., J.P., and Mrs Goddard), residents and children of Weymouth and Melcombe Regis.'

The central depot was to be opened on 9th March, and the Mayor had decided to earmark a float of books for units of the Services stationed locally.

On the 24th February, the Mayor and Mayoress were part of a large crowd which witnessed the presention of a mobile canteen by the B.W. Club to the Weymouth Salvation Army, it being dedicated "for the use of H.M. troops and the benefit of our fellow citizens in any time of distress." The Mayor said he knew of nothing better to which the club could devote its surplus funds.

Beginning on 27th February was Weymouth Y.W.C.A. Week,, planned to raise funds to secure the upkeep of the Y.W.C.A. centre at the Sidney Hall. The Mayor on the first Saturday presided at a Caledonian Market in Weymouth shopping centre, opened by the local M.P., Lord Hinchingbrooke, who was thanked by the Mayoress. She was also a guest at other events during the Week, as well as presenting prizes - some of which she had donated.

The Mayoress was to preside at a meeting of the W.V.S. at the Guildhall on 10th March. According to the *Southern Times* on 12th March, she 'expressed regret that no men had accepted their invitation to attend. "I must put it down to shyness," she laughingly observed.'

The *Southern Times* on 2nd April published a letter from Mayor Goddard, thanking everyone who had generously contributed the thousands of books during the recent Borough book collection (which the author remembers participating in). The same newspaper reported that he had agreed at its meeting on Sunday, 27th March, to become patron of the Weymouth Channel Islands Society. He 'said the Society would strengthen the comradely ties between Weymouth people and the Channel Islanders' in exile.

On the evening of 12th April, the Mayor was one of those watching a First Aid Competition between Junior members of two Civil Defence Depots.

The front page of the *Southern Times* on 16th April, carried this item:

'MAYOR'S APPEAL This is Aid for China Week in Weymouth, and in an interview with the Mayor (Coun. J. T. Goddard) this morning the "Southern Times" was given this message for its readers:

"The Mayor appeals to Weymouth people not to be deterred from giving generously this week to the China Fund. The stirring address by Miss Wong and the great effort China is making must appeal to all people, and you can show your gratitude by giving freely to Lady Stafford Cripps's Fund to send badly needed medical supplies to the Chinese armies.

"Last year Weymouth's China Week raised £450, and I hope at least a similar sum will be raised this week. Already through the generosity of a few people £60 has been given, and the flag day tomorrow will be the crowning effort of the week. I hope when you purchase your emblem you will remember China's urgent need. . ."'

This appeal was alongside an article about a meeting the previous evening, Thursday, 15th, presided over by the Mayor, which had been addressed by Miss Diana Wong, Chinese M.o.I speaker

Mrs Winston Churchill, wife of the Prime Minister, unofficially spent Easter at the *Royal Hotel*, Weymouth. On the Thursday morning, 22nd April, after her arrival, she received the Mayor and Mayoress. Mrs Churchill said she was pleased to note that Hilda Goddard was wearing W.V.S. uniform. This organisation was the chief topic of conversation, with Mrs Churchill remarking she was proud of it. When the Mayoress presided at the monthly meeting of Weymouth W.V.S. at the Guildhall on the 28th, she spoke of the earlier reception with Mrs Churchill.

The Mayor presided at a concert of choral and vocal music given by a 'famous' military male voice choir on Thursday evening, 13th May, at Maiden Street Methodist Church. Although the *Southern Times* did not name the choir, it reported that it was voluntary and had raised £500 for charities.

22nd-29th May inclusive was Weymouth's "Wings for Victory Week", with the aim of providing 50 Typhoon aircraft, each costing £5,000. The Mayor was naturally deeply involved in the various activities. The event opened on the morning of the 22nd with him and Service chiefs inspecting contingents from the three Services. Then mounting the saluting base, the Mayor (according to the *Southern Times* of 28th May)

'read three inspiring messages to the townspeople, which he said had been flown to Weymouth from London by carrier pigeons, which were present at the ceremony in a basket . . . [He] said he felt certain that what Weymouth aimed at would be achieved.'

One speaker then went on to say that Weymouth people had already saved £3½ million, and he felt they would make it a round £4 million before the end of the campaign. The Mayor then opened a basket and carrier pigeons sped away to Wimborne, bearing his good-will message for their own Wings Week. He, then accompanied VIPs to inspect the Weymouth A.T.C. at the Co-operative Hall, before opening the R.A.F. exhibition. Then in the afternoon the Mayor and Mayoress were hosts at a tea party at the *Clinton Restaurant*, where they entertained Service members who had taken part in the parade. Both were also at a Wings Week Dance on the 26th, at the *Regent Dance Hall*. Many other events had been planned, including a bowls match between the Corporation officials and councillors (including the Mayor) and Civil Defence wardens.

On the Friday night, the Mayor and Mayoress were again to be guests, this time at a successful "Wings" fund-raising Dance at the *Burdon Hotel*. At a "Wings" whist drive organised by the Women's Section of the British Legion, amongst the prizes presented by the Mayoress was one of a savings certificate which she had donated. On the last day of the Week, Saturday 29th, the Mayor kicked-off at a football match on the Recreation Ground between an R.A.F. XI and a Royal Navy side - which ended in a 5-5 draw.

The *Southern Times* of 4th June further reported the glad tidings:

'Weymouth has won its Wings. At noon on Monday, [31st May], the Mayor of Weymouth raised the indicator on the Statue [of George III] amid loud cheers to nearly £190,000 - £185,604 to be exact - and proudly announced that the town's "Wings for Victory" Week had been a complete success. The target of £150,000 for the Week had been exceeded . . .

'Addressing a large gathering of children, from every school in the town, the Mayor thanked them for their efforts, and appealed to them to go on with the good work, not just during the "Wings" campaign, but to keep it up every day till victory, as the country needed planes to win the war.

"Be loyal to your teachers," he advised, "and obedient to your parents, and one day the siren will sound for the last time, and then we shall say 'Thank you' to the youth for what they have done to bring the war to a successful conclusion."'

At the end of May the Mayor and Mayoress were amongst the guests at the first social and dance arranged by the Weymouth Company of the Girls' Training Corps.

The Mayor was one of the VIPs and guests at a combined annual inspection and drum-head service of local S.J.A.B. Ambulance, Nursing, and Cadet Divisions on Sunday, 6th July. Also present was one of the Mayor's two daughters who were in the W.R.N.S. The *Southern Times* of 16th July went on to say that the Mayor expressed his pleasure at attending the parade and being permitteed to accompany the county commissioner when he carried out the inspection. The "children" as he called the cadets, particularly impressed him. He was glad that youth was so keen to embellish the ranks of the brigade as they grew up.

'[He] referred to the S.J.A.B. as "old friends", referring to the time when he was an air-raid victim, and when he was taken to hospital by them.'

In the *Southern Times* of 6th August there was a photograph of all five of the Goddard women in uniform - headed 'Civic Family In Uniform'. It depicts Mrs Hilda Goddard in her W.V.S. uniform, surrounded by her three daughters - Writer Audrey Goddard, W.R.N.S., Mrs Eleanor Woodford, W.V.S., Beryl Goddard recently promoted Leading Wren, and niece Ethel Gerrard in the N.A.A.F.I.

As well as the Goddards' daughter Beryl having joined the W.R.N.S. at the outbreak of war, their daughter Eleanor's husband, Reginald Woodford was also in the Royal Navy. On return from a trip to Philadelphia in the U.S.A. he was to tell the family in the *Royal Adelaide Hotel* all about supermarkets, unknown as yet in the U.K. A nephew of the Mayoress, John Elliott, of the Union Defence Force, South Africa, was to be taken prisoner at Tobruk.

Sometime during the year the Freemasons' United Service Lodge No. 3473 (of which Joe Goddard was a member) changed its place of meeting from Portland to that of All Souls Lodge No. 170, Weymouth, whose Masonic Hall is on the corner of St. Thomas Street and School Street.

A front page report in the *Southern Times* of 13th August said:

'When a large gathering of "Weymouth's over 60's" were the guests of the Mayor and Mayoress at the Sidney Hall on Wednesday [11th] the possibility of the establishment of "Eventide Houses", comfortable places for old people, was visualised by His Worship.

'[He]] said that they had been in the habit of speaking and acting for the Youth Movement in the town, and quite rightly so . . . But while they had been doing this, they had forgotten the old folks. Now they wanted to do something for those who had once been young, but were not so young any longer. . .

"I welcome you all on behalf of the [Old People's Welfare] committee," the Mayor concluded, amid grateful applause from the crowded hall of over 60's.'

That same afternoon the Mayor and Mayoress attended a whist drive organised by the Rotarians, in aid of the British Sailors' Society and Royal National Lifeboat Institution, in advance of a pending Weymouth Seafarers' Week. As seemed to be the usual custom on these occasions the Mayoress presented the prizes.

The *Southern Times* on 27th August similarly reported the Mayor as spearheading Weymouth's 'Aid to Russia Week', to be held 2nd-10th October. He had presided over a civic meeting in the Guildhall, supported by the Mayoress, and the chairman of Portland U.D.C. who would co-operate by also having a Week. Some 60 organisations and churches would take part, with a target of £1,500, sufficient to cover the cost of a ward in the new Stalingrad Hospital. This sum could be easily attained with a shilling from each resident.

'After welcoming [the delegates], the Mayor said they all appreciated the valuable effort the Russians were making towards winning the war.

"When Mrs Churchill was here," he added, "she expressed her admiration of what had been done in Weymouth, especially by the children, for her Aid to Russia Fund. She said that this country was sending out medical supplies by the ton."

'Now to show the British people's appreciation of the heroic defence of Stalingrdad the Dean of Canterbury, Dr. Hewlett Johnson, had launched a £75,000 appeal for a new hospital in Stalingrad as a living symbol of Anglo-Soviet friendship.

'Weymouth had already sent £150 to this fund for a bed, and now it was suggested the town should aim at the cost of a ward. "£1,5000 seems a huge sum of money," said Coun. Goddard, "but I feel it can be done." There was already £35 on hand from the recent Caledonian Market.'

This Caledonian Market had been organised by four young Weymouth girls, which was opened by the Mayor,

'who paid tribute to the children's initiative, and said that by helping Russia they were helping to shorten the war, as well as making a fine gesture to a gallant people.'

The Mayor presided at the opening on Friday, 27th August, of a two-days' produce show at the Sidney Hall, in aid of the Red Cross Agricultural Fund. The *Southern Times* of 3rd September, reported him saying that he was certain it was a better show than last year's, and he hoped it would be an annual effort.

On Monday, 6th September, John Goddard attended the funeral at Weymouth crematorium of his old comrade-in-arms from the 14th Hussars, 70-year old John Spring, who he had rescued and carried injured off the battlefield at Bloemfontein in 1900. They were both members of the Freemasons' United Service Lodge No. 3473 at Portland, of which Spring had been a founder in 1910, and Past Master; and had thus probably been the one to introduce Goddard. As the *Southern Times* of 10th September reported, Spring had died as a result of a fall down some stairs whilst putting up the black-out when fire-watching at the *Clinton Restaurant*.

The King had approved a proposal that Sunday, 26th September, should be observed to commemorate the Battle of Britain, and all those whose services had helped in its success. The *Southern Times* of 17th September further announced that the Mayor and Corporation of Weymouth, etc., would attend church at St. Mary's Church in the afternoon, followed by a march past of all three Services and associated organisations. The Mayor was anxious that this parade should be the best so far held, and asked hotels, boarding-houses, traders and private residents along the route to decorate their premises. The salute would be taken from a dais between the *Gloucester* and *Royal Hotels*.

On a lighter note, it was noted that the Mayor had recently presented cups and prizes to the winners of competitons run by Greenhill Bowling Club.

A large area of advertising space was generously donated in the *Southern Times* of 24th September to allow the Mayor, as part of the Stalingrad Hospital Appeal, to call for literally 'Articles of Every Description' for a Caledonian Market on 2nd-9th October in St. Mary Street. Those who had already given everything they could spare to the many previous war markets were urged to collect from friends!

The advertised Battle of Britain parade on 26th September was reported by the *Southern Times* of 1st October as being 'Weymouth's Biggest Wartime Parade'. After the church service, where the Mayor read the lesson, he subsequently inspected a guard of honour formed by a Home Guard unit on the Esplanade, before taking the salute from a dais.

At its annual Changeover meeting on 7th October, Brother Goddard, Sub Chief Ranger, reached the pinnacle of the Honorary Court Highclere of the Ancient Order of Foresters of Weymouth by being elected Chief Ranger. As well as yet another change of initials on his Collar, it would now bear two red tassels.

Fund-raising during Stalingrad Hospital Week was being most successful, according to the *Southern Times* of Friday, 8th October, with the target £1,500 already exceeded by some £600, and another day or so still to go. The big event of the Week had been the mass meeting addressed by the Dean of Canterbury, at which the Mayor presided. Whilst at a tea party at the *Clinton Restaurant* on the 6th, nearly 130 Certificates of Honour published by the Mayor were presented by him to the savings committee and group secretaries who had achieved their targets in the recent 'Wings for Victory' campaign. The Mayor (who was accompanied by the Mayoress), in turn, was presented with a plaque provided by the Air Ministry commemorating the town's efforts.

'Accepting the gift, the Mayor said: "Some day in the not so far distant future when the new Municipal Offices are built, this plaque shall have a place of honour."
'They already had a plaque at the Mayor's Parlour, commemorating War Weapons Week and Warships Week.
"I trust this will be the end of plaques, and before we have another peace will be in the world," he added, amid applause.'

Both the Mayor and Mayoress had attended a military band concert in the *Regent Theatre*, and a concert given by Southern National Bus. Co. employees, and many other such events. Meanwhile, for her own part the Mayoress had opened the Caledonian Market at the beginning of the Week. Fund-raising continued after the Week's official end on Saturday, 9th, when there was a Great

Youth Rally in the Sidney Hall, where (according to the *Southern Times* 15th October) the Mayor addressed the 700 young people present:

"I cannot understand why it is that we have to press some boys and girls to join a youth organisation." [He was later to comment] " I have often wondered why all boys and girls are not in some organisation. I wonder what those outside feel like. All those present that night seemed so happy and healthy, and showed a desire to perform a service."

Following the Mayor's address the Mayoress and other organisers received purses handed up by representatives of public organisations, when the amount donated was £334. There was applause when the Mayor announced that one organisation had already raised sufficient for a bed.

On a more personal note, 'Joe' Goddard had agreed to continue as Mayor of Weymouth for a record sixth year, having given his decision at a meeting of the Town Council sitting in committee on Monday, 3rd October.

Acutt was to describe in his book:

'In the St. John Hall [in Westwey Road, Weymouth] on Sunday afternoon, October 17th, 1943, ambulance and nursing cadets were enrolled and a number of certificates distributed. . .

'The Mayor of Weymouth (Councillor J. T. Goddard) presided over a large gathering [which included County officials].

'The Mayor in opening the ceremony, said he regarded it not only as an interesting one, but a serious one as well. Cadets had certain obligations, and he hoped they would fulfil them to the best of their ability.'

On Saturday, 22nd, *The Southern Times* announced that the Mayor would be amongst those taking the salute next afternoon of a march as part of a recruiting campaign for the Training Corps for Girls. In the same edition it was stated that less than £450 was needed to double the Stalingrad Hospital target of £1,500 - for which the Mayor was still being handed donations. The newspaper also contained a letter from the Mayor, asking for volunteers to donate books listed by the Librarian for a Town Reference Library, or those with experience in obtaining such books.

Meanwhile, as a measure of the changing fortunes of the Allied Forces, Weymouth Town Council was now contemplating contingency plans for attracting and entertaining tourists once the war was over.

Yet once again, on Tuesday, 9th November, Mayor 'Joe' Goddard was to be re-elected at the annual Mayor-choosing ceremony in the *Hotel Burdon* for a

municipal record sixth term, as reported in the *Dorset Daily Echo* of 9th and
10th November. The proposer said in eloquent praise:

"We have had a wonderful captain on the bridge. It had not been an easy job, but
at all times Councillor Goddard had displayed tact, besides upholding the dignity
of the office. The public of Weymouth owed a deep debt of gratitude to the
Mayor for the services he had rendered and the finest compliment which could be
paid him was unanimously to re-elect him that day.

"Those who knew realised to the full that the Mayor had had a wonderful
companion in life. Mrs Goddard had been a tower of strength in all the services
the Mayor had rendered. The duties of a Mayor were extensive and he could not
be expected to fulfill all appointments. Mrs Goddard had often deputised for him
in an able manner. Often she had rolled up her sleeves and worked like a trojan,
especially in the cause of charity."

The Councillor seconding was to be equally fulsome in praise:

"One aspect of the work not known to the general public was being an *ex-officio*
member of every committee, and Councillor Goddard had availed himself of that
privilege by attending nearly every meeting. Every morning of the week he
devoted practically the whole of his time to his public offices, and even on
Sundays he received deputations on occasions from members of the council to
consider affairs of state.

"Everything Councillor Goddard had done had been *pro bono publico*.

"To quote the words of the Prime Minister [Winston Churchill], Councillor
Goddard had gone through "blood, tears and sweat" and they hoped that during
the coming year he would taste the sweets of victory.

"Mrs Goddard had been an indefatigable worker in every good cause, espceially
the W.V.S. She carried out her duties in a quiet unassuming manner with a charm
that endeared her to one and all."

'He felt the Mayor and Mayoress must miss very much the help of Miss Audrey
Goddard, who was now in the 'Wrens' and stationed in one of the far-flung
outposts of the Empire.'

The Mayor in his speech of acceptance said:

"For myself, and the small part I have been fortunate to take in the 'ups and
downs', I should be ungrateful if I did not deeply appreciate the honour you have
seen fit to bestow on me year after year to continue in office. The one thing that
has induced me to accept is the fact that continuity while the present

circumstances prevail may have certain advantages in dealing with the many problems that from time to time appear, the solving of which has been made easy by the ready and great assistance I have received from everyone. . . The town has been honoured by many disinguished guests, whom it has been my privilege to meet on your behalf, amongst them may be mentioned Mrs. Churchill, the wife of our great leader, who personally thanked me for the continual support we are giving to her Aid to Russia Fund.'

The Mayor at the same time welcomed Weymouth's three repatriated prisoners of war - who had been specially invited to attend - and said the occasion was a fitting opportunity of expressing the gratitude of the townspeople to them and all the officers and men they represented.

Weymouth was now to become in a hectic state of preparation for a pending invasion of mainland Europe, with a continual input and build-up of mainly American troops. Even so, a certain discretion was observed by the local Press, as exampled by the *Southern Times* of 3rd December:

'An appeal to the residents to throw open their doors to American Servicemen was made by the Mayor of a South Coast town on Wednesday [1st] at a meeting called by the local W.V.S. to arrange a hospitality scheme for United States troops.
'The Mayor said the object was to make arrangements for the soldiers, and appealed to the residents to endeavour to make their stay in the area as happy and comfortable as possible.
'While the chief object of the men's stay in the district was to enable them to train for battle, it was realised they were also in need of social facilities in their off-duty hours.'

There was still time for normal war-time social activity. At Christmas 1943 the local W.R.N.S. put on a stage show in the Theatre Ballroom of the *Burdon Hotel*, to which Town and Service dignitaries and top brass were invited, together with their wives, etc. The Mayor's Christmas Relief Fund was again launched, whilst the P.O.W. Fund was two years or so old.

The Mayor took space in the *Southern Times* on 24th December to pass on Christmas Greetings from himself and the Mayoress, which included the following:

". . . Although we know the end is not yet, we are confident that the hostilities, which have caused so many separations and so much suffering, are nearing cessation, and it is our earnest hope that the year of 1944 will bring that peace for which we all have so great a longing."

Alas, even this cautious optimism was not to be realised until some five months into 1945.

   The year was to close with the Mayor paying tribute to the work the W.V.S. had done during the war. The tenacity and continuity they had displayed were a feature of the British people. During 1944 they looked forward to victory and the triumph of their labours. This was expressed at a W.V.S. party to some 250 local members, whose leader appealed to them to double their numbers. He and the Mayoress also attended a party the Weymouth Services Club gave to members of Forces and friends; and a W.V.S. party to "homeless" mothers of Weymouth, women living in the town on war work from all, parts of the country, and their children; and also the party for the Health Centre staff children. They also arranged, with the Weymouth Caledonian Society, a party for the London evacuees at Bowleaze. The Mayoress alone was present at another party for Weymouth's youngsters whose parents were on war work.

1944

The year opened with expectation of an Allied landing in mainland Europe, with an increasing influx of American troops and vehicles of all descriptions.

At a New Year's party on 5th January, for 100 children and their mothers, whose fathers were prisoners of war, Mayor 'Joe' Goddard distributed two toys from the Christmas tree to each child, and afterwards presented useful gifts to the adult helpers. According to the *Southern Times* of 7th January this was organised by Weymouth Relatives of Prisoners of War at the St. John Ambulance Hall.

The following day, at the quarterly meeting of the Honorary Court Highclere of the Ancient Order of Foresters of Weymouth, Chief Ranger Brother Goddard unexpectedly became Past Chief Ranger. The biographer does not know the reason for this, but it may possibly have been due to pressure of Mayoral duties concerning the massive build-up in Weymouth of the invasion forces prior to D-Day in June. As Past Chief Ranger, his collar would have been modified by reverting back to one tassel, and having a centre white stripe to indicate a Past Chief Ranger.

The *Southern Times* of 14th January reported that during the course of consideration by Weymouth Town Council of a Home Office tribute paid to the Fire Guard and N.F.S. in Weymouth, scorn was passed on the Chief Warden's criticism of the alleged inferior and cheaper style of Civil Defence beret badges requisitioned by the County Council. The Mayor hoped the Council would not use that recommendation (to delete the Chief Warden's comments) as an excuse on which to criticise the men who were doing a really good job. The Emergency Committee was very grateful to them, he said.

As president of the Weymouth Division of the St. John Ambulance Brigade, the Mayor distributed the awards at the Division's annual award presentation, on 2nd February. He paid tribute to the work of the brigade, saying that it was only very recently that the public had begun to realise the value of the work of the Order, which had been carried on through the centuries. He later inspected a scroll of the names of Division members on active service, of whom one had died of wounds.

The Mayor as its president chaired the annual meeting of the Weymouth and District War Savings Groups, at the *Clinton Restaurant* on 9th February. It was suggested that the aim for 1944 should be for Weymouth to raise a £1,000,000 (£820,000 in 1943). The Mayor declared that the savings movement was only able to carry on its good work because of the ready assistance of keen supporters. He was sure the townsfolk would make every endeavour to reach the one million pounds target.

At the Town Council's Emergency Committee meeting the next day, whilst it was authorised that old age pensioners should only pay 6d for their British

Restaurant meals, equal facilities should be provided for parishes on the outskirts of the town. The Mayor said they had made a good start, and in course of time they would endeavour to improve it.

The *Southern Times* of 11th February further reported that on the previous Sunday afternoon the Mayor had presided at a crowded meeting of Salvationists and their friends at the Weymouth Citadel.

'In welcoming the Mayor, the Divisional Commander said that many of their supporters, including the Mayor, would make excellent Salvationists, "but they have missed their way," he added amid laughter.

'The Mayor said that during his long term of office the people of Weymouth had had to bear many difficulties. But, like all Britishers, they had been able to stand the test because of their belief in God and Christianity. He was always pleased to be associated with the Salvation Army, and he wished the local corps every success in the forthcoming self-denial week.'

On Wednesday, 23rd February, the Mayor as its president attended the Weymouth Services Club's fourth birthday celebration party, where he cut a birthday cake suitably inscribed.

Tuesday, 21st March, saw the funeral of Mr H. J. Wrate, the oldest member of Weymouth's Honorary Court Highclere, Ancient Order of Foresters. In attendance was the Mayor - 'Chief Ranger Honorary Court Highclere'! At the Honorary Court Highclere meeting of 6th April, it was minuted that Acting Chief Ranger Brother Bell, the Hon. Secretary, was directed to convey to Brother Goddard an expression of the sympathy of the officers and bretheren, in his illness, and to express the earnest hope that he would soon regain his usual good health and strength. From newspaper reports, however, it would seem that Mayor Goddard continued his duties unabated.

There was another salvage and book recovery drive in Weymouth during the period 15th-19th April. The decision had been made during a committee meeting at the beginning of March, when according to the *Southern Times* of 3rd March,

'The Mayor said that in spite of the very successful drives they had had in the past he was certain that many hundreds of Weymouthians had all sorts of salvage tucked away in their cupboards and drawers. Appealing to householders to do what they could, the Mayor declared "I am as pleased as Punch that the Second Front is about to be opened." In view of the forthcoming large-scale operations, salvage was more important than ever.'

The Mayor was at a meeting prior to the opening ceremony of Weymouth's new reference library, reported in the *Southern Times*, 31st March:

'"Today is the happiest Weymouth has ever had", the Mayor declared amid applause.

'The idea of Weymouth having a library had been mooted for years, he went on, and there had been a lot of criticism of the fact that a town of this size had not got a public library. The delay had largely been due to the difficulty of finding suitable accommodation. . . "I hope that in the not-so-distant future a public library will be an accomplished fact," he added.

'The Mayor said he sincerely hoped that the reference library would be made good use of, and appealed to everyone, especially youth, to take advantage of its facilities.

'Alderman Attwool, chairman of the Library Committee, paid tribute to the Mayor for his part in making the library an accomplished fact, and said that he had "fathered the scheme".'

Sunday, 23rd April, being St. George's Day and a national day of prayer, a special civic church service was held at St. Mary's Church, attended by the Mayor, and representatives of armed and civilian services. The Rector of Weymouth, Rev E. L. Langston, expressed confidence that "God would be with us when the Second Front was opened, and that He would give us the victory over Fascist tyranny" in the same way as he had answered other similar calls during the war.

The next day, the 24th, was the first air-raid since 1942, probably trying to ascertain the extent of, and attack, the build-up of the American invasion force.

The Mayoress presented the prizes at a successful dance on Wednesday, 26th April, in aid of the 'Salute the Soldier' campaign, attended by some 700 people. She was in turn presented with a bouquet of irises and tulips by the band leader.

6th-13th May was a special Week, with the object of Weymouth organising a number of varied events in order to raise £200,000 to equip and maintain a Battalion of Infantry for six months. A full-page advertisement in the *Southern Times* of 5th June, included this message from the Mayor:

'We are on the eve of great events in which our soldiers will play a major part. As an expression of admiration and gratitude to these gallant lads, and as a tangible proof of our determination to afford them unqualified support, I appeal to my fellow Townspeople to make our "Salute the Soldier" Week and outstanding success.'

The Week was officially opened on Saturday afternoon, 6th May, by the Lord Lieutenant of Dorset, the Earl of Shaftesbury, who took the parade salute in front of the *Gloucester Hotel*. In introducing him, the Mayor read telegrams of good wishes from Sir John Anderson, the Chancellor of the Exchequer, and Sir James Grigg, Minister for War. A joint "Salute the Soldier" and Red Cross service on Sunday was attended by the Mayor and Mayoress.

The *Southern Times* of 19th May carried this happy report:

'Mayor Gives Niece Away At Wedding

'The Mayor of Weymouth gave away his niece at her wedding last week at St Mary's Church. . .

' Miss Ethel Mary Gerrard, the bride, is the only daughter of Mr and the late Mrs W. Gerrard, of Ashdene Road, Ash, Surrey, and the bridegroom was Mr Ernest Arthur Heasman, Royal Irish Fusiliers, only child of Mr and the late Mrs A. Heasman, of Fulham.

'The bride wore a gown of white satin, a veil loaned by her cousin, Mrs Woodford, and carried a bouquet of lilies of the valley. Miss Marie Bell, A.T.S. (step-sister), was her only attendant, Miss Beryl Goddard (cousin), who is serving in the W.R.N.S., being unable to be present. Miss Bell wore a gown of blue figured satin, with a headdress of blue feathers and carried a posy of anemones.

'Best man was Mr Ernest Bonny, Royal Irish Fusiliers. The bride had been staying with the Goddards since 1937.

'The honeymoon was spent at Lyme Regis, the bride's travelling outfit being a dress of Air Force blue with a light-blue coat and accessories.'

On the night of 27th/28th May was the final bombing air-raid on Weymouth, with damage and loss of life.

On Sunday, 4th June, the Mayor was present at the final round of the Dorset S.J.A.B. county competitions in St. John Hall. He was to express his pleasure that the County Commissioner had allowed the competitions to be held at Weymouth; and he moved a vote of thanks to Lady Ellenborough (County Vice-President) who had presented the prizes.

Tuesday, 6th June, saw the eventual D-Day departure of the thousands of U.S. invasion troops from Weymouth (and vehicles from Portland), who had been arriving over the past many months for the invasion build-up. During the stay in Weymouth of the American forces Mayor Goddard must obviously have had both official and unofficial contact with them. One unsubstantiated story is that the Americans could obtain short-supply Scotch whisky from the *Royal Adelaide*.

There then followed a reverse influx of American battle casualties, and civilian war refugees from freed France, and returning prisoners of war.

One sombre occasion for the Mayor (accompanied by the Mayoress) was when as a fellow member he attended the semi-military funeral of the President of Weymouth British Legion, Lieutenant-Colonel W. Puxley Pears at Holy Trinity Churche. This took place on Monday, 12th June. Both has served in the Boer War and later in Mesopotamia, but their paths had apparently not crossed.

By July, with the invasion of Europe now apparently consolidated more than a month after D-Day, the Weymouth Town Council was turning its mind even more to catering for expected returning holiday visitors to the resort.

The Mayor and Mayoress attended a Scout Day luncheon in the *Clinton Restaurant*, to mark the official opening of the new headquarters in Old Parish Lane on Wednesday, 16th August. When the Mayor spoke he said that he had had the pleasure and privilege to know the first Chief Scout, Lord Baden-Powell, as long ago as 1904-5 when as General Sir Robert Baden-Powell he was Inspector of Cavalry and he himself was in the Hussars. He had had many opportunities of seing him and admiring his qualities. The *Southen Times* of 18th August then went on to report that after the luncheon the official opening of the new Scout headquarters was performed by the Mayoress, who said:

"This must be a very happy day both for you Scouts and for those who will be following you."

The Mayor (accompanied by the Mayoress), after inspecting the several fire station contingents), took the salute at a parade of Dorset Firefighters on Sunday, 20th August. This was to celebrate the third birthday of the National Fire Service, and took place in front of a large gathering of people on Weymouth College playing-field. There was a poor quality photograph of the Mayor addressing the assembly in the *Southern Times* 25th August, when he was reported as saying:

"'I have often wanted to have the opportunity to express my appreciation of the sservice rendered by the N.F.S. There are many organisations with which I am familar through this war, and I remember the time when it was even difficult to clothe the N.F.S. They were lucky if they got a pair of rubber boots.

"A fireman's duty is not as spectacular as the other three services, but you have done it with valour when you have been called to do so. Your job is to fight a relentless foe, fire. That foe spares no one, but spreads until it has devoured everything in its path. We have seen how that foe has been fought by you men.

"Today we have the finest fire fighting service in the whole world. One day the history of this war will be written, and your part will be one of which you may be justly proud.'"

During the following week the Mayoress opened a bring and buy sale in aid of the Citizens Advice Bureau at its headquarters on the Esplanade. The same newspaper reported her expressing her pleasure at being associated with the effort to raise funds for the continued good work of the C.A.B., which is kept busy with the large number of people wanting advice on all kinds of subjects.

On Wednesday, 23rd August, the Mayor and Mayoress, with their daughter Miss Beryl Goddard, were present at the Broadwey and Upwey Garden Society Summer Show, at the Reynolds Institute, Broadwey. Again, the *Southern Times* reported the Mayor's opening speech:

"The show has two objectives. It is a form of competition and it is also a form of education. It is a very good type of competition, the harmless sort which nobody minds. It is up to all expert gardeners to help along those who are 'just learning'."
'He also spoke with appreciation of the wonderful collection of fruit, vegetables and flowers.'

Wednesday, 30th August, saw both the Mayor and Mayoress at St. Gabriel's bazaar (which the latter opened) in the grounds of St. Paul's Vicarage. Both spoke of the good work done by and for St. Gabriel's Home; and local children presented the Mayor with a buttonhole, and the Mayoress with a bouquet.

On the same day, as a departure from appeals for the war effort, at a meeting held in the Guildhall, the Mayor launched an appeal for £10,000 for Weymouth and District Hospital, recently damaged by enemy action. It was to be a month long campaign, 5th September-5th October. The *Southern Times* reported on 1st September:

'The Mayor, presiding, said: "There has never been a local scheme more ambitious than the present one, and never one more deserving. The hospital was badly damaged, but even so several people desired to get a fund going to make the place a good deal better than before.
"A small committee has met and decided to launch this appeal for £10,000. I know it seems a colossal figure, but it isn't, if you remember the huge sums this town has raised in the past.
"We are apt to lose sight of the fact that charity begins at home, and during five years of war we have contributed magnificently to many deserving causes. Now we have reached the stage when we should do something for ourselves."'

There was a 4-day Caledonian Market at 108 St. Mary Street, opened on Monday, 4th September, by the Mayor and Mayoress. This was one of the events to be held in aid of the Weymouth & Portland Hospital Re-establishment Fund. At a series of fund-raising dances, girls would be chosen to go forward to a final to choose a Beauty Queen. The organiser hoped that the Mayor and Mayoress would consent to be judges. According to the *Southern Times* of 20th October, the final was at a dance held at the *Regent Dance Hall*, on the 18th, with the Mayoress one of the judges. Money for this appeal, and for others during the war, was raised in a manner of different ways. Audrey Judge (née Burden) recalls how she, her sister and a friend held a pavement jumble sale on the corner of Emmerdale Road and Abbotsbury Road, Weymouth. Afterwards they had to go along to the *Royal Adelaide* to give the money they had raised to Mayor Goddard. Audrey's father, Eddie Burden, was an A.R.P. warden and had been on duty the night the *Royal Adelaide Hotel* was bombed in 1941.

Again on a lighter social note, the *Southern Times* on 15th September noted:

'Greenhill Bowling Club held the finals of the Red Cross pairs competition on Wednesday [13th. The speaker who] introduced the Mayor at the close of play, and spoke of the Mayor's generosity to the club, especially regarding repairs to the pavilion and the presentation of six woods [one of the prizes].
'The Mayor . . . hoped that now the Red Cross effort was completed the club would help with the Hospital Re-establishment Fund.'

At the Weymouth British Legion Branch's Annual General Meeting in the Guildhall, on 25th October, it was agreed the Mayor be invited to become a Vice-President.

According to the *Southern Times* of 3rd November, the annual meeting of Weymouth and District Hospital on 27th October was a contentious one regarding proposed amendments to rules. The proceedings had been opened by the Mayor presenting prizes to nurses.

On 9th November Mayor 'Joe' Goddard was re-elected for a seventh term in succession as Mayor of Weymouth. After several years being held in the *Burdon Hall* instead of the Guildhall, this was the first time the ceremony was held in the *Clinton Restaurant*. According to the *Dorset Daily Echo* of 10th November, the proposer was again to eulogise:

"At the time when he was first appointed in 1938 there were rumblings of world conflict and before his year of office was completed the war was upon them, changing the entire range of their activities. It was quite natural and in accordance with precedent that the Mayor should be asked in November 1940, a time of real danger and anxiety, to undertake another year of office. . .
"Through those early years, the Emergency Committee, headed by the Mayor, managed what was still being done of ordinary business, and shaped, welded and

encouraged the Civil Defence Service.

"A great responsibility fell upon the Mayor and the stream ran far too fiercely even to contemplate 'swapping horses'. I know we are all agreed the Mayor has proved a good war horse, unshaken by the whirlpools of national anxieties or eddies of local difficulties.

"The council had driven the Mayor hard, year after year, attending meetings of the Emergency Committee at least once a week, and, not infrequently, more often; his duties had demanded daily attendances at the Municipal Offices for prolonged periods. Few could gauge the full extent to which the Mayor had been engaged upon work of local and even national importance.

"When the war situation came to the point where the Prime Minister could say, 'We are now masters of our own destiny,' they had still kept the Mayor in the chair, because, through the years of grinding toil, he had come to possess qualifications for that important position, and no other person could obtain those qualifications because those early, almost devastating years, were not to be lived through again.

"Living through those years in his important position moulded the Mayor and gave him the personality and experience to lead us through dark days, to see the brightness of dawning victory, as one may see the roseate hues of the sunrise after a long winter night. And so we desired and were privileged to retain the Mayor.

"Not only in connection with the war had the Mayor earned their gratitude; numberless social functions had been supported and encouraged by his presence; he had shown the benefit of people getting together in friendship and recreation.

"Our heartfelt thanks are due to him for all this self-sacrificing work, and we show it by electing him to another term of servitude - for that it certainly is - but this time we hope that his year of office will see the dawn which has given us so much promise, brighten and strengthen, until, like the sun at high noon in a cloudless sky, it sends down upon us the warming rays of a glorious peace which will enter the hearts of every one of us.'"

Mention was also made of the Mayor's £10,000 appeal for the Hospital, which had reached £8,000 so far, adding that one way in which appreciation of him could be shown was by exerting their utmost to ensure the fund's success.

The Mayoress, Mrs Goddard, was also to receive her due of praise for all her work and support during the past year.

According to a fulsome report in the *Dorset Daily Echo* of 11th November:

"'A Great Guy" was elected Mayor of Weymouth on Thursday . . . [said] a young American sailor from the city of Weymouth, Massachusetts, who occupied a place of honour at Weymouth's Mayor-choosing ceremony.

'It was an *Echo* reporter who, thanks to Mrs. Nicholson, now working at the American Red Cross Club, found 18-years-old Lloyd Edwin Nash, jnr. of 68 Lake-street, East Weymouth, Mass., and made arrangements with his commanding officer, through the Mayor and the Director of the American Red Cross here, for this Weymouth boy from overseas to witness our Mayor-choosing ceremony . . .

"This is a swell town and bigger than ours. We have no hotels like yours, and nothing like your bay and promenade. What I want particularly to take back home is a picture of your new bridge."

'Young Nash had been told that there is a stone in that bridge which was the gift of his own home town and as a child he remembered being told about the swell things that went on in Weymouth, Mass., when the civic deputation from Weymouth, England, went over there about 15 years ago.

'The picture of the bridge is secured to him, as he was photographed with the Mayor and Town Clerk and others near the stone from Weymouth, Mass., . . .'

The *Dorset Daily Echo* of 15th November went on to publish one such photograph, which showed the young "bashful" Nash standing between Mayor and Mayoress Goddard, along with Percy Smallman the Town Clerk. The caption said this photographic session took place after the mayor-choosing ceremony. It is interesting to note that with the war now coming to a close there is no longer any obvious newspaper censorship.

From 15th November, weekly meetings of the Weymouth British Legion's Service Committee were held at Mayor 'Joe' Goddard's *Royal Adelaide Hotel*, basically arising from the burning-down in May 1941, by German incendiary bombs, of the Legion's headquarters. Presumably the *Royal Adelaide* had by now been repaired from its own bomb damage.

As the *Southern Times* of 8th December reported:

'On a grey, December Sunday morning [3rd], Weymouth Home Guard assembled for their last parade, stretching all along Westwey Road. . .

'The Mayor then addressed the assembled men as follows:-

"I am honoured today in two ways. Firstly, to express my own and the townspeople's thanks for your magnificant response to the call made on you in the dark days that have now passed, and secondly, to take the salute at your standing-down parade.

"The years I have held my office have given me a chance to keep in touch with you throughout the whole period of your service, and I have observed you grow to a high state of efficiency that reflects great credit on yourselves and your officers. . .

"We can speak more freely now than in the past of the conferences we used to attend regarding the defence of our town and in particular the anti-tank island. The efficient manner in which everything was arranged and the enthusiasm that was aroused, makes me think sometimes that you were sorry that the Germans never attempted their parachute invasion.

"Tonight your colonel-in-chief, H.M. the King will speak to you and tell the whole world how proud he was and still is of the millions of men like yourselves, regardless of previous rank, who were ready to enlist in the defence of our country. . . .

"Today we may stand down. I say we, because although I may only have been a back room member I have, in spirit, always been in your ranks. We are at least left with the great comradeship created in the Home Guard, which I hope and trust will continue for many years."

'Lord Hinchingbrooke, M.P. for S. Dorset, thanked the men for their past endeavours, and said it was fitting that the Mayor should be taking the salute in a ceremony to say hail and farewell. As Mayor, he was greeting those who were returning to civil life to take up the tasks of reconstruction. As one of themselves, he was saying farewell to them as soldiers.'

The subsequent saluting base was, as seemed to be usual, again outside the *Gloucester Hotel.*

At about the same time the Mayor, at a Town Council meeting, had to very reluctantly move a resolution that Dr. Gordon Wallace be released by the Weymouth Corporation as its Medical Officer of Health, at the request of the Ministry of Health. This was to enable him to become an expert hygienist in the Civil Affairs branch of the Army on the Continent. The resolution was carried.

At the Weymouth British Legion's Finance Committee meeting of 6th December it was mentioned that 'Councillor J.T.Goddard O.B.E., M.C., J.P.' was a Branch Trustee.

On Tuesday, the 12th, the Mayor presided over the first meeting of the newly formed Town Council Citizens' Committee at the Guildhall. This was composed of representatives from various influential organisations in the borough, who put forward such proposals as housing for old people, and improvement of harbour facilities. The Mayor claimed that it was an extraordinary meeting, with extraordinary work to do. If it did what it set out to do, then some good should be the outcome.

The *Southern Times* on the 15th also noted that as the Hospital Appeal total of £10,000 had been reached, the appeal would close on the 31st December.

Mayor and Mayoress Goddard sent out printed Christmas cards from the Mayor's Parlour, which included the sentiment '*Hearty Greetings for Christmas and every Good wish for a Victorious New Year'*. One such was sent to their son-in-law Lieutenant R. Woodford R.N. at H.M.S. *Excellent*, Whale Island, Portsmouth.

1945

In the New Year's Honours List, an O.B.E. had now been awarded also to Mr. Percy Smallman, the Weymouth Town Clerk, for his wartime services. It was thus natural that at the Town Council meeting on Thursday, 11th January, the Mayor led Council members in congratulating him.

At the same Town Council meeting the Mayor, as chairman of the Emergency Committee, submitted its report recommending that the British Restaurant at Wyke Regis be closed. This was on the basis of insufficient people using it, and it making a loss. It was agreed however that it be kept open a further three months.

On Tuesday, 23rd January, the Mayor travelled across to Portland Council Offices. This was for him to be presented with a cheque for £1,277 as Portland's final contribution towards his Weymouth & Portland Hospital Appeal. He expressed gratitude for the great help which the Portland community had given to the Appeal Fund, and that relations between Portland and Weymouth had never been more friendly than they were then.

At the annual meeting of Weymouth Chamber of Commerce, the proceedings opened with the Mayor being further presented with a cheque for £1,140 towards his Hospital Appeal. The Chamber's president said that the presentation was a tribute also to the Mayor himself. Another speaker said that the result showed in what high regard he was held in the town.

In the East Wing corridor of the Weymouth Community Hospital, Melcombe Avenue, Weymouth, there is a horizontal rectangular plaque, headed by the Borough Arms:

> THIS TABLET RECORDS WITH GRATITUDE
> THE SPECIAL APPEAL BY
> COUNCILLOR J. T. GODDARD O.B.E., M.C.
> (MAYOR OF WEYMOUTH AND MELCOMBE REGIS)
> TO WHICH £12,098. 5.11 WAS SUBSCRIBED
> BY THE PEOPLE OF
> WEYMOUTH, PORTLAND AND DISTRICT
> 1944

See also 1958 below.

The Mayor, as its vice-president, presided at the annual meeting of the Weymouth and District branch of the N.S.P.C.C., held in the *Clinton Restaurant*, on Wednesday, 31st January. He was thanked for his sincere and obvious interest in the work of the Society.

Royal Adelaide Hotel, Weymouth c. 1930 with possibly some
Goddard children in porchway.

Corner of the Coffee Room, Royal Adelaide Hotel c. 1930

WEYMOUTH CELEBRITIES IN CARICATURE

Weymouth celebrities in caricature by "Matt" of the Sunday Graphic,
September 1933

Councillor John ("Joe") Goddard on first being elected Mayor of Weymouth, 9th November 1938, with his wife Mayoress Hilda Goddard.

Mayor "Joe" Goddard at foundation stone ceremony at Weymouth British Legion's new headquarters 11th March 1939.

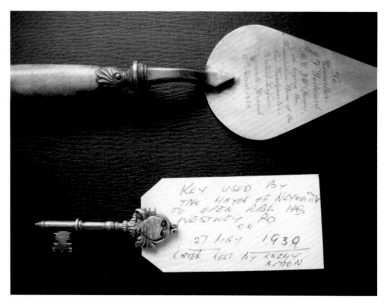

Inscribed trowel used by Mayor John Goddard to lay foundation-stone at Weymouth British Legions new headquarters; and the key used at the subsequent official opening.

Mayoress Hilda Goddard at official opening of Weymouth British Legion's new headquarters, 27th May 1939, receiving a bouquet from her granddaughter Ann Goddard.

Mayor and Mayoress Goddard with King George VI, Queen Elizabeth and
Princesses Elizabeth and Margaret at Weymouth, talking with local centenarian
Mrs Wallis. 22nd July 1939.

Mayor John Goddard with King George VI at Weymouth 9th August 1939

Mayor and Mayoress Goddard (with WVS badge in her hat), with Canadian gift of a Mobile Kitchen on Weymouth Esplanade.

Mayor and Mayoress Goddard, Town Clerk Percy Smallman and young American serviceman from Weymouth, Massachusetts on the Town Bridge, Weymouth, Dorset. November 1944.

November 1st, 1941 - The Adelaide Hotel

"Adelaide Court" in 2003

Mayor John Goddard with Lady Louis Mountbatten at annual inspection of Weymouth's St. John's Ambulance Brigade, 24th October 1942.

Mayoress Hilda Goddard (WVS) with her daughters and niece, from left: Audrey Goddard (Wren), Eleanor Goddard (WVS), Ethel Gerrard (NAAFI) and Beryl Goddard (Leading Wren).

Mayor and Mayoress Goddard collecting money, possibly at a
Licensed Victuallers event.

VE Street Party with
Mayor Goddard sitting
on extreme right.

THIS TABLE RECORDS WITH GRATITUDE
THE ... ... APPEAL BY
COUNCILLOR ... GODDARD, O.B.E. M.C.
(MAYOR OF WEYMOUTH AND MELCOMBE REGIS)
TO WHICH £12098. 5.11 WAS SUBSCRIBED
BY THE PEOPLE OF
WEYMOUTH, PORTLAND AND DISTRICT
1944

IN RECOGNITION
OF THE EFFORTS OF THE LATE
ALDERMAN JOHN GODDARD, O.B.E. M.C., J.P.
(MAYOR OF WEYMOUTH & MELCOMBE REGIS 1938·1945)
THIS REBUILT OPERATING THEATRE
WAS OPENED BY
MR. JOHN VINCENT, J.P.
ON 8TH MAY 1958

THIS ROOM WAS GIVEN IN MEMORY OF
... AMY ROSE SWAFFIELD ...
FOR THE USE OF THE STAFF NURSES OF THIS HOSPITAL
1939

Plaques in Weymouth Community Hospital

The Weymouth British Legion's
'Goddard' Snooker Challenge Cup

Mayoress Hilda Goddard

Mayor John Goddard

John Goddard's decorations and medals with his O.B.E. and M.C. at top.

Her Honour Judge Ann Goddard, Dougie McMeeken M.B.E. in the Goddard Room at Weymouth Royal British Legion's headquarters. 15th September 2001.

The annual meeting of the Weymouth Local Savings Committee was held on Wednesday, 14th February, at which the Mayor presided. He was reported in the *Southern Times* of the 16th as saying that it was essential that everybody should realise that this work could not stop. General Sir Henry Jackson, representing the Secretary of State for War, presented 'Salute the Soldier' plaques to the Mayor (as president) and to Mr. John Vincent (chairman), saying that Weymouth had truly saluted the soldier. The Mayor moved that the meeting demand that the chairman, hon. secretary, and hon. treasurer continue in office for another year. It was carried unanimously.

Reported in the *Southern Times* of 9th March were the warm tributes to the Mayor for his work on behalf of service men and women. This was a feature of the opening ceremony of the B.W. Club Thanksgiving Market which was inaugurated at the Club's premises in Chelmsford Street, on Tuesday, 6th March. One speaker said he had been to many towns during the war, but never had he seen such a splendid lead given by the chief citizen as in Weymouth. Opening the market the Mayor announced that the idea was not his, and he hoped that people would support the market generously to raise funds for local servicemen. A 2lb. box of chocolates was bought by the Mayor at auction for 16s.

In March the Mayor attended the 21st annual meeting of South Dorset Ladies' Auxiliary League of the Licensed Trade at the *New Bridge Hotel*, Weymouth. He said the licensees of Weymouth were like a happy family and they had the brewers amongst them, which was an advantage. There was little problem with under-age drinking; and as they had voluntarily given up the extra half-hour, he did not anticipate much difficulty in its restoration. He added that there were endeavours to re-establish the British Legion. The Legion had lost its home and the men needed a place where they could meet and talk. It would be a fine gesture if the licensed victuallers could arrange this.

Thursday, 12th April, at the Weymouth Town Council meeting, consideration was given as to how to celebrate V-Day, and welcome back servicemen and others who had been in the forces. According to the *Southern Times*, 13th April, the Mayor pointed out that a certain amount of exploratory work had already been done. Also that the troops would be coming home in small batches, so that it would be difficult to arrange a welcome for all these people, however good the intentions might be. A special service of thanksgiving had been suggested. He said there were tremendous difficulties with regard to an offer of freedom of the Borough to the Dorsetshire Regiment. A better way would be to present some trophy to the regiment. Forms of a war memorial were also to be considered.

Following a night and morning of 'VE-Day Jollity' [Victory in Europe] and celebration around Weymouth, in the afternoon of Tuesday, 8th May, a crowd began to gather for a Service of Thanksgiving for Victory, to be held in front of the *Gloucester Hotel*, The Esplanade. Mayor Goddard, resplendent in scarlet gown, gold chain, decorations and medals, led the proceedings, attended by some 10,000 people. As the notes of Big Ben struck three, silence fell, and the voice of the prime minister, Winston Churchill, formally announcing the end of the war, was relayed by loud speakers so that everyone could hear. There then followed the Thanksgiving Service for Victory. Exhuberant celebrations then continued, all of which were detailed in the local Press.

This was followed on the following Sunday morning, the 13th, with a Victory March Past and the Church Parade of all the fighting Services. This was again at the *Gloucester Hotel*, when Mayor Goddard was one of the dignitaries taking the salute. According to Acutt:

'As a Squadron of fighter planes roared low overhead, the Mayor Goddard brought his hand smartly to the salute, paying his Official tribute to the men and women of Weymouth whose united efforts had helped to bring victory to Europe. The parade took 12 minutes to pass the saluting base. . . The Mayoreess [and other V.I.P.s] were in the Hotel verandah lounge. The Mayoral party then joined the great congregation at St. Mary's Church where the townspeople offered humble thanks for the Divine guidance which had led them to victory.'

On the same Sunday the Mayor and Mayoress attended a service of thanksgiving by Channel Islanders in Weymouth.

From VE-Day +1, the Mayor and Mayoress had a busy time attending several celebratory street parties for children and their parents, where they would be photographed. For example, it is known that on 27th May the Goddards attended two such parties at Ferndale Road and Maycroft Road. The Mayor also looked in at the dancing on the Pier Bandstand. He had apparently also been known to look in unannounced at such functions as a 21st birthday party.

Back in 1938 'Joe' Goddard had become one of the guarantors, each for £25, in regard to the then British Legion Weymouth Branch's new premises, since destroyed in 1941. On 22nd May 1945 all such guarantors were thanked and released from their undertaking.

Acutt was to also describe the following:

'The Farewell Parade of Weymouth Civil Defence Services was held on [Sunday]. . . May 27th [1945] . . . The parade on the Recreation Ground was watched by a large crowd in brilliant sunshine . . . The parade numbered nearly 500.

'Headed by a contingent of special police and the mace-bearers, the Mayor (Councillor J. T. Goddard) and corporation, fully-robed, walked from the Sidney

Hall, and while the inspecting party went to the platform the rest of the Council took their seats in the stand to watch the inspection. . . Also present . . . the Mayoress. . .

'The ceremony of inspection was then carried out by the War Emergency Committee - the Mayor, Alderman A. Biles, Alderman Percy Boyle, and the Controller, Mr Percy Smallman.

'Addressing the company, the Mayor said: "The purpose of this parade is to enable me, on behalf of the Town Council and the Emergency Committe, and through them, on behalf of the townspeople generally, to say "thank you" for all the work that you have done during the past few years for the care and welfare of the people of the borough.

"My long term of office has enabled me to know from the inside your work, in every branch of the service. The Emergency Committee have, of course, dealt with every detail as it presented itself, and Civil Defence work was a new work for us as it was for you. Duties were not only new, but in many respects difficult and have only been efficiently performed because of your excellent co-operation. Your rapid attendance at incidents during air-raids brought comfort and support to the people who were most closely concerned in such incidents, but far wider was the effect of your influence on the townspeople from the mere knowledge that your services existed and was in a state of constant readiness to render help under all circumstances that might arise owing to the war.

"As you settled down into your stride in A.R.P. activities you have in many directions taken interest in other work for the benefit of the community, and not the least of this kind of work was your effort for the hospital £10,000 fund.

"The Civil Defence organisation has for long been accepted as an organisation of service, self-sacrificing and efficient in its performance of duty, and long suffering under the strain and sometimes criticism to which it has been subjected.

'In Civil Defence there were no classes: all banded together in comradeship to give help to citizens injured in body or estate by enemy action.

"The Emergency Committee watched the organisation grow, and when the time came to go into action the committee's confidence in the service was justified. The Emergency Committee were proud to have been associated with the service and he was convinced that the council and the people were grateful for the services rendered and greatly admired the efficiency which had marked the work.

"We have, unfortunately, suffered fatal losses, and to-day we mourn for the loss of members of the Civil Defence who, in the discharge of their duty, and indeed owing to the very fact that they were hurrying to rescue work while bombs were still falling, lost their lives. I know how deeply their loss affected the branch of service of which they were members, as, indeed, it affected all branches of the service. They will always be in our minds whenever our activities in the Civil

Defence are talked about in future years.

"Your service, created by the greatest war which has afflicted mankind since the world began, met and dealt with every situation which arose, whether in hot action or in administration, in a manner which has always called forth our greatest admiration.'"

Much of this presumably was copied from reports in the local Press. The Mayor would doubtless have appreciated the band playing on this occasion - that of the 13th/18th Hussars, being an ex-14th/20th Hussar himself.

Between June 1940 and April 1944, the alert had sounded in Weymouth 787 times; 481 high explosive bombs, 2 magnetic mines, 9 oil bombs, and 4,300 incendiary bombs were dropped. There were 83 fatalities; 7,417 properties affected, of which 414 were destroyed or had to be demolished.

Reported in the *Southern Times* of 15th June was that on Monday, 11th June, Weymouth became host for two days to Britain's 15-years old 'Railway Queen' on a special visit which included the Red Cross and St. John Ambulance exhibition railway coach which was touring the country. Special mention was made of the Penny-a-Week Fund, which enabled clothing and other essentials to be sent to Russia, and parcels, etc., to British prisoners-of-war. The Mayor (accompanied by the Mayoress) said that the Fund was now drawing to a close, and asked his listeners to visualise all that had been achieved. Of the sixteen million pounds raised, he was proud to say Weymouth had contributed £18,580. He recognised and thanked all the local organisers and collectors for their efforts. He in turn was thanked by the county chairman of the Red Cross and St. John for his work as chairman of the local committee of the Fund, and that few knew the amount of work he had done during the previous six years. He had been a wonderful chairman, and he and others had done a marvellous job.

V.E. parties had continued at least to the end of May, including one in the Mayor's own Westham ward. This was held for the children of Cromwell Road in St. Paul's school playground. It was opened by the Mayor and Mayoress, with the latter being presented with a bouquet of roses and then cutting a huge iced Victory cake. Such parties were sometimes with entertainment, and competitions which they were expected to judge. Together, or separately, they attended parties not only in the town of Weymouth itself, but in the Borough's outlying villages. The one held at the *Ship Inn* in Upwey was apparently only attended by the Mayoress. But both attended a later Victory Sports held for 200 children from Upwey and Broadwey, where they judged various competitions, including fancy dress. The Mayoress was normally always presented with a bouquet. As reported in the *Southern Times* of 15th June, at the Weymouth Town Council meeting on

Thursday 14th, the Mayor appreciatively referred to the magnificant manner in which the mothers organised these parties:

'He said they carried out an extraordinary job of work, and while it was the Emergency Committee's job to do something to celebrate the cessation of hostilities in Europe, it would have been difficult for the committee or any other body to have done what these people did. They did it ungrudgingly, and where the food came from was no concern of anybody. (Laughter)

"I attended 35 street parties and the manner in which the children enjoyed themselves was a credit to the organisers and lady friends in the town. I said I would report it to the Council, and I hope you will express your pleasure to those people who carried out this good job of work."

'The Mayor's tribute was warmly applauded. A vote of gratitude was conveyed to the Mayor and Mayoress for attending what was believed to be every such occasion, even to outlying parts of the borough as Upwey.'

At the same Town Council meeting, a letter sent on behalf of the United States' 14th Port United Kingdom to the Mayor was read out. This paid tribute to the part Weymouth and outlying districts had played for more than a year in providing the mass of facilities, co-operation and hospitality for the U.S. Navy and Army leading up to D-Day.

"Hundreds of thousands of American vehicles and many times that number of specially trained troops have passed over your roads."

In reply, the Mayor wrote:

"I can assure you it has been a great pleasure to extend what help has been within our power, and more so at a time when our two nations have been fighting for our lives and liberties in the greatest war effort ever known.

"The port of Weymouth was proud to bear an important part receiving and sending forward great numbers of men and vast forms of armour which came from the U.S.A. to fight for the British Empire. With the material help thus forged by the U.S.A. the war has been won, and once more those principles of liberty so dear to your nation and ourselves were established.

"I am convinced our close association during those war years has more friendly moulded the happy relations of our two countries."

The meeting learned that discussion had already started between the Mayor and the U.S. port commander of Weymouth to perpetuate this alliance.

Once the war was over the British prisoners-of-war started to come home. On the evening of Monday, 25th June, the Mayor led a Civic welcome to returned P.O.W.s in the *Clinton Restaurant*. The *Southern Times* of 29th June reported:

'The evening was devoted to the enjoyment of an excellent meal, informally chatting, and entertainment. In a short speech the Mayor said it might have seemed to the man in the street that the entertainment had been delayed, but in waiting for the last man to arrive they might have missed a few who had had to go back to their units. Although it might be difficult, the intention was to entertain every Serviceman in Weymouth. They all realised what the men had gone through, and the entertainment that evening was to show in some small manner appreciation of what they had done. Some might have suffered greater hardships than others, but it was gratifying to all that they were back. It was also intended to form a British Legion that was worthy of them. Premises had already been located, though at the time requisitioned, to make a worthy home where they and their wives could meet and talk about old times. He bade a hearty welcome on behalf of the Corporation to the 57 Servicemen who were present.'

According to the *Southern Times* of 20th July, among visitors at a Girl Guide Festival and Brownie Revels held at *Springfield*, Weymouth, on Saturday the 14th, was the Mayor, deputising for the Mayoress who was ill. He told the girls he had thoroughly enjoyed himself, and by living up to their rules they would become good citizens.

On Wednesday, 1st August, the Mayor inspected the first of Weymouth's 200 pre-fabricated houses to be completed. He told the *Southern Times* reporter he considered they would make ideal temporary homes for young married people. He pointed out, however, that they were unsuitable for people with large families.

Under the banner headline 'MAYOR'S INSPIRING SPEECH OF THANKSGIVING' the *Southern Times* of Friday, 17th August, reported on Weymouth's response to VJ-Day (Victory over Japan :

"The war is won, gloriously and completely won; the war drums throb no longer and the battle flags are furled. We look for the safeguarding of liberty through the Parliament of Man, the Federation of the World."
'It was with these inspiring words that the Mayor of Weymouth concluded his address to the thousands of people who congregated on the Esplanade, opposite the *Gloucester Hotel*, for a service of Thanksgiving for Victory and Peace on Thursday afternoon.
'Six years ago, said the Mayor, the course of political destiny was sweeping European countries into war, a conflict which we knew, once started, was bound

to involve the whole world.

'We were anxious and apprehensive; we were unprepared, and knew that our enemies were fully armed and brutally vain, strutting about Europe with an arrogance born of easy victories of strength over weakness.

'Deficient in every material that wins wars, the nation went unitedly into the conflict, throwing its whole energies into building up defence and striking power.

'After Dunkirk, Britain alone stood in the path of the victorious Huns, and almost her only weapon was her indominatable spirit.

'Undoubtedly that was Britain's finest hour in this conflict, when the country in its love of freedom rose to far greater heights than she reaches now in the hour of final and complete victory.

'How well our great leader in those dark days, with his unerring instinct, knew this, said the Mayor, and how he encouraged us and imparted to us his own magnificent spirit of fight and endurance.

'And so the nation fought and endured, until the long process of defeat after defeat was first slowed down, then halted.

'And then came the time when we fought back with fury born of the valour of all our Services, and the tireless work of our factories, sharpened by the devastation caused by the enemy in so many of our towns.

"And now the war is over - we can hardly believe it - and the nation's thoughts and energies must be turned to dealing with the difficult problems that the war created." he said.

"I thank our townspeople for their splendid patriotism and patience during the years of war, and ask that we pledge ourselves, each of us according to our ability and opportunity, to strive to make our town a happy community in the years of peace which lie ahead.

"Today we give thanks for victory, and whilst many show their thankfulness and relief in joyful celebration we shall all keep in remembrance, quietly and in gratitude, those who have given their lives or their health to make this possible, and our hearts go out in sympathy to relatives and friends who have suffered bereavement in this terrible conflict.

"It is now finished, and we hope for peace, unity and concord, and through these three to promote happiness and properity.'"

The appearance of the Mayor on the dais had been heralded by a fanfare. The service concluded with the National Anthem, after which the Mayor, Mayoress and guests took tea in the hotel.

It was further reported in the same newspaper that following a day of festivities, on the night of VJ-Day:

'Feeling that the Mayor, whose courage, fine example and hard work have played such a large part in keeping Weymouth cheerful during the worst of the war years, should not be out of all the fun, a party marched to his home and called for his appearance.

"We want the Mayor! We want the Mayor!" they shouted, and, hastily putting on some clothes, his Worship went out into the street and talked to them.'

Whether there were many VJ children's parties as there had been VE ones is not known, but the Mayor and Mayoress attended at least two. The first was on Friday, 24th August, when

'With banners and flags fluttering in the breeze, and to the singing of popular wartime songs, almost a hundred children from [streets in Westham] marched in procession down Abbotsbury Road and across Westham Bridge to a grand Victory tea and celebration at the Co-op Hall...

'The Mayor, who was accompanied by the Mayoress, told the children how pleased he had been to see their victory march.

'He though special thanks should go to all those who had helped to make the celebrations a success.'

The *Southern Times* report of the event carried a poor quality photograph, which seems to depict the Mayor seated closest to the camera, at the head of one of the tables full of happy children.

The other party was that at Chelmsford Street, Weymouth, on Wednesday afternoon, 29th August. After tea the Mayor said it was the "nicest and homeliest party" he had been to, and said he felt that a party should be held every year in this way. He added that they had a lot to be thankful for, and that was a good way to show it. The Mayoress was presented with a button-hole.

The Mayor presided over the opening of a bazaar held on 29th August, in aid of funds of St. Gabriel's House, Weymouth, in the grounds of St. Paul's vicarage, Westham. He introduced the official opener, and later both he and the Mayoress were presented with nosegays.

The *Southern Times* of 21st September carried a full-page advertisement for Weymouth's 'Thanksgiving Week', to be held 22nd-29th September, with a National Savings target of £150,000. As well as bearing a message from King George VI, there was also this one from the Mayor:

'In our Thanksgiving Week commencing on Saturday next we remember with gratitude the courage and devotion of all those who made Victory possible. In wishing our local Savings Movement every success I feel that resolve for the future should be coupled with Thanksgiving for the past.

'Weymouth has done nobly in its Savings Campaigns and our townspeople have, on each occasion, attained their target, and I am convinced that aim will be achieved again next week.

'The war with Japan, the last of our aggressor Nations, having been brought to an end, we are now free to begin the task of Re-construction.

'I extend to our local Committee my best wishes and appreciation of their excellent work.

J. T. GODDARD, Mayor.'

One returning P.O.W. was the Mayoress's nephew, Gunner John Hamilton Elliott, Royal Artillery, of Cape Town, South Africa. He had been taken prisoner at Tobruk in Libya, and was to spend 1½ years in Italy, and the same again in southern Germany. He had come to visit the Goddards at the *Royal Adelaide Hotel*, particularly Mrs Goddard, his aunt. The taxi-driver who drove him from Weymouth railway station refused to take his fare when he heard his story. According to the *Dorset Daily Echo* of 5th October, a month later he became engaged to the Goddards' youngest daughter, Leading Wren Jessie Beryl Goddard. They were subsequently married on Wednesday, 3rd October at St. Mary's church, Weymouth. Both were 25 years old. It was a rather watery sun which shed its rays on the bride, who was given away by her father. She wore a gown of white marocain, with veil and orange blossom head-dress lent by her sister, and a pearl necklace, gift of the bridegroom. She carried a bouquet of carnations and white heather. Her 9-year old niece Ann Goddard was bridesmaid, in a gown of blue taffeta, cut in old-world style, and wreath of rosebuds in her hair. She carried a posy of deep pink carnations. The bridegroom's gift to her was a brooch. A happy omen was the appearance of a black cat which strolled across the porch as the ceremony was drawing to a close and jumped on to the church wall. The happy couple left the church through a guard of honour of fellow Wrens from HMS *Attack*, Portland - as shown in *Dorset Daily Echo* photograph. The reception was held at the *Clinton Restaurant*, where 80 guests assembled. The honeymoon was to be in Edinburgh, with the bride travelling in a brown and yurquoise suit and fur coat with brown and turquoise accessories. They were then going to live in South Africa, where the groom would be in banking. The groom's best man had been a fellow South African prisoner-of-war.

Presumably John Goddard, as Past Chief Ranger of the Honorary Highclere Court of the Ancient Order of Foresters, would have been at the Court meeting and Supper afterwards at the *Crown Hotel* on 4th October, where 48 Bretheren attended.

At the 17th October meeting of Portland Council, tributes were paid to Mayor Goddard. The chairman said: "Before we next meet Councillor Goddard will have relinquished the term of office which he has held in such a distinctive manner for so many years." The Council agreed to send him a letter of good wishes.

One of the Mayoress's last engagements was as guest at the annual meeting of the Weymouth Women's British Legion, held at the *Borough Arms* at the end of October.

At the Mayor-choosing ceremony on Friday morning, 9th November, again at the *Clinton Restaurant*, Mayor 'Joe' Goddard was at last allowed to retire from that position after being in continuous tenure since November 1938. There were some notable speeches, including the tributes to the outgoing Mayor and Mayoress in full accord with public sentiment and which would be universllly endorsed. The retiring Mayor extended a warm welcome to new councillors. As the *Dorset Evening Echo* of 10th November was to report:

'Alderman B. Biles [who throughout had been Mayor Goddard's Deputy-Mayor], moving a vote of thanks to the retiring Mayor and to Mrs Goddard, said he did so with mixed feelings. After he had been elected to the office for the second year the war thrust him headlong into into greater responsibilities, which he had shouldered in a marvellous way. He had figured in many outstanding events before the war and he referred to the visit of the King and Queen and the two Princesses, the opening of the Pier Bandstand, Crematorium and British Legion headquarters. He spoke of his almost daily work on the Emergency Committee, and the part he had to take in the preparation for defence and the formation of "Tank Island". He was himself blitzed one Sunday morning in 1941 and was brought from the nursing home in that year to be re-elected Mayor. If the Germans had ever landed, their first question would have been "Where's the Mayor?" "And it wouldn't have been a 'courtesy call'" said the Alderman.

"The VE-Day and VJ-Day celebrations crowned seven years of self-sacrificing service, nor do we forget how he performed the least exciting routine duties of his office in so many ways, and rallied the townspeople in a magnificent effort for the Weymouth and District Hospital, which reached over £12,000" he said. He spoke, too, of Councillor Goddard's work for National Savings and how he was one of five representatives from the non-county boroughs on the General Purposes Committee of the Association of Municipal Corporations - "a singular personal honour."

'During his Mayoralty he was installed Chief Ranger of Hon. Court Highclere [of the Ancient Order of Foresters], being the second Mayor to hold that office in 50 years. Among the distinguished visitors he received was Mrs. Winston Churchill, and it was said that he smoked a cigarette which the then Prime Minister brought home from Turkey.

'Summing up, Alderman Biles observed, "Weymouth has been nobly served by its war-time Mayor," and he added a warm tribute of appreciation for the Mayoress, who had won the respect and admiration of the whole of the townspeople.

'Councillor C. E. Pye, who was Head Warden in the war, in seconding, spoke of the Mayor's position as chairman of the local War Emergency Committee, and of the local Defence Committee, which was responsible for the building up, training and equipping of Civil Defence, providing air raid shelter accommodation, rest centres, Cookery Nooks, and plans to meet any possible invasion. "I also know how deep was his anxiety and that of Mrs. Goddard for the welfare of the townspeople and those in distress and I have seen them both on the scene of air raid damage at all hours of the day and night.

'Their calm and unruffled disposition re-acted on the Civil Defence Service, and the morale of Weymouth people, always at a high level, was due in no small measure to the fine example set by both. Of the Mayoress, he said, "Never flagging, never tiring, she was always ready by example and counsel to take her rightful place, either along or alongside Councillor Goddard, in the forefront of the town's activities." Councillor Pye paid tribute to the W.V.S., in which Mrs. Goddard was foremost, and in conclusion he wished the retiring Mayor and Mayoress peace and happiness during their well-earned rest.

'Councillor Goddard met with an ovation when he rose to reply. Praising the speech of the Mayor-elect, he said it was comforting to know that the continuity of service they had endeavoured to give to the town was now in the hands of one who had expressed himself so finely.

"There have been many anxieties and work of a troublous nature, but there have been many pleasant asides," he said. He expressed his acknowledgement of the great assistance given him by the Town Clerk and the other executive officers, and he could say that the whole of the townspeople had co-operated with him. Singling out the Women's Voluntary Service, Councillor Goddard mentioned the late Mrs. Shewell and her magnificent work. He also spoke of Councillor T. F. E. Jakeman and his work for the Savings Movement. He thanked his deputy (Alderman Bert Biles) and members of the Emergency Committee, and added, "Whenever a word of comfort was required I always received it from the Mayor's Chaplain [Rev E.L.Langston].

"If I have left out anyone I know you will forgive me." said Cllr. Goddard, who concluded: "We are looking forward to the future and with all pulling together for the prosperity of this town let us try and forget the ravages of war and make it a much better town than it ever was before." (Applause.)

'Here came a surprising and spontaneous tribute from the assembly when they

sang "For He's a Jolly Good Fellow." In the memory of the oldest present there was no parallel for this at Mayor-choosing.
'The new Mayor announced that he had appointed Cllr. Goddard as deputy-Mayor.'

For his services to the Borough, Councillor 'Joe' Goddard was subsequently nominated for election as an Aldermen. But this honour must have been soured somewhat by its method of attainment. Several alderman vacancies were up for election, with Councillor Goddard one of the candidates, during which he chose not to vote during the ballot. There being a tie for the final position, it was only on the casting vote of the chairman that 'Joe' Goddard was elected. This elevation caused a bye-election in his Westham West ward.

He was subsequently appointed chairman of the Watch Committee, and thus spoke in favour of its report before the Town Council on 13th December. One proposal was to make representations to the railway stationmaster to increase the number of taxis allowed to stand in the station yard. This was at the request of the public (including visitors) who complained that during certain hours no taxis could be obtained.

THE END

At the Weymouth British Legion Branch's Annual General Meeting on Wednesday, 28th November 1945, it was noted that amongst those present was "Vice-President Alderman J. T. Goddard", who was to take a lively part in the meeting, including proposing the election of the new Branch President, Lieut.Colonel E. W. C. Sandes (of Kut fame). He was also to be re-elected a Vice-President. According to the minutes of the meeting:

'The Chairman called upon the President to perform the very pleasant duty of presenting Alderman J. T. Goddard with a Life Membership of the Legion. This was done with honour & distinction. Mr Goddard suitably replied.'

The *Dorset Daily Echo* of 29th November was to further report on the occasion:

'Calling upon the president to present a certificate of life membership to Alderman Goddard, the chairman said it was for the great amount of work he had done for the Legion. Few members would ever know all that he had done.
'The president said Ald. Goddard had been of great value to the legion in every possible way and especially during the seven years of his Mayoralty. He believed that the present excellent membership was largely due to the deputy-Mayor's efforts. It gave the president particular pleasure in making the presentation because they had been comrades in arms in Mesopotamia in the last war.
'Responding, Ald. Goddard said he regarded this as a signal honour. One of the most pleasant duties of his Mayoralty was to lay the foundation stone of the club in Westwey-road, when he was presented by that great Legionaire, Captain Hamblin, with a silver trowel, and another was when he opened the premises and was presented with a silver gilt key. Both of these gifts he treasured.
'The recipient assured the members that this did not mean that his efforts had finished. He was confident that they were going to establish a branch worthy of the town. Recently he had had an interview with Major-General Hawkins, Regional Officer of the Ministry of Works, and after discussing other matters he had pointed out that the continued requisition of the King-street premises was retarding the efforts of the Legion. Shortly it was to be derequisitioned and now it was up to all of them to get down to brass tacks and make Legion House a place worthy of those who had done so much for them all.'

At the Branch General Committee Meeting on Wednesday, 5th December, it was noted that 'Joe' Goddard was still one of the Branch's six Trustees.

1946

On Wednesday, 7th August, Deputy-Mayor 'Joe' Goddard, accompanied by Mrs Goddard, opened the British Legion's fete at *Springfield*, Rodwell, the home of Major J. H. C. Devenish, of the Weymouth brewing family. According to the *Dorset Daily Echo* of 8th August 1946: 'The Deputy-Mayor stressed that they had only one more stile to get over', with only another £1,000 to find to complete purchase, renovation and furnishing their new headquarters. A bouquet was presented to Mrs Goddard.

The Weymouth British Legion Branch's Service Committee meeting of 6th March was the last one to be held at 'Joe' Goddard's *Royal Adelaide Hotel*.

There had been a report in the local Press on 7th February that

'A letter is to be sent from Weymouth Civic Society to the Town Clerk [of Weymouth Council], asking him to put before the council a proposal that the borough should bestow upon Weymouth's war-time Mayor, Alderman J. T. Goddard, O.B.E., M.C., the freedom of the borough in recognition of the work he had done for the town.

'A resolution on these lines was unanimously approved at a meeting of the society at the Guildhall, Weymouth, last night [6th].

'Captain H. G. Jackson, C.B.E.. R.N., who presided, said that for seven years Alderman Goddard was Mayor of the borough. He had borne the burden of the work throughout the war and at the end, when he might well have been a tired man, and unable to do more than absolutely necessary, he and his wife turned out again and again for parties given in the streets for children to celebrate Victory Day.

'Alderman Goddard had worked for the borough in a wonderful way and he (the chairman) felt that the borough in return should do something to show their recognition of what he had done for them.

'It was true Alderman Goddard had been made an alderman since retiring from the Mayoralty "but personally I feel that it is insufficient," he continued. "There is one thing the borough can do and that is make him an honourary freeman - (hear, hear). It has been a very rare award. Since 1929, 17 years ago, nobody has been made a freeman of the borough and my personal opinion is that we might well press the Council to award the freedom to him."

'Mr. A. E. Cox, seconding, commented that he had been closely connected with the Civil Defence in Weymouth and he knew personally the enormous amount of work the former Mayor had done for which he thoroughly deserved recognition.'

This proposal was eventually to be approved at a special Town Council meeting on 31st October.

On 9th November, at the Mayor-choosing ceremony held at the Queen's Hall of the *Royal Hotel* on The Esplanade. According to the *Dorset Daily Echo* of 11th November, the Mayor, Councillor C. H. J. Kaile,

'made feeling reference to the illness of the deputy-Mayor (Alderman J. T. Goddard) . . . and re-appointed [him] as his deputy.'

Ex-Mayoress Mrs Goddard was however present and seated on the special dais.

At the Weymouth British Legion Annual General Meeting at the Guildhall on Tuesday, 26th November, the President

'expressed regret that our Senior Vice-President ['Joe' Goddard] was prevented from attending the meeting owing to illness & it was hoped that he would soon be restored to better health.'

Later in the meeting 'Joe' Goddard was re-elected a Vice-President.

Regrettably, before he was able to be ceremonially admitted an Honorary Freeman of Weymouth he was to sadly die. As the *Dorset Daily Echo* of Thursday, 28th November 1946, was to front page headline and report:

'*DEATH OF ALDERMAN*
J. T. GODDARD
Weymouth Freeman, But Did
Not Live To Receive Scroll

'A month ago Weymouth Town Council agreed to appoint Alderman J. T. Goddard O.B.E., M.C., Mayor of the town for seven consecutive years, a Freeman of the borough. Alderman Goddard never received that honour, for he died to-day at his home, the *Royal Adelaide Hotel*, Weymouth. His health first showed signs of breaking down following his long period in office as Mayor. . .

'In due course he was elected chairman of the South Dorset Licensed Victuallers' Association and in that capacity served for 15 years. Pressure of duties compelled him to give the office in the first two years of the war, but he took on the office again after that.

'Outstanding among his public and social obligations in the months that preceded World War II was the privilege of welcoming the King and Queen and the two Princesses to Weymouth, and on another occasion the King alone, when his Majesty travelled to Weymouth to inspect the Reserve Fleet in Weymouth Bay.

'That same year witnessed a massed bands concert in the Alexandra Gardens on behalf of the victims of the submarine *Thetis*, by which he was able to raise the sum of £100. An audience of 1,000 were alarmed that night to see the Mayor lose his balance and fall over the edge of the stage into the empty orchestra pit. Fortunately he was none the worse for his fall and a moment later, smiling and treating the incident lightly, he again mounted the stage.

'His biggest money-raising achievement came during the year 1944-45, when he launched his £10,000 Hospital Fund. When the fund closed it had reached a total of £12,125. It has since been managed by a Committee of Control.

'It was characteristic of his public spiritedness that Alderman Goddard, when Mayor in 1940, was among the early enrolements in the L.D.V. (later the Home Guard).

'During his Mayoralty Alderman Goddard was installed Chief Ranger of Honorary Court Highclere No. 1 Weymouth, Ancient Order of Foresters.'

The cause of death according to a Certified Copy of an Entry of Death, which had been registered by his son Graham from London, on the 29th November, was:

'1a. Carcinoma Ventricula.
1b. Pulmonary tuberculosis.'

The *Dorset Daily Echo* of 30th November reported that:

'Weymouth British Legion women stood in silent tribute to the late Mr. J. T. Goddard, chief vice-president of Weymouth British Legion (men's section) . . . at their annual meeting held at the *Old Borough Arms*, Weymouth.

Mrs. Jolly (chairman) referred to the great work Mr. Goddard had done for the Legion generally, and Mrs. House (secretary) was instructed to send a letter of condolence from the branch to Mrs. Goddard. It was decided that there should be a collection for a Goddard memorial.'

In the best part of four columns the *Dorset Daily Echo* of 3rd December reported the funeral service which must have taken place in a packed St. Mary's Church:

'WEYMOUTH MOURNS
A SELFLESS MAN
Hundreds Pay Tribute To
Alderman J. T. Goddard
"To all of us he was a man greatly revered; an outstanding man who has selflessly

devoted his life to the service of King and Country, as well as to our local community," commented the rector of Weymouth, the Rev. E. L. Langston, at a memorial service at St. Mary's Church, yesterday, to Alderman J. T. Goddard, O.B.E., M.C. The service was attended by the Mayor of Weymouth (Councillor C. H. J. Kaile) and members of the corporation with representatives of many organisations in the town. . .

'Covering the coffin was a Union Jack and resting on top were the medals won by Alderman Goddard. Throughout the service bearers were on either side of the coffin with the standards of the Weymouth British Legion and the men's and women's sections.

'The hymns were "For all the saints who from their labours rest," and "How bright these glorious spirits shine!" Psalm 23 was chanted and as the coffin was leaving the church on its way to the crematorium the congregation joined with St. Mary's choir in the Nunc Dimittis. . .

'In his tribute the Rev. Langston said the town had suffered a severe loss by his death. "Alderman Goddard," he said, "fought in a crack regiment, the 14th Hussars, in the South African War, and in the first world war in Mesopotamia and Persia, and after being 27 years in His Majesty's service he devoted himself to the communal interest of the town and borough.

"Service above self has always been his motto. None of us will ever forget his faithful and magnificent leadership during the years of the recent war. Shall we ever forget his wise and statesmanlike leadership and inspiration during the war years as chairman of the Emergency Committee and the friend of all those who suffered as a result of the raids? No man ever before has served as mayor for seven years in succession. The crowning joy of his life and service was the offering to him of the freedom of the borough which, alas, he has not been able to receive publicly.

"From our hearts to-day we thank God for the life, service and comradeship of Joe Goddard," continued the Rector. "What was there in him that made him the man that he was? I think if we study the ideals of Christianity, Freemasonry with its first charge that you shall be true men to God and the Holy Church, and Rotary with its motto 'Service above self', we shall understand something of the inward and secret power of his life and influence.

"To-day we are needing men and women of Joe Goddard's ideals of service. Our deepest sympathy goes out to his dear widow and family who have won a place of love and respect in all our hearts, and especially to his youngest daughter, Beryl, who is in South Africa and unable to be with us to-day."

'Principal mourners were: Mrs Goddard (widow); Mr Graham Goddard (son); Mrs R. Woodford and Miss Audrey Goddard (daughters); Mrs G. Goddard (daughter-in-law); Lieut. R. Woodford, R.N. (son-in-law); Mr & Mrs Fred

Goddard (brother and sister-in-law); Mr and Mrs Heaseman (nephew and niece);
Mr Jack Elliott (nephew); Mrs Clark, Mrs Ilott, Mr James Ilott, Mr Tamblyn and
Mr Charles Woodford (friends); . . .

'Lieut.-Colonel J. A. T. Miller, Brigadier General G. Browne, and Brigadier
General Norton represented the Hussars in which Ald. Goddard served for many
years; Colonel V. Mocatta, late of his regiment also attended.

'Accompanying the Mayor were the macebearers carrying draped maces [plus
many council members, officers and representatives of the British Legion, South
Dorset Licensed Victuallers' Association, Ancient Order of Foresters, Weymouth
Rotary Club, United Services Lodge and Brunswick Lodge 159 [Freemasons] . . .'

His ashes were apparently scattered in the Weymouth Crematorium garden, with
no permanent memorial being placed there except a simple entry in the Book of
Remembrance.

No photographs have so far been found covering this event, which was
obviously something of a civic occasion.

'Joe' Goddard had made his hand-written Will back in 1935:

"This is the last Will and Testament of me John Thomas Goddard (commonly
known as John Goddard) of the Royal Adelaide Hotel Weymouth in the County
of Dorset Licensed Victualler I revoke all Wills or other testamentary dispositions
at any time heretofore made by me I appoint my Wife Hilda Constance Margaret
Goddard sole Executrix of this my Will I direct payment of all my just debts
funeral and testamentary expenses and subject thereto I give to my son Graham
Elliott Goddard all my prize cups medals and trophies & also my war medals To
my daughter Eleanor Pearl Catherine Woodford my Silver Tea and Coffee service
with Tray To my Daughter Audrey my large Persian Rug and to my Daughter
Jessie Beryl my Piano by Ibach All the rest residue and remainder of my Estate of
whatsoever nature or [limit] and wheresoever situate or over which I may have a
power of disposition by Will I give devise and bequeath unto my said Wife
absolutely In witness whereof I have hereunto set my hand this fourteenth day of
November One thousand nine hundred and thirty five
Signed by the said John Thomas Goddard   (
the Testator as and for his last Will and   )
Testament in the presence of us both present (J.T.Goddard
at the same time who at his request in his   )
presence and in the presence of each other   (
have hereunto subscribed our names as   )
witnesses.   )

-W.-.Holland.
>   56 Cromwell Road, Weymouth.
>   Clerk.

C. J. Austen
89, Corporation Rd
>   Weymouth.
>   Spinster."

The Will was subsequently sworn by *H. C. M. Goddard. Executrix.* before *William D Furness, A Commissioner for Oaths.*

The Principal Probate Registry proved and registered this Will on 22nd February 1947, with Administration being granted to the said executrix,, at the Royal Adelaide Hotel. The gross value of the said Estate was £ 9333-11-1, with a net value of the personal estate amounting to £ 6225-6-0. Estate Duty of £ 357-9-2 was paid.

EPILOGUE

At the General Committee meeting of the Weymouth Branch of the British Legion, held at the *Crown Hotel* on 6th December 1946, it was minuted:

'THE GODDARD MEMORIAL
'The Chairman [Mr A. J. G. House] suggested that a room in Legion House be dedicated to the memory of Alderman Goddard and this to be called The Goddard Room. The cost of this project would be borne by individual subscription. Mrs Goddard had been tentatively approached regarding this matter and had presented to the Legion a portrait in oils of Alderman Goddard in full mayoral regalia. This picture would be hung in the proposed Goddard Room. A picture of the Cutty Sark, a Silver Trowel and a Mayoral Golden Key had also been given and these latter would be placed in a glass case with a suitable plaque and would be situated in the Memorial Room. Proposed by Mr White, seconded by Mr Russell, that the sum of one guinea in lieu of a wreath be subscribed from branch funds towards the Memorial Fund.
'An immediate collection was held amongst members present. This realised the sum of fifty shillings which was placed to the Memorial Fund.
'The Chairman then put his prior suggestion to the meeting. This was carried unanimously.
'One minute's silence was observed in respect of the late Alderman Goddard.
'In passing from this matter, the Organising Secretary suggested that monies subscribed to the above fund be placed in a separate account and be handled by the Committee.'

The *Southern Times* 13th December carried the item:

'COUNCIL HAVE EMPTY CHAIR

"He was a good colleague, a sound adviser, and a very amiable friend" said the Mayor at the opening of the Council meeting on the 12th [when Alderman Goddard's death was officially reported to the Council]. After dealing with the late alderman's record the Mayor said his magnificent service to the town during the war was so fresh in the memory that no amplification was necessary. His capabilities were recognised far beyond the borough. On October 31st they had passed a resolution admitting him to the Honorary Freedom of the Borough. His name would be inscribed on the roll and the scroll would be presented to Mrs Goddard.
'They had seen Alderman Goddard in rapidly failing health, and at times in pain,

and knew that for him the sands of time were running out, yet they marvelled at his bright spirit.'

1947

At its January meeting, Weymouth Town Council elected the Mayor, Councillor C. H. J. Kaile an Alderman, to fill the vacancy caused by the death of 'Joe' Goddard. Then the *Dorset Daily Echo* of Monday, 17th February 1947, was to poignantly report:

In Recognition Of Eminent Services

'At the Mayor's Parlour on Saturday the Mayor of Weymouth (Alderman C. H. J. Kaile) handed to Mrs. Goddard the casket and certificate of freedom, which would have been presented to Alderman J. T. Goddard but for his death before the ceremony could be carried through. Alderman Goddard was Mayor of the town for seven years.

'The presentation was private and informal. With the Mayor were the Deputy-Mayor (Alderman B. Biles), the chairman and vice-chairman of the Finance Committee (Alderman F. W. H. Peaty and Percy Boyle), the Town Clerk (Mr. Percy Smallman), and the Mayor's Chaplain (the Rev. E. L. Langston).

'Mrs. Goddard was accompanied by several members of her family.

'The silver inscription plate on the inside lid of the dark oak polished casket (12ins. by 6ins) bears these words: "Borough of Weymouth and Melcombe Regis. Certificate of admission of Alderman John Thomas Goddard, O.B.E., M.C., J.P., as an Honorary Freeman of the Borough by resolution of the Town Council of the 31st October 1946."

'Mounted on the top of the casket, which has silver column corners, silver ball feet and hinges and which is lined with white satin are the Borough Arms in oxidised silver. The recipient's initials, "J.T.G." also in oxidised silver, are mounted on the front of the casket. The certificate of freedom, illuminated and beautifully ornate, bears the wording:

"Borough of Weymouth and Melcombe Regis. At a meeting of the Council of the Borough of Weymouth and Melcombe Regis, specially called for the purpose, held on Thursday, the thirty-first day of October 1946, the Mayor (Councillor Charles Henry James Kaile) in the chair, it was unanimously resolved that in recognition of his eminent services to the Borough, and in pursuance of Section 250 of the Local Government Act, 1933, Alderman John Thomas Goddard O.B.E., M.C., J.P., be admitted an Honorary Freeman of the Borough of Weymouth and Melcombe Regis and that the Common Seal be affixed to the

Certificate of Admission."
'The certificate also bears the borough arms on one side and the common seal
with the signatures of the Mayor and Town Clerk on the other.'

It is not known when the British Legion actually started using its new premises,
but a Management Committee meeting was held there on Friday, 18th April. Part
of the meeting was concerned with the pending official opening to be held on the
3rd May, when arrangements for the opening of the Goddard Room were also
confirmed.

Thus on the afternoon of Saturday, 3rd May, was the official opening by the
Mayor of the Legion's fresh Weymouth Branch premises. These were at the old
Eye Infirmary, 6 King Street, Weymouth, adjacent to the old Christ Church
building. The occasion was extensively reported in the local Press. It was an apt
day, being six years to the day that the previous headquarters had been destroyed
by enemy action. The Mayor observed:

"I feel that I am deputising for a very great patriot and keen lover of the British
Legion, the late Alderman J. T. Goddard." ...
'Mrs Goddard received a bouquet. . .
'Mrs Goddard opened the Goddard Room - a moving memorial to her late
husband whose portrait looked down on the assembly.'

This room was situated in the north-west corner ground floor, i.e. facing onto
King Street. The blue double-doors facing King Street, but no longer in use, used
to be the main entrance to the building. Thus the Goddard Room would have been
entered from the right-hand side of the passageway inside these doors. As
intimated back in 1946, Mrs Goddard duly presented a portrait in oils of
Alderman Goddard in full mayoral regalia. Also given had been a picture of the
Cutty Sark, the Silver Trowel and Mayoral Golden Key (of the old Westwey
Road premises), all placed in a glass case with a suitable plaque.
A large mounted brass plaque was also presented to the British Legion:

IN GRATEFUL REMEMBRANCE OF
ALD. J. T. GODDARD, O.B.E., M.C.
FOR 18 YEARS CHAIRMAN OF THE SOUTH DORSET
LICENSED VICTUALLERS ASSOCIATION
THIS PLAQUE IS PRESENTED BY ASSOCIATION
MEMBERS TO THE BRITISH LEGION IN
RECOGNITION OF HIS SERVICES TO THE ASSOCIATION
AND THE TRADE IN GENERAL

A group of subscribers subsequently enabled a large silver cup to be engraved:

SNOOKER CHALLENGE CUP
PRESENTED TO THE
BRITISH LEGION WEYMOUTH BRANCH
AS A PERPETUAL MEMORIAL TO
CAPTAIN "JOE" GODDARD. O.B.E. M.C.
LATE 14th HUSSARS
BY A FEW FRIENDS

There is only a photograph of this cup whose whereabouts are still not known, despite widespread enquiries. However, there is luckily also in the Weymouth British Legion Branch archives a

'LIST OF SUBSCRIBERS TO THE GODDARD CUP.
1947

MR. L. GODFREY.	MAJ. R.S.FEARON.
" G. HUSSEY.	MR. F.A.PAY.
" W. HURDLE.	" E.A.BAKER.
" A.S.LOVE.	" J. MC.LAUGHLIN.
" H.A.BELL.	" BRYER ASH.
" J.JOYCE.	" W. WHITTLE.
" N.GRAHAM.	DR. GORDON WALLACE.
" A.E.JACKSON.	MR. E.C.BROWN.
" E.A.WINZOR.	" H.A.MEDLAM.
" A.E.WHETTAM.	" C.H.J.KAILE.
" H.WOLFF.	" E.W.HUTCHINGS.
" E.D.PHILLIPS.	" R.CLEVERTON.
" R.WYATT.	" A.REDDELL.
" W.BURT.	" J.L.JAMES.
" R.GUY.	MRS. H.GODDARD.

. . . .

FRAMED. MOUNTED. LIST COMPILED FOR REFERENCE
BY BRANCH CHAIRMAN 1949'

The Branch Chairman at the time was Mr. A. J. G. House. Both the photograph of the Cup and subscription list had also been preserved from clearance disposal by Branch member Mr. W. J. Roper - who was later in 2001 to be presented with a Branch 'Certificate of Appreciation' for his considerate actions.

At the Weymouth British Legion Annual General Meeting, at Legion House, on 19th November, according to the minutes:

'The Mayor [Councillor A. P. Burt] went on to remind members of another Mayor of Weymouth, Alderman 'Joe' Goddard, both the Town and the Legion could be grateful to him who rendered such fine work in their respective interest.'

1948

By 1948 Mrs Hilda Goddard is shown in *Kelly's Directory* as living at 284 Chickerell Road, Weymouth. It is a detached house two hundred yards or so from the *Royal Adelaide*, just around the corner of Chickerell Road's junction with Abbotsbury Road.

On Tuesday, 3rd August, the *Dorset Daily Echo* announced the death early that day of the widowed Mrs J. T. Goddard, having been taken ill the previous night. She was aged 69, and living with her son-in-law and daughter, Reginald and Eleanor Woodford, at 'East Wyld', Chickerell Road, Weymouth. She had only returned from South Africa about five weeks previously, having been to visit her brother and her married daughter Beryl. She was said to have performed outstanding work during the war as Mayoress and a member of the W.V.S. For many years she was a member of the South Dorset Ladies Auxiliary of the Licensed Trades, and also a longstanding member of the Weymouth Branch British Legion Women's Section. She was also a member of the Inner Wheel. South Dorset Licensed Victuallers Association had arranged for their president, Mr. E. C. Hunt, to present a plaque in memory of her husband and she was to have handed it to the British Legion for erection in the Goddard Room at Legion House, but the function had to be cancelled. This plaque, however, is now happily on display in Legion House.

A Certified Copy of Hilda Goddard's *Death Certificate* gave the cause of death as:

'1 a. Hemiplegia
 b. Cardiovascular degeneration'

Present at her death, which took place at her home at Chickerell Road, Weymouth, had been her son, Graham, of London, who registered the death. It is of interest that her third Christian name is correctly given as 'Margaretta' when it was 'Margaret' that was generally quoted.

Her funeral took place in what must have been again a packed St. Mary's church, Weymouth, on Thursday, 5th August, being reported in detail next day in the *Dorset Daily Echo*. In his address the Rector, the Rev. M. Garner, paid tribute to her life and work.

"For seven years the late Alderman Goddard was your Mayor. They were no ordinary years, but years of special stress and strain when you had to maintain a strong centre of life here in the front line, years of great responsibility under the splendid leadership you had from Alderman Goddard and his kindness, hard work and hospitality.

"I have heard so many times of the quality of that work, but, of course, he could not have done that had it not been for his partner. We are gathered here as a representative body because we desire to pay tribute to her as you paid tribute to Alderman Goddard 18 months ago. She was there by his side and his inspiration in public life, and there to sustain him so that he was able to carry on in the splendid way he did."

'The Rector mentioned particularly Mrs Goddard's work for the Women's Voluntary Service, and the British Legion and said he only wished that his predecessor, the Rev. E. L. Langston, could have been there to pay this tribute because he had told him how he valued their friendship.". . .

'On the coffin was a full length cross of flowers from the family.'

Family members were Mr. Graham Goddard (son), Mrs Woodford and Miss Audrey Goddard (daughters), Mr Anthony Goddard (grandson), Lieut. R. Woodford R.N. (son-in-law), Mrs Graham Goddard (daughter-in-law), Mrs E. Heasman (niece), Mr Robert Elliott and Mr Ray Elliott (nephews). Amongst the friends were Mrs Ilott and Mr J. Ilott. Also in attendance were the current Mayor and Mayoress, members of the Town Council, and representatives of the various organisation with which she had been associated were in the congregation, including the Ladies League. Unfortunately family members from South Africa were unable to be present. Among the many wreaths was one "In appreciation of her greatness, worth and sweetness from all her 14th King's Hussars' friends."

Her ashes were scattered in the Weymouth Crematorium garden, as had been her late husband's, with again no permanent memorial being placed there except an appropriate entry in the Book of Remembrance.

1958

Also situated in the East Wing corridor of the Weymouth Community Hospital is (in 2007) a horizontal oval plaque, which has obviously been repositioned since its original installation:

IN RECOGNITION
OF THE EFFORTS OF THE LATE
ALDERMAN JOHN GODDARD O.B.E., M.C., J.P.
(MAYOR OF WEYMOUTH & MELCOMBE REGIS 1938-1945)
THIS REBUILT OPERATING THEATRE
WAS OPENED BY
Mʳ JOHN VINCENT J.P.
ON 8ᵗʰ MAY 1958

1970

During the year was the death of Joe and Hilda Goddards' married son Graham, aged about 62.

1990

This year saw the death of 'Joe' and Hilda Goddard's daughter Eleanor, aged 86, who had married Reginald Woodford in 1931. They had a son Anthony John in 1931, and a daughter Pamela Hilary in 1945.

2001 *et seq*

Saturday, 15th September 2001 saw the re-dedication of a GODDARD ROOM at Legion House, Weymouth, by his granddaughter, Her Honour Judge Ann Felicity Goddard Q.C. She had been photographed as a small girl in 1939 when presenting a bouquet to her grandmother, the then Mayoress. The event was hosted by Major G. D. McMeeken M.B.E., Chairman of the Weymouth Branch of The Royal British Legion, and the author as Branch Secretary. Others present included Mr Anthony Woodford, a grandson, and Mrs Pamela M. Tull, another grand-daughter; plus Mrs Helen Bruce, Deputy Mayor of Weymouth & Portland Borough Council, with her husband and Escort, Mr Ian Bruce; Mr Mick Arnold, Chairman of the Dorset County Royal British Legion, and Mrs Arnold.

On display were brief biographical details of 'Joe' Goddard, consisting of photographic and other artifacts, etc. Further photographs and memorabilia were kindly donated at the same time to the Weymouth Legion by his family. A framed sepia photographic portrait of John Goddard in mayoral regalia has since been on display in Legion House, with the silver trowel, golden key, and Victuallers brass plaque in its archives; but alas there has been no trace of the *Cutty Sark*.

This room on the ground floor, the Club's LOUNGE, had at some time been constructed out of two original small rooms, one of which had previously been the dedicated GODDARD ROOM. Thus, as the current Lounge incorporated the original room, a degree of continuity still existed.

Unfortunately, in early 2006 the Royal British Legion Club at Weymouth had to cease trading, due to lack of sufficient support. However, the Weymouth Royal British Legion Branch remains operational, and as owners of the premises, ensures the Goddard Room remains *in situ* for the time being. It is the intention now to find more suitable premises in Weymouth, with presumably keeping in mind to subsequently dedicate a new Goddard Room within.

In the more than 100 years since John Goddard's early years in Wednesbury there would inevitably have been changes. The author witnessed just how much during his visits there in 2003 and 2006; and in the study of then-and-now maps and photographs. Gone were the 'dark satanic mills'. There was large-scale slum clearance in 1933, including the area which contained the various addresses of the Goddard family. The Sandwell Community History & Archive Service at Smethwick has a photograph showing St. James Church and School in splendid isolation surrounded by a vast area of razed and cleared housing. Most of the subsequent re-development was to be of industrial estates, although street names were retained, e.g. Great Western Street and St. James Street. Dudley Street is now a busy dual-carriage road. In addition, several railway lines and sidings were similarly to be covered over with industrial and warehousing units, etc., and roads.

There is still some family continuity with a distant descendant family member living in adjoining Tipton, who the author was pleased to meet in 2006.

APPENDIX I

THE GODDARD FAMILY GENEALOGY

An early informal Goddard Association existed in London in the 17th century. A surviving printed invitation dated 1664, to those with the surname Goddard, asked them to meet monthly at the *Red Bull* in "Mount Goddard Street". This address was destroyed in the Fire of London in 1666.

The present Goddard Association of Europe was formed in 1985. At time of writing the address of the Secretary was: 2 Lowergate Road, Huncoat, Accrington, Lancashire BB5 6LN.

The best documented branch of the 'family' is that said to be settled in Wiltshire for several centuries; but other long established branches exist in most counties, especially Hampshire, Derbyshire, Yorkshire, East Anglia, and London.

The Goddard Association is one that considers the name Goddard to have a Viking origin. Various branches of the Goddard Family have used a coat of arms, but not apparently 'Joe' Goddard's branch.

As well as the author of this work, other peripheral members of Joe Goddard's line are currently researching its genealogical aspects. Direct family descendants have also been most helpfull, especially with the provision of reminiscences, family photographs and momentoes. It is with all their kind assistance that I have been able to draw up something of a Family Tree. Because of the computer system used by the author, and the constraints of space in this biography, the details as set out in the following pages do not conform to the usual 'Tree' shape. Also it does not contain as many 'twigs' as it could do. Nevertheless, it is hoped the six generations shown in the 'Tree' may be followed without too much difficulty - and may even prove useful to others.

The number after each name is just purely for unique identification purposes within this, the author's particular family's genealogical profile. The dates are for births only: there not being provision for additional dates of death. s = spouse.

It will be noticed that the Goddard Tree only starts with John Goddard's grandfather. It was not considered relevant for this biography to delve any further backward. As regards the ancestry of John Goddard's wife Hilda (née Elliott), a little of that can be ascertained in the MARRIAGE chapter.

The author would appreciate being advised of any errors, and of appropriate additional family members.

```
1-  William GODDARD-85 (1810)
    2-  William GODDARD-1 (1837) BORN-HOUNSLOW. DIED-WEDNESDAY 1896
    s-  Catherine CLARK(E)-2 (1846) BORN-LEAMINGTON. DIED-WEDNESDAY 1896
        3-  William GODDARD-3 (1868) BORN-LEAMINGTON. DIED-1901+
        s-  Emma INGRAM-32 (1867)
            4-  Fanny GODDARD-33 (1887)
            4-  Maud GODDARD-34 (1889)
            4-  Edward GODDARD-35 (1891)
            4-  Alfred GODDARD-36 (1895)
            4-  Catherine GODDARD-37 (1900)
        3-  Frances Louisa GODDARD-4 (1870) BORN-BIRMINGHAM. DIED-1905+
        s-  George (John) COOMBES-25 (1867) BORN-PERSHORE,WORCS. DIED-1905+
            4-  George William COOMBES-26 (1913)
            s-  Harriet Ann UNKNOWN-88 (1916)
                5-  Irene COOMBES-89 (1940)
                s-  John BEVIN-96 (1940)
                    6-  Robert John BEVIN-97 (1969)
            4-  Henry COOMBES-27 (1893)
            4-  Harold COOMBES-28 (1895)
            4-  (Frances) Louisa COOMBES-29 (1896)
            s-  Albert KAYE-66 (1896)
                5-  Margaret (Peggy) KAYE-67 (1921)
                5-  Jack KAYE-68 (1922)
                5-  Gordon KAYE-69 (1923)
                5-  Frank KAYE-70 (1924)
                5-  William KAYE-71 (1925)
                5-  George KAYE-72 (1926)
            4-  Kate (Katie) COOMBES-30 (1897)
            s-  Frank BEARDMORE-73 (1897)
            4-  John (Jack) COOMBES-31 (1900)
            4-  Elsie May COOMBES-42 (1902)
            s-  Horace LOYNES-46 (1904)
                5-  Barbara LOYNES-47 (1938)
                s-  William HARRIS-52 (1936)
                    6-  Debora Dawn HARRIS-53 (1962)
                    6-  Claire Suzanne HARRIS-54 (1973)
                5-  Terence LOYNES-48 (1930)
                s-  Joyce PASKIN-55 (1930)
                    6-  Marcel LOYNES-56 (1956)
                    6-  Richard LOYNES-57 (1957)
                    6-  Kerry LOYNES-58 (1958)
                5-  Bryan LOYNES-49 (1934)
                s-  Jean TELFORD-59 (1934)
                5-  Horace Anthony LOYNES-50 (1942)
                s-  Elaine Patricia BRADLEY-60 (1943)
                    6-  Anthony LOYNES-61 (1966)
                    6-  Garry LOYNES-62 (1967)
                5-  Graham LOYNES-51 (1946)
                s-  Brenda HARPER-63 (1946)
                    6-  Kim LOYNES-64 (1971)
                    6-  Paul LOYNES-65 (1972)
            4-  Gladys COOMBES-43 (1903)
            s-  William COX-74 (1900)
            4-  Ellen (Nell) COOMBES-44 (1904)
            s-  Walter DOWNS-75 (1900)
                5-  Walter DOWNS-76 (1926)
```

```
              5-  Colin DOWNS-77 (1927)
          4-  Charles (Sonny) COOMBES-45 (1905)
     3-  Harry (Henry) GODDARD-5 (1873) BORN-READING. DIED-1901+
     3-  Moses GODDARD-6 (1875) B-WEDNESBURY. DIED-1917 SOMME FRANCE
     3-  John Thomas GODDARD 0-7 (1879) BORN-WEDNESBURY. DIED-1946 WEYMOUTH
     s-  Hilda Constance M ELLIOTT-10 (1879) B-ALDERSHOT. DIED-1946 WEYMOUTH
          4-  Eleanor (Nell) P GODDARD-11 (1905)
          s-  Reginald WOODFORD-38 (1901)
              5-  Anthony John T WOODFORD-123 (1932)
              5-  Pamela Hilary P WOODFORD-124 (1945)
              s-  Alvin TULL-127 (1945)
                  6-  Tristan Owen William TULL-138 (1972)
                  6-  Sarah Louise TULL-139 (1975)
                      7-  Charlotte Austin FEMALE-233 (2005)
          4-  Ethel (Queenie) L GODDARD-87 (1907)
          4-  Graham ELLIOTT GODDARD-12 (1908)
          s-  Margaret Louise H CLARK-39 (1908)
              5-  Ann Felicity GODDARD J-86 (1936)
          4-  Audrey GODDARD-13 (1912)
          s-  Cornelius J UNGERER-40 (1913)
          4-  Jessie Beryl GODDARD-14 (1920)
          s-  John Hamilton ELLIOTT-41 (1920)
              5-  Susan Lesley ELLIOTT-83 (1947)
              s-  Anthony WESTOBY-140 (1946)
                  6-  Bruce WESTOBY-141 (1972)
                  s-  Joy UNKNOWN-234 (1972)
                      7-  Timothy WESTOBY-235 (2004)
                      7-  William WESTOBY-236 (2006)
                  6-  James WESTOBY-142 (1974)
                  s-  Sarah UNKNOWN-144 (1973)
                      7-  Dylan WESTOBY-237 (1997)
                      7-  Clyde WESTOBY-238 (1999)
                  6-  Clare WESTOBY-143 (1978)
              5-  Graham John ELLIOTT-84 (1947)
              s-  Louise UNKNOWN-145 (1947)
                  6-  Catherine Cathy ELLIOTT-146 (1975)
                  6-  Tara ELLIOTT-147 (1977)
                  s-  Stuart BLAKE-239 (1975)
                      7-  Tristan BLAKE-240 (2000)
                  6-  Nicola ELLIOTT-148 (1979)
     3-  Charles GODDARD-8 (1881) BORN-WEDNESBURY. DIED-1918, BELGIUM.
     3-  Frederick GODDARD-9 (1884) BORN-WEDNESBURY. DIED-1901+
```

APPENDIX II

WAR-TIME GOODWILL MESSAGE TO THE U.S.A.

This is a transcript of the recorded Goodwill Greetings from Weymouth, Dorset to Weymouth, Massachusetts, U.S.A., on Wednesday, 12th November 1941. It was taken from an original 10-inch double-sided 78 r.p.m. gramophone record, in the ownership of Mr. Jack West, who kindly loaned it for transcription. It was in good condition, with clarity of sound. For the sake of posterity, in keeping a less fragile copy of the recording, the author had it further copied onto a C.D.

Serious consideration was given as to whether to print the transcription as it would have been in the written script, or as it was actually spoken. Bearing in mind that few readers would have the opportunity of hearing the recording, it was eventually decided to do the latter alternative, as it best faithfully shows how John Goddard for one seems to have spoken. He shows no discernible trace of any West Midlands-type accent - understandable after some 40 plus years mixing with people from all districts and walks of life. He does not, however, seem to have picked up anything of a Dorset accent during his subsequent 16-years living in Weymouth, unlike Percy A'Court who spoke with a mild Dorset accent. Percy Smallman, the Town Clerk, spoke in a very clear, precise manner, as befitted his position! To a certain extent, though, each speaks somewhat stilted as if reading from a script.

JTG = Councillor John Goddard (Mayor)
PS = Mr Percy Smallman (Weymouth Town Clerk)
PJA = Councillor Percy A'Court (Former Mayor[1])

JTG   A month ago, 'ere in Weymouth, we were listenin' to your message of goodwill. The air-raid sirens 'ad sounded 'alf-an-hour before. And we could 'ear the planes purring over'ead. So you can guess what it meant to us to 'ear your voices at that moment; and to know that, just as Britain can rely on the support of your great nation, so we in Weymouth can be assured of the sympathies of our own daughter town. Your broadcast came over extremely well, and we 'eard every word of it. Some of you will remember our Town Clerk, Mr Smallman, who accompanied Mayor A'Court on his visit to you in 1926[2]. He 'eard your message at 'is post in the Civil Defence control room.

PS   Yes. We were all listening that night, with one ear on the radio, and one ear open for the sound of bombs. None fell that night. But the night after we did get some. One bomb was a direct hit, that destroyed part of the Mayor's house, and buried him in the debris.

JTG   I was in bed at the time. The bedroom collapsed, and I went down with it. I thought I was dreamin' at first.

PS   You didn't sound as if you were dreaming, Mr Mayor, when the rescue party finally dug down to you.

JTG   Well, they got down so far, and I 'eard one of them say: "'e is alright. And the other chap said: "'e's swearing a bit, so 'e must be alright."

PS   I was told the Medical Officer gave you a shot of morphia to keep you quiet, when he heard the language you were using.

JTG   Well, so would you be using language if you 'ad your arm trapped between two beams.[3]

PS   All the same, I don't think I could compete with an old soldier like you, Mr Mayor. How many years did you tell me you'd been in the army?

JTG   Twenty-seven. Wars make no difference to me.

PS   I'll say they don't. Well, the rescue squad dug the Mayor out of the ruins in an hour or so, and he was taken to a nursing-home, in an ambulance that had been presented to us by the American Red Cross. And I think you'll agree that that's the best symbol you can find of the sympathy and the material support that you people in America are giving us. But it takes more than a German bomb to keep our Mayor in hospital. And he was at his job again in a few days.

JTG   Well, there's plenty of work to be done. Before the war we used to get thousands of 'olidaymakers 'ere in Weymouth. The town 'as been a popular sea-side resort ever since George III started coming 'ere for his summer 'olidays in 1789. But nowadays, with the Germans just across the Channel, the beaches are all covered with barbed wire, and machine gun posts.

SIDE 2

PS It was here in Weymouth that the Battle of Britain started last year. On August 11th, 1940, Weymouth saw its first daylight air-battle, and many German planes were brought down that day.

JTG And we've 'ad other excitements 'ere as well. There was the thousands of British and French troops passing through after Dunkirk.

PS And later, we coped with 35,000 refugees from the Channel Islands, when the Islands were evacuated. You never know what's going to turn up next. Weymouth is in the front-line alright.

JTG That's right. But I'll tell you why I'm especially glad to be 'ere on this occasion. The room I'm speaking from is one of the rooms in the Royal Suite of Gloucester Lodge, that George III used to occupy during 'is annual visit to Weymouth, a few years after the American War of Independence. I suppose in those days 'e was the best 'ated man in America. And I think it is in improved friendships between the two British and American people that we can use this room to send a message to you. Just as in the same way as you invited the Mayor of Weymouth to attend your 4th of July celebrations a few years ago. Mr A'Court was then Mayor. Many of you will remember 'is visit. And 'ere 'e is to speak to you now.

PJA Well, I am very glad to have had this chance of speaking again to my old friends in Weymouth, Mass. It was a real pleasure to 'ear your voice, Mr Phillips, and to 'ear news of Mr [O'Donnell][4] and his Selectmen[5]. And I'm sure Mr Smallman 'ere feels the same.

PS I certainly do.

PJA *(Cough, cough.)* I think that it was the first time anyone from these parts have gone to America in an official capacity to join in your 4th of July celebrations. We couldn't have 'ad a warmer reception than we got in Weymouth, and I faithfully appreciated the honour that your Moderator[6], Mr Barnes[7], paid me in inviting me to conduct your Town meeting for a short time. The first time an Englishman had conducted a Town meeting in Massachusetts since the days of George I. And I'd like to recall to you the closing words of the Resolution that was adopted at that meeting. They were: 'Such demonstration of goodwill as the best kind of guarantee of permanent and abiding peace between the two countries.'

JTG   I think that expresses it perfectly. And now when we are fighting for our lives, and liberties, in the greatest war the world has ever seen, we look forward with confidence to the future. For we know that with the material help that will be coming from you in ever increasing quantities, we shall win this war, and establish once more those principles of liberty that are so dear to you as they are to ourselves.

NOTES

(1). A'Court had been Mayor of Weymouth for the period November 1925-November 1927.

(2). For details of this visit see *Dorset Daily Echo*, 16th July 1926.

(3). According to a family member, 'Joe' Goddard was to be somewhat upset by what Percy Smallman said during the recording about his language when being dug out after the bombing. He apparently admitted to only saying "Damn!". Someone who was on the scene within a few minutes of the bomb falling has related to the author that he could hear 'Joe' Goddard shouting away in the ruins.

(4). Mr Daniel O'Donnell - see report of the American broadcast in *Dorset Daily Echo*, 30th October 1941.

(5). According to *Webster's Third New International Dictionary* 1993, Selectmen were 'Persons chosen to exercise special powers in a system of government, especially of a board of officers chosen usually in three-year terms in towns of all the New England states (except Rhode Island) to transact and administer the general public business of the town.'

(6). According to *Webster's* a Moderator is 'The nonpartisan presiding officer of a town meeting.'

(7). Senator George L. Barnes, Town Moderator of Weymouth, Mass. - see *Dorset Daily Echo*, 16th July 1926, for report on visit.

APPENDIX III

ANCIENT ORDER OF FORESTERS

In 1934 John Goddard became a member of the Honorary Court Highclere of the Ancient Order of Foresters at Weymouth. The following is taken from a *Souvenir Guide Book*, titled on the cover:

ANCIENT ORDER OF FORESTERS
HIGH COURT
WEYMOUTH
AUGUST, 1929

WITH THE COMPLIMENTS
OF
HONORARY COURT HIGHCLERE

On the inside title-page is:

ANCIENT ORDER OF FORESTERS

HIGH COURT
WEYMOUTH

———

Forestry in Weymouth
and District

———

THE
HONORARY COURT HIGHCLERE
No. 7634

(No. 1 OF HONORARY COURTS)

There then followed this historical narrative:

'The Ancient Order of Foresters has been known in Weymouth and District since 1859, when the first Court was opened. By 1929 the Weymouth District consisted of 32 Courts, with a voluntary membership of 1,670 of both sexes and a National

Health Insurance membership of 2,400. The total funds of the District Branch and its Courts amounted to £38,000 - exclusive of National Health Insurance Funds.

'Unique in Weymouth is the largest and most active Honorary Court in the Order, Court Highclere (Hon. Court, No. 1) whose membership is restricted to influential townsmen. The High Court was to be held in Weymouth in 1929.

'The story of the origin of Honorary Court Highclere started in 1882, when the High Court of the Order was held in Weymouth - the only time it had been held in the town prior to that of 1929. The proceedings apparently touched the imagination of the then Town Clerk, Brother Pelly Hooper, a solicitor in the town. The High Chief Ranger in 1882 was Bro. W. C. T. Hounsell, a prominent townsman of Weymouth, including being a Town Councillor. Bro. Hooper conceived the idea of forming an Honorary Court, and in 1887 he founded the Honorary Court Highclere, the Dispensation being dated 24th September 1887. The number of members was limited to 50, which limit was subsquently increased to 100.

'The objects of this Honorary Court were:

(a) To promote the principles of Forestry, whereby a large number of members may be induced to take an active part in the administration of the affairs of the Order, Districts, and Court respectively, by the discussion and consideration of any matter that may in any way affect the constitution of the Order or its Branches.

(b) To raise a fund for relieving poor and necessitous Foresters or their families resident within "The Weymouth United District", where, from want of funds or other causes their own Courts are unable to sufficiently relieve them, also to subscribe to any Hospital or Sanitorium whereby admission may be availablle for members of the Weymouth United District or their immediate relatives.

(c) When the Court is not sitting, a Committee, consisting of the Chief Ranger, Sub-Chief Ranger and Treasurer, be empowered to make a grant of a sum not exceeding £5 5s. to any necessitous and deserving case that in their opinion requires immediate relief, such action to be reported to the Members of the Court at their next meeting for discussion and confirmation.

'Each year at the Dinner following the Annual Meeting of the Honorary Court Highclere, there is a silent toast to the memory of the late Brother Pelly Hooper, decribed as "To the pious memory of our Founder."

'Honorary Court Highclere, No. 7634, is one of the few Honorary Courts working throughout the country, and has been granted permission by the High Court to be designated No. 1 of the *Honorary* Courts.

'The meetings of the Court are held quarterly in the Council Chamber at the Guildhall, Weymouth, by permission of the Mayor and Corporation. At these meetings applications for assistance from any necessitous Foresters, or their dependents, are considered and dealt with - all the income of the Court, with the exception of necessary business expenses, being available for this purpose. The Members of Honorary Court Highclere do not themselves benefit, except from the satisfaction of knowing that service has been rendered to Brethren in need outside the Court.

'During the Great War, Honorary Court Highclere entertained on several occasions, wounded soldiers, among whom were many Foresters, and the Court is a Life Governor of the Foresters War Memorial Benevolent Fund.

'On the 13th April 1920 the Weymouth United District of the A.O.F. honoured Honorary Court Highclere by inviting Bro. H. J. Groves to unveil the War Memorial at Oddfellows Hall, Market Street, Weymouth, to Foresters who had fallen in the Great War, and the proceedings were attended by a goodly number of Officers and Brethren of Honorary Court Highclere.

'Under the stained-glass Memorial Window in the South Aisle of St. Mary's Church, Weymouth, to the memory of the parishioners who fell in the Great War, are two tablets inscribed with the names of the illustrious dead, which were subscribed for and presented by members of Honorary Court Hichclere on 9th March 1924.'

A more updated history of Honorary Court Highclere No. 1 may be found in F.R.Jakeman's booklet of 1987; and a well-illustrated history of the A.O.F. in general up to 1984 by W.G.Cooper - see the Bibliography.

Members of the Honorary Court Highclere in 1929, who seemed to continue to be prominent business and political members of Weymouth society, included Bro. E. C. Hunt of a local brewing business and who was a senior officer in the Weymouth Branch of the British Legion; and Bro. Percy A'Court who had been the Mayor who had visited Weymouth, Massachusetts in 1926.

The Court's annual subscription in 1940 was 10s 6d. An annual Banquet was apparently held during each January, but this was cancelled shortly after the outbreak of war, and was restricted to a Supper, as first seen in January 1940.

Since it was founded Highclere has always met four times a year. The Annual Dinner has similarly been held in October, preceeding the Changeover [of officers] Meeting. Ladies were invited for the first time to the Centenary Dinner in 1987, which is now held a few days after the Changeover Meeting.

Subscriptions remained at 10s. 6d. until the mid-1950s, and have since risen in accordance with inflation. The basic aims and rules of the Ancient Order of Foresters Friendly Society (as it is now called), and Highclere in particular, have not changed a great deal over the years. Membership numbers of Highclere have been increased since its foundation, as had its range of membership from all walks of life.

BIBLIOGRAPHY

Acutt, D. G. F. *Brigade In Action* Sherren & Son, Weymouth 1946

Ancient Order of Foresters *Souvenir Guide Book* Honorary Court Highclere
Weymouth 1929

Anglesey, The Marquess of *A History of the British Cavalry 1816-1919,*
Volume 6: 1914-1918 Mesopotamia Leo Cooper 1995

Attwooll, Maureen & Harrison, Denise *Weymouth and Portland at War*
Dovecote Press, Wimborne 1993

Attwooll, Maureen *The Borough of Weymouth and Portland: A Mayoral*
History D.F.Hollings 2004

Bott, Ian M. *Wednesbury in Old Photographs* Alan Sutton Pub. Ltd 1998

Browne, J. Gilbert *Historical Record of the 14th (King's) Hussars 1900-1922*
Volume II Royal United Service Institution, London 1932

Chambers, Graham *A Soldier's Diary* The Pentland Press Ltd, Bishop
Auckland 1999

Chappell, Mike *British Cavalry Equipments 1800-1941* Osprey 2002

Cole, Howard N. *The Story of Aldershot* Gale & Polden, Ltd. Aldershot 1951

Cooper, Leonard *British Regular Cavalry 1644-1914* Chapman & Hall 1965

Cooper, Walter G. *The Ancient Order of Foresters Friendly Society 150*
Years 1834-1984 AOFFS 1984

Cox, Henry *The Red Cross Launch 'Wessex' on the River Tigris-1916: The*
Diary of Sydney Cox MBE Natula Pubns 2002

Dorset Daily Echo newspaper - various dates.

Fry, Des *A Teenage View of Wartime Weymouth* Private pub. 1993

Garnett, David (ed.) *The Letters of T.E.Lawrence of Arabia* Various editions

Hackwood, Frederick W. *Newspaper Cuttings, Volume 14. The Boer War*
1899-1902 Sandwell M.B.C. Archives, Smethwick

Hamilton, Henry Blackburne *Historical Record of the 14th (King's) Hussars*
from A.D. 1715 to A.D. 1900 Longmans, Green & Co. London 1901

History of Dorset Freemasonry Revealed 1736-2000 Provincial Grand Lodge
of Dorset 1999

Holmes, Richard *Redcoat* Harper Collins 2001

Kelly's Directory for Weymouth and District - various dates

Jakeman, F.R. *Honorary Court Highclere Number 7634 of the Ancient Order*
of Foresters Number 1 of the Honorary Courts 1887-1987 Weymouth 1987

Kruger, Rayne *Good-bye Dolly Gray* Cassell 1959

Lewis, Samuel *A Topographical Dictionary of England* 5th edition 1844

Lewis, Samuel *A Topographical Dictionary of Ireland* 2nd edition 1846

Linaker, David & Dine, Gordon *Cavalry Warrant Officers' and N.C.O.s Arm Badges* Military Historical Society 1997

McDonald, Ian *The Boer War in Postcards* Wrens Park Pub'ng. 2001

Pearson, Robin & Wade, Jean *Black Country Pubs* Alan Sutton Pub. Ltd 1998

Pharo-Tomlin, John *The Rammuggur Boys: 14th/20th King's Hussars 1715-1992* Museum of The King's Royal Hussars in Lancashire, Preston 2002

Pope Family *A Wessex Family and the Great War (The Popes of Wrackleford, co.Dorset)* Privately printed 1919

Price, W.H. *One Man's War* Weymouth & Portland B.C. 1997

Reaney, P.H. & Wilson, R.M. *A Dictionary of English Surnames* Routledge 1991

Ryder, Robert (ed.) *Wednesday Faces, Places and Industries* Wednesbury Herald 1897

Sandes, E.W.C., *In Kut And Captivity With The Sixth Indian Division* John Murray 1919

Southern Echo newspaper - 5th September 1904

Southern Times newspaper - various dates.

Sandwell M.B.C. *Historic Wednesbury: A town trail* 1993

St. James' Boys' School, Wednesbury *Diary or Log Book* from 1884

The Times newspaper - various dates.

Virgin, Sue *Upwey:Life in the Dorset Village 1920-1950* Private pubn 1999

Watt, Steve *The Battle of Vaalkrans 5-7 February 1900* Ravan Press 1999

Wednesbury Herald Editor *Wednesbury Faces, Places, And Industries* 1897

Wilkinson-Latham, Christopher *The Boer War* Osprey 1977

"   "   "   'Queen Victoria's Chocolate Box' Antique Arms & Militaria

Weymouth Reference Library:

 Illustrations Collection L.352.0934.GOD2;

 'Scrapbook of the Life & Times of Mayor Goddard', oversize document file L.921.GOD1;

 Newscuttings Box 1, L.942.331.LE3, page 100;

 Local Newscuttings Index, Vol. 10, pages 105 & 154.

Websites, etc.:

14th (King's) Hussars: <www.website.lineone.net/ royal.hussar/14hww1.htm>

14th/20th Hussars: <www.1420h.org/uk/home.html>

Commonwealth War Graves Commission:
         <www.ancs.ac.uk/postgrad/bracewel/hawksrest/Uniforms.htm>

Cuckfield village details of 14th Hussars men in South Africa:
                              <www.cuckfieldcompetition.co.uk>

Genuki UK & Ireland Genealogy - Wednesbury

Goddard Association of Europe, 2 Lowergate Road, Accrington, Lancashire BB5 6LN: <goddard-association.co.uk>
Museum of Lancashire, Preston, Lancashire : <www.lancs.ac.uk>
O'Dwyer, Patrick 'Hussars Research' e-mail: <hussars@which.net>